NARRATIVE AND DESIRE IN
RUSSIAN LITERATURE, 1822–49

By the same author

*WRITERS AND SOCIETY DURING THE RISE OF RUSSIAN REALISM

*RUSSIAN WRITERS AND SOCIETY IN THE SECOND HALF OF THE NINETEENTH CENTURY

*WOMEN IN RUSSIAN LITERATURE, 1780–1863

THE STRUCTURAL ANALYSIS OF RUSSIAN NARRATIVE FICTION (*editor*)

POETICS OF THE TEXT: ESSAYS TO CELEBRATE TWENTY YEARS OF THE NEO-FORMALIST CIRCLE (*editor*)

THE FUTURISTS, THE FORMALISTS AND THE MARXIST CRITIQUE (*translated with Christopher Pike*)

**Also published by Macmillan*

Narrative and Desire in Russian Literature, 1822–49

The Feminine and the Masculine

Joe Andrew
Senior Lecturer in Russian Studies
Keele University

© Joe Andrew 1993

All rights reserved. No reproduction, copy or transmission of this publication may be made without written permission.

No paragraph of this publication may be reproduced, copied or transmitted save with written permission or in accordance with the provisions of the Copyright, Designs and Patents Act 1988, or under the terms of any licence permitting limited copying issued by the Copyright Licensing Agency, 90 Tottenham Court Road, London W1P 9HE.

Any person who does any unauthorised act in relation to this publication may be liable to criminal prosecution and civil claims for damages.

First published 1993 by
THE MACMILLAN PRESS LTD
Houndmills, Basingstoke, Hampshire RG21 2XS
and London
Companies and representatives
throughout the world

ISBN 0-333-52122-6

A catalogue record for this book is available from the British Library.

Printed in Great Britain by
Ipswich Book Co Ltd
Ipswich, Suffolk

For Barbara

Contents

1	Introduction	1
2	Pushkin's Southern Poems	11
3	V.F. Odoevsky and the Two Princesses	50
4	Elena Gan and *A Futile Gift*	85
5	Mariya Zhukova and Patriarchal Power	139
6	Alexander Herzen: *Who Is To Blame?*	184
7	The Law of the Father and *Netochka Nezvanova*	214
	Notes	227
	Bibliography	251
	Index	255

1
Introduction

The present volume is intended as a sequel of sorts to my earlier *Women in Russian Literature: 1780–1863*, which was one of the first books in any language to investigate issues of gender in Russian literature.[1] That book had as its aim readings, from a feminist perspective, of a number of major works of Russian literature primarily from the first half of the nineteenth century, with a view to arriving at an understanding of the purposes of the ways women were represented in that culture. My hope was that the enterprise would not merely shed new light on the works of fiction concerned, but would also alter our perception of the tradition which produced the works. Quite deliberately I chose for my analysis those works which formed the canon of early Russian Realism, the ones which established the themes and plots of that age and of later periods, namely, *Evgeny Onegin*, *A Hero of Our Time*, *The St Petersburg Stories*, *Home of the Gentry*, *On the Eve*, as well as some others. (These were also the texts with which I grew up as a student of Russian literature and which, on the whole, still form the 'core curriculum' in schools and universities, both in Russia itself and outside the old Soviet Union.) As *Women in Russian Literature* was intended to break new ground in terms of the applicability of a body of critical theory it seemed to me that the best place to start was with the works that would be most familiar to any reader, myself included.

Narrative and Desire is, then, a sequel of sorts. Not, however, in any chronological sense, because, in fact, the present work actually covers much the same period, and over an even shorter time-span (1822–49, to be precise). It is, though, a sequel in at least two particular ways. Firstly, I have moved, as it were, one layer downwards. Apart from the first chapter proper which concerns itself with three early works by Pushkin (his Southern Poems), all my analyses are of works from outside the canon, whether an early work by a major writer (Dostoevsky's *Netochka Nezvanova*) or, more usually, works by writers who have not commonly been studied from a purely literary perspective (Odoevsky and Herzen). Even less familiar to most readers will be the works by Mariya Zhukova and Elena Gan, two of the cohort of women writers who began to publish in the 1830s, but who have been scarcely republished since, and have had almost no critical writing devoted to them. Secondly, my own critical concerns have moved on somewhat. I now concentrate more specifically and directly on gender issues, looking at masculinity as well as femininity, and have tried to incorporate some of the most recent developments of feminist literary criticism, especially those to be found at the interface of semiotics and psychoanalysis. At the same time I have attempted to utilise a more typological approach to narrative (and to narrativity), to unearth the ancient patterns and models which underlie even relatively sophisticated works of fiction.

I begin with Pushkin because it seems always necessary to begin with Pushkin. This truism, however, has a particular resonance for the present work. Pushkin not only stands as an enormous presence throughout nineteenth-century literature (and twentieth-century literature for that matter) but is also, by common consent, the *father* of modern Russian literature.[2] Given that many of my ensuing discussions will deal with familial relations, as well as symbolic fathers, Pushkin's status as the engenderer of what followed is of peculiar importance. And, indeed, virtually all the texts here discussed, especially those of the 1830s, are deeply influenced by Pushkin. To a greater or lesser extent they can be read as rewritings, whether explicitly or implicitly, of *Evgeny Onegin* and other similar works by Pushkin. Each author was, as it were, at pains to prove herself or himself to be a dutiful daughter or son.[3] Pushkin may or may not be the 'first Russian feminist'[4] as has been claimed: either way, he certainly was concerned, both in *Evgeny Onegin* and in the works discussed here, with notions of gender, with images of masculinity and femininity. The three Southern Poems can be seen as harbingers both of *Onegin* and of the later narratives in that many of the principal plot and character types of Russian Romanticism–early Realism are introduced here. *The Prisoner of the Caucasus* gives one of the first adumbrations of the 'superfluous man', the educated young Russian who is unable to respond to the test of love or to act decisively. The figure of the unnamed Circassian Woman can also be seen to prefigure both the 'strong heroine' and, at the same time, the self-sacrificing victim. Many of the society tales of the 1830s, and particularly those by Gan and Zhukova, construct their narrative architectonics on the principle of contrastive heroines. This desire can be traced back (in Russian literature, at least) to the second of the Southern Poems, *The Fountain of Bakhchisaray*, and to the conflict between dark, passionate Zarema and virginal Mariya. Equally, we see in this work the looming, punishing figure of the 'Stern Father', Khan Girey. A different version of the father appears in the final poem, *The Gipsies*, in which the emblematically entitled The Old Man acts as *raisonneur* and moral arbiter. This work also offers a more developed version of the proto-superfluous man in Aleko, while Zemfira is a variation of Zarema. Despite the differences between the three works it should also be noted that all four heroines die (three of them murdered and one suicide): the themes of the suffering and/or punished heroine are firmly established at the very beginning of modern Russian literature.

After Pushkin my main consideration is with prose fiction of, roughly speaking, 1835-45, a period during which nearly all the works discussed were published. I have chosen this particular period and these specific writers for a variety of reasons and the period has claims to our attention on several different fronts. On the most general level the 1830s and 1840s can be characterised as the 'Rise of Russian Realism',[5] the decades during which the pioneering ground-work was laid down and which led to the full flowering of the Russian novel in the 1850s and 1860s. This period has also been called the 'Remarkable Decade',[6] a time of intense intellectual debate around the so-called 'accursed questions' of Russia's destiny and which led to the formation of the groups known as the Westernisers and Slavophiles. Another sign of the intensity of development in the Russian cultural world during the 1830s and 1840s is the emergence for the first time in any numbers of women writers.[7] Gan and Zhukova have been chosen because they are probably the best but there were many others. In turn, the appearance of women on the cultural scene was a mark of a more general democratisation of literature, in terms both of the producers of literature and of its subject matter.[8]

In more specifically literary terms, the 1830s and 1840s were a time of great generic experimentation, which is a signal feature of many of the works I will be discussing (most notably those of Gan, Odoevsky and, albeit to a lesser extent, Zhukova). The paradigm for those developments is Lermontov's *A Hero of Our Time* which saw the fusion of lesser genres into a large work, while also displaying great inventiveness within the temporal scale. While Odoevsky, Gan and Zhukova did not approach this level of sophistication, they also reveal a conscious concern with discovering the most appropriate format for discussing the central theme they share with their great contemporary and which was first developed by Pushkin, namely, the role of the individual within (patriarchal) society. This theme finds its sharpest focus in the dominant genre of the 1830s, the Society Tale, which was utilised by Gan, Zhukova and Odoevsky (as well as by Lermontov, of course). In this instance the source of inspiration is once more Pushkin, the Pushkin of *The Queen of Spades* to an even greater extent than of *Onegin*.

In concentrating almost entirely on lesser, 'non-canonical', fiction in this formative period I had in mind a number of questions and projects. In such works, it can be argued, we see the themes of the period in a clearer light. That is, in *Onegin* and *Hero*, for example, the sophistication of Pushkin and Lermontov lead to a great degree of ambivalence: the jury will always be out on the moral issues raised in these major novels. Like their eighteenth-century 'grandfathers', however, Gan, Zhukova and Odoevsky tend to make the authorial position more clear-cut. Equally the issues around gender tend to be presented more starkly. This is certainly true in the case of the two female writers, which leads on to further issues I have wished to raise *en passant* in this book. Did women authors in this period attempt to write 'as men', or was their response to these early formulations of the 'woman question'[9] profoundly different from that of their male contemporaries? It seems to me, as I will argue more fully in later chapters, that Gan certainly did approach these issues differently from her contemporaries, particularly in her handling of plot paradigms and in her treatment of the creative woman, whereas Zhukova's 'femaleness' is much less apparent. Be that as it may, it is certainly the case that *all* of the writers considered in the following pages adopted the 'woman question' as one of their central concerns (and this includes even the young Dostoevsky). This issue, it seems to me, should be ranked high amongst the 'accursed questions' which exercised and energised the intellectual and literary milieux of the 1830s and 1840s.

In these regards, these seven Russian writers (along with many others, of course) were creating a uniquely indigenous tradition. At the same time, however, they were being deeply imitative in that the paradoxical place of woman in (male) culture is, of course, an ancient theme. That is, although excluded from the mansions of power, woman has been one of the central themes of art, precisely, indeed because of her problematical place in society. 'What does woman want?' was a question formulated long before Freud found this particular expression of the puzzle.[10] Consequently, the supposedly enigmatic, mysterious nature of women has been a near universal myth of 'human' (that is, male) cultural expression, from the Bible to the *film noir* and beyond. The obverse of this proposition is that coherence of female characterisation is relatively rare. As we shall see, all too often the heroine in Russian literature is a composite of irreconcilable opposites, or else the pair of contrastive heroines presents a deeply fissured perception of femininity. This arises from the fact that women are perceived and then represented within an alien culture, that of the dominant code of men. As Judith Fetterley has argued, concerning such characterisation:

> Mirrors for men, they [women] serve to indicate the involutions of the male psyche with which literature is primarily concerned, and their characters and identities shift accordingly. They are projections not people.[11]

Central to these paradoxes and dilemmas, and central to Russian fiction during the period under consideration, is female sexuality. As Teresa de Lauretis has argued, 'What Freud's question really asks, therefore, is "what is femininity – for men?" In this sense it is a question of desire: it is prompted by men's desire for woman, and by men's desire to know'.[12] And these questions underlie most narratives, whether of this period or earlier (and later) ones, even in stories authored by women. The female principle has been seen as desirable but therefore dangerous: it is a curse, disruptive, destructive. Indeed, both the mirror images – the *alter egos*, the sisters of Virgin and whore, Mother and Seductress – are defined by their sexuality. Woman is both (and not uncommonly, simultaneously) angel and demon. But here too we are dealing with 'projections', *signs* of the male psyche.

In the novels and stories of the eighteenth and nineteenth centuries sexuality remained the cornerstone of woman's being. As Foucault has shown, 'an entire machinery for producing true discourses concerning'[13] this issue was set in motion, and the novel played an important, hegemonistic role in the creation of these discourses, in Russia as much as in Western Europe. The nineteenth century perpetuated the ancient tendencies of the dangerous sexual woman, in the *femme fatale*, La Belle Dame Sans Merci, or of her contrastive type, 'The Angel in the House'.

For both types, love and marriage, seduction and adultery were the principal plot paradigms. The typical situations (which are repeated in most works discussed in the present volume) find women waiting for their lives to be filled by love and marriage, or experiencing the destruction of their sanity or their very being by seduction and betrayal. Women remain in these works as elsewhere in the century intimately aligned with the worlds of feeling and love. As Nancy K. Miller has argued, 'experience for women characters is still primarily tied to the erotic and the familial. The sexual *faux pas* is still a fatal step,'[14] as Zhukova's Baroness Reykhman, for example, will discover.

Rarely do women escape these discourses of sexuality and, consequently, a female *Bildungsroman* is a rarity for many reasons. (Gan's *A Futile Gift* and Dostoevsky's *Netochka Nezvanova* offer extremely different treatments of this difficult theme.) Women are partial creations, stereotypes, projections. Even when they do figure as the central protagonists (which is the case here in nearly all the stories by Gan, Zhukova and Odoevsky which I will be discussing), and are represented as characters rather than as mere images, their development is severely circumscribed. Only in Gan of the seven writers is there a real sense of possible lives for women beyond the patriarchal system. Dostoevsky's Netochka may have gone on to great things as an artist but the work remained unfinished. Indeed, it is curiously significant that both Gan's and Dostoevsky's attempts at a female *Bildungsroman* remained incomplete, even if for very different reasons. (Gan died and Dostoevsky was arrested, imprisoned and exiled.)

Central to all of this, and to my analyses of the fifteen works which follow, are of course, conceptions of gender. Many possible definitions and discourses now circulate around this term. My main debt in this area is to the work of Teresa de Lauretis, especially her 'Desire in Narrative', from which I derive my own title, and her later *Technologies of Gender*.[15] The single most important theme of the present book is that for me, as for de Lauretis, narrative is one such 'technology of gender'. But how should we see gender, in the light of her deeply important work?

De Lauretis begins her lead article 'The Technology of Gender'[16] with a number of propositions. The most important for me are as follows:

(1) Gender is (a) representation – which is not to say that it does not have concrete or real implications, both social and subjective, for the material life of individuals. On the contrary, (2) The representation of gender *is* its construction – and in the simplest sense it can be said that all of Western Art and high culture is the engraving of the history of that construction.[17]

In other words, gender should not be considered something a male or female person is born with, but rather a construct that is absorbed *subjectively* in the process of socialisation. This absorption is achieved, maintained and perpetuated by means of what Althusser terms the 'ideological state apparati' or, as de Lauretis herself will term them, the 'technologies of gender'. Narrative, simple story-telling (or 'all of Western art and high culture') is one such technology and one of my central projects in the following pages (as it was in *Women in Russian Literature*) will be to attempt to show how gender is inscribed in and by the architectonics of plot and in and by the representation of male and female characters. Implicit in my argument will be the proposition that gender is *the* organising principle or discourse of narrative fiction. The texts, to use Foucault's phrase, are 'saturated with sexuality'.[18]

Probably central to de Lauretis's argumentation (and to mine) is the notion that gender is not only a construct but a *relational* term: 'Gender is the representation of a relation'.[19] Moreover, she argues, this relation speaks to and derives from, 'political and economic factors in each society'. The materialism (some would say determinism) of de Lauretis is important in that some practitioners of gender analysis (feminist or not) tend to take a rather a-historical, essentialist view of gender, which leads to reductionism. It is always important to locate a particular relational representation of gender in the specific historical and cultural environment which produced this representation. Thus, the iconography of femininity to which I return time and again in the following pages should be seen as the product of a particular moment in the development of Russian literature (late Romanticism/early Realism). In locating it (or any such instance) in all its specificity, we also learn more about the more general evolution of modes of representation in Russian culture: it is a two-way process. To return to de Lauretis's discussion, we should recognise that 'The sex-gender system, in short, is both a socio-cultural construct and a semiotic apparatus, a system of representation which assigns meaning . . . to individuals within the society'.[20] In this sense, and returning to Althusser, the sex-gender system is precisely part of the ideology of a given society and, thus, representations of gender relations are (or certainly can be) an 'ideological state apparatus'.[21] Consequently 'Gender has the function (which defines it) of constituting concrete individuals as men and women.'[22] And this also is a two-way process in that this function 'applies both to fictional men and women' and to the 'real' men and women who read (and are formed by) these representations.

From a feminist perspective, these propositions are not neutral or value-free. Given the relational nature of gender, femininity is not an essentialist term but rather a contrast to masculinity, which invariably is valorised, and consequently femininity is denigrated. Masculinity is the given or norm, while femininity is constructed as other, or Other, even if some radical feminist theorists stand these propositions on their head.[23] De Lauretis encapsulates the tensions and contradictions of these constructs and I end this section with her words:

> This negativity of woman, her lacking or transcending the laws and processes of signification, has a counterpart, in poststructuralist psychoanalytic theory, in the notion of femininity as a privileged condition, a nearness to nature, the body, the side of the maternal, or the unconscious. However, we are cautioned, this femininity is purely a representation, a positionality within the phallic model of desire and signification; it is not a quality or property of women . . . in the phallic order of patriarchal culture and in its theory, woman is unrepresentable except as representation.[24]

And this is why so many of the images of women that I will be discussing are not representations of characters but a series of imbricated and irreconcilable images, pure representation, even pure sign.[25]

Given the relationality of gender which de Lauretis so convincingly argues for, it is clearly important in any discussion of gender to consider both polarities, the images of masculinity as well as of femininity. To a certain extent my earlier *Women in Russian Literature* touched upon masculinity, but in the present volume this aspect of representation will be much more of a constant. The images of masculinity which I will be discussing are much the same as those I have already sketched in my consideration of Pushkin's ground-laying work in his Southern Poems. The Old Man of *The Gipsies* is followed by the eponymous Baron Reykhman and, even more directly, by

Dr Krupov in *Who Is To Blame?* while Efimov in *Netochka Nezvanova* is a fascinating portrait of the abuses made in the name of the Father. The educated, but ineffective young Russian of Pushkin's Southern Poems was, of course, to have many heirs, most notably Pushkin's own Onegin and Lermontov's Pechorin. Beltov is the most notable superfluous man dealt with here while the rake's economy finds expression in Anatoly in Gan's *The Ideal*, in Zhukova's *Dacha* and Odoevsky's *Princess Zizi*. In terms of images of femininity, the passionate heroines (Zemfira and Zarema) are followed in different guises by Princess Zizi herself and Zoya (again in *Dacha*). The innocent, persecuted heroine (a type which, of course, predates Pushkin's Mariya) receives many treatments in the period: versions of this type are Zizi and Zoya (already we see imbrication at work), as well as Olympia in Gan's *The Locket*. A particularly striking aspect of all these heroines as well as many others (indeed, nearly *all* the heroines) is the physical iconography, denoting spiritual torment, which is attached to them, almost indiscriminately. Indeed, one could argue that such iconography is the *dominanta* of femininity in this period:[26] to be female is to suffer, to be vulnerable.

New images also make their appearance. The issue of female power is treated both negatively and positively. The destructive force of gossip[27] finds its fullest expression in Princess Mimi and *Society's Judgement* but we also see it as a background theme in *Who Is To Blame?* Not surprisingly, perhaps, the two female authors considered depict the theme of the creative woman most fully although her position is seen as deeply problematical: Gan's *Society's Judgement* and *A Futile Gift* are especially important in this regard. Zenaida and Anyuta (the respective heroines of these two works) could also be seen as adumbrations of a type that was to find full expression only twenty years later, namely, the 'new woman'. Lyubov Krutsiferskaya in *Who Is To Blame?* is a fuller rendition of this theme, although, like many other heroines, she bears traces of other types and, indeed, has her fair share of dysphoric iconography.

What unifies all these fifteen works with the exception of *A Futile Gift* is the thematics of plot. As already noted, love and marriage were virtually the only possible plot lines in this period, and the absence of this plot is one of the aspects of *A Futile Gift* which make it such a remarkable, innovatory work. *Netochka Nezvanova* is also something of an exception, although even here the politics of romance are a vital ingredient, even if treated in a highly individual light.

As is implied in all these remarks, my approach to the fifteen works to be analysed is largely oriented towards discussions of, to use traditional terminology, character and plot. The methodology employed is much the same as in *Women in Russian Literature* and is a (highly) modified version of that originally compiled by Michael O' Toole, which in turn goes back to that of the Russian Formalists.[28] On this occasion, the method is even further refined, so that I usually deal only with setting, plot and character (under the guise of male and female images). As before, I have not sought to discuss the theoretical implications of such a method, but have rather used these categories as useful tools of analysis, to help me unpack the relationship between gender and narrative and narrative and desire.

I concluded the Introduction to *Women in Russian Literature* by noting that

> very regrettably[,] there is a marked dearth of feminist analysis of Russian literature, for political reasons perhaps in the Soviet Union, and for slightly less apparent reasons in the West.[29]

Since I wrote those words in 1986 the political situation has, of course, seen a change of seismic dimensions in the 'Soviet Union' and both there and in the West feminist analysis is very much on the agenda, so that the last few years have witnessed a welter of interesting work, conferences and debates, especially in America, and the future for feminist Slavic studies now looks very promising. There is much to look forward to, both in the discovery of women writers who have been, like Gan and Zhukova, 'hidden from history' and in the development of new approaches.

Indeed, there are many individuals and organisations to which I am indebted for assistance in the preparation of this book. Two periods of research leave from Keele University have enabled me to begin, and now to end this work; Mercia Publications gave me a generous award to assist me in my researches, as did the British Academy. On a personal level Stephanie Sandler, Cathy Popkin, Barbara Heldt, and Neil Cornwell have all shown great support, advice and encouragement, while Catriona Kelly has been particularly helpful. In a different way I am very indebted to Alison Roscow. Above all others I must thank Barbara Andrew, without whose unfailing support, encouragement, advice and enthusiasm my life and work would be very much the poorer.

2
Pushkin's Southern Poems

The main focus of the present volume is prose literature of the 1830s and 1840s. Pushkin's Southern Poems, therefore, stand apart from the main body of the book, as they are, of course, poetic in form and because they appeared about ten years before the period concerned. A consideration of them, however, provides a good prelude to the main discussion. As Stephanie Sandler argues 'These are stories of sexual involvement, extended anecdotes about coupling and separation'.[1] In other words, at the very beginning of his artistic maturation (and, therefore, at the inception of modern Russian literature proper), Pushkin placed issues of gender at the centre of his preoccupations. These three works, then, can be seen as a meditation on sexual relations which led into the central issues of *Evgeny Onegin* which, in turn, exerted a profound influence on the literature of the 1830s.

1. *THE PRISONER OF THE CAUCASUS* (1822)

The first dozen lines of the poem proper (after the Dedication)[2] depict off-duty Circassian braves reminiscing about military exploits, their houses and the like, and conclude with the lines

> [They remember . . .]
> As well the caresses of black-eyed captive women.
>
> (1.56)

I shall begin my discussion of Pushkin's first Southern Poem with an attempt to decode the paradoxes and contradictions of this line, which are symptomatic of the work as a whole, before outlining the theoretical and methodological underpinnings of my overall analysis.

As an instance of the somewhat periphrastic language that Pushkin increasingly eschewed after the Southern Poems 'caresses' may be read as a rather coy poeticism, a euphemism for sexual favours: moreover, it implies that these are voluntary on the part of the unnamed women. The next word, however, forms an oxymoron and thereby contradicts the voluntary element in the caresses. If the women are 'captives' the giving of their favours is surely forced: there is at least a suggestion of rape.[3] 'Black-eyed' is a recurrent epithet of the Southern Poems, applied to both Zarema (in *The Fountain of Bakhchisaray*) and Zemfira (in *The Gipsies*), and is a motif which is borrowed from Byron's Eastern Poems.[4] These captive women are therefore delineated as stereotyped instances of the Eastern/Southern beauty, noted for their passionate eroticism. Consequently, women are introduced into the text as enthusiastic recipients of male pleasure, which is simultaneously forced upon them. Women are presented as existing for the violent pleasure of men, although, in a coded form, it is suggested that they enjoy this. This line, then sets the scene for the sexual politics of the work, and, consequently, the dysphoric resolution of the love plot is immediately pre-determined.

That domination is a central theme of the poem has already been demonstrated by Stephanie Sandler. In the present section I will seek to make a number of similar (as well as different) points about the poem, but starting from a rather different perspective. My approach will be mainly in terms of plot typologies and is based on the work of Lotman (who in turn derives, in this instance, from Propp) and feminist reworkings of his arguments by Teresa de Lauretis.[5]

In his article 'The Origin of Plot in the Light of Typology' Lotman outlines the central features of narrative, many of which are exactly applicable to the characters and plot-lines of *The Prisoner of the Caucasus*. Lotman sees characters typologically as either 'mobile' or 'immobile':

> It is not difficult to notice that characters can be divided into those who are mobile, who enjoy freedom with regard to plot-space, who can change their place in the structure of the artistic world and cross the frontier, the basic typological feature of this space, and those who are immobile who represent, in fact, a function of this space.[6]

He then goes on to refine this typology to an even simpler and more fundamental model:

The elementary sequence of events in myth can be reduced to a chain: entry into closed space – emergence from it (this chain is open at both ends and can be endlessly multiplied). Inasmuch as closed space can be interpreted as 'a cave', 'the grave', 'a house', *'woman'* [my italics] (and, correspondingly, be allotted the features of darkness, warmth, dampness) . . ., entry into it is interpreted on various levels as 'death', 'conception', 'return home' and so on; moreover all these acts are thought of as mutually identical. The birth – resurrection consequent upon death – conception is linked with the fact that birth is thought of not as the act of the emergence of a new, previously non-existent personality, but *as the renewal of one which has already existed* [my italics].[7]

Apart from the inclusion of 'woman' in the interchangeable list above, Lotman does not really approach this typology in terms of gender. Later in the article, however, he does move closer to the gender implications of his own argument, in regarding 'death – sexual relations – re-birth' as 'the most archaic mythological complex'.[8]

If Lotman largely ignores gender in his argument, the implications for a feminist analysis are brilliantly developed by Teresa de Lauretis in her seminal paper 'Desire in Narrative', and later work. In her view 'the connection between narrative and the Oedipus, desire and narrative . . . appears to be incontestable'.[9] In asking what is the *purpose* (and effect) of narrative (or rather narrativity) she proceeds to argue that, in narrative, the subject is engaged in 'certain positionalities of meaning and desire'.[10] Whose desire can be said to speak in narrative; to what extent can the work of narrative be seen to be the mapping of differences, especially sexual differences? In the end, is the main function (or, at least, effect) of narrative, therefore, to establish and codify gender?

In response to these questions I would endorse de Lauretis's proposition that the kernel of narrativity can be construed to be a reformulation of Freud's celebrated question about women: 'what does a woman want?' becomes 'what is femininity – for men?'.[11] And, indeed, this question is precisely the one which provides the impulse for narrative, and is one of the questions answered by the text of *The Prisoner of the Caucasus*.[12] It is at this stage of her argument that de Lauretis moves to her perceptive and highly persuasive rereading (and rewriting) of Lotman to establish the role allotted typologically to female and male characters in underlying narrative structures and models. Women, as Lotman has noted, are interchangeable, synonymous with the 'cave', the 'grave' and so on, and are, generally speaking, merely inscribed in hero narratives, places and topoi through which the hero and plot move to accomplish meaning; they are obstacles (or Donors[13]) in the path of the questing hero, to be slain and/or defeated (The Sphinx, Medusa). In reverse, of course, narrative typically, or rather typologically, concerns male destiny, the process of quest for a truly human (*that is* male) identity. Indeed, returning once more to Lotman, de Lauretis argues that the hero *must* be (at least morphologically) male, because the space, the obstacle is morphologically female:

> the mythical subject [,] is constructed as human being and as male; he is the active principle of culture, the establisher of distinction, the creator of differences. Female is what is not susceptible to transformation, to life or death; she (it) is an element of sub-space, a topos, a resistance, matrix and matter.[14]

De Lauretis does not leave it at that, however. Insistently and persuasively she returns to the quotation with which her article opens to argue that the formulation by Lotman, of 'entry into closed space – emergence from it' conceals another, rather darker proposition about the establishment of difference that is the work of narrative. Laura Mulvey has argued that 'Sadism demands a story, depends on making something happen, forcing a change in another person, a battle of will and strength, victory/defeat, all occurring in a linear time with a beginning and an end'.[15] For de Lauretis this proposition is remarkably similar to common definitions of narrative. Indeed, the opening words can be reversed, so that we read '*Story demands sadism*', and the rest. And, of course, given the preceding argument concerning the inherent maleness of the narrative process, typologically the change forced will be in a woman; narrative tells of her defeat, his victory. This paradigm can be applied to *The Prisoner of the Caucasus* and, with variations, to the other Southern Poems.[16]

In terms of gender, these propositions have profound implications, given that narrative can be viewed, as I have already argued in Chapter 1, as one of the 'technologies of gender'.[17] De Lauretis regards gender as a prime instance of Althusserian ideology, and, in extending Foucault's proposition that sexuality is produced by discourse, she applies his argument to gender (a category, as de Lauretis convincingly argues, that Foucault generally overlooked, if not dismissed). Gender, she maintains, is a relational term: it represents 'not an individual but a relation, and a social relation'.[18] Moreover, female sexuality/gender is invariably constructed as *other*,[19] 'both in contrast and in relation to the male'.[20] Consequently, femininity is not a biological or in any other way an inherent quality, rather it is 'purely a representation, a positionality within the phallic model of desire and signification'.[21]

Bearing all these propositions in mind we may return to the concluding sentence of Yury Lotman's article, which reads: 'By creating plot-texts, man [sic] learnt to distinguish plots in life and thus to make sense of life'.[22] My project, in the ensuing discussion of *The Prisoner of the Caucasus* (and the other Southern Poems) is to rephrase this statement in the following terms: *by analysing plot-texts we understand how narrative constructs and defines desire and constitutes gender.*

Like the other two Southern Poems *The Prisoner of the Caucasus* concerns itself centrally with sexual involvement[23] and sexual identity, or gender, and the relative roles and narrative expectations of the male and female characters. In the present work the expectations and, especially, the plot-resolution is sharply differentiated in terms of gender, along lines which conform, remarkably precisely, with Lotman's typology. Before examining the narrative and plot structures, however, I begin the central sections of my analysis with a consideration of gender as it is constructed in the work.

1.1 Images of Women

I look first at femininity, recalling Sandler's remark 'That women enter the narrative as captured cannot be unimportant'.[24] Equally significant, however, is the fact that this reference to 'captive women' is one of the very few to women (other than the Circassian Woman) in the text, which is androcentric to a profound degree. There is, for example, only one reference in the text to family life in the village where The Prisoner is held. This is the 'peaceful family' (1.352) to which the lone Circassian returns to rest between his heroic military exploits. No mention is made of a wife, sister, daughter: by implication, women do not really exist in this military patriarchy or, at least, they are not worth mentioning.[25] Almost the only other reference to women in general is the 'young maidens' (1.603) who sing their song near the end of the poem proper.

In general terms, then, women are engendered as 'captive' 'maidens' or as absent even from that most feminine of locations, the domestic interior. The Circassian woman, who, like her male counterpart, The Prisoner, remains unnamed is, then, the only female character,[26] although 'character' is a rather misleading concept to use, given that she, like many of the heroines of Russian Romanticism, is rather a collocation of imbricated images and projections of male fantasy.[27]

Her appearance in the text (ll.157ff.) presents her as 'immediately a wonderfully nurturing figure',[28] in returning to life the corpse-like Russian, by her offer of *kumys*. This image, however, presents the first paradox connected with her. On the one hand, the offer of fermented mare's milk denotes her as 'well within the most universal of all feminine stereotypes, the provider of life, the mother figure'.[29] On the other hand, however, this equine association links her inextricably with the surrounding military patriarchy by which, as we shall see in more detail later, she is both defined and circumscribed.

Other paradoxes and clashing stereotypes emerge almost immediately. Anticipating Zarema and Zemfira and, harking back to the Byronic tradition, the Circassian woman is portrayed as deeply sexual,[30] and this is a motif that is to be intensified as the narrative unfolds, gradually accruing other implications. In her first appearance, when she revivifies the 'dead' Prisoner, he notices, amongst other things 'the fire of her cheeks' (l.173), surely another euphemism, this time for sexual passion. Assuming this to be so, the Circassian woman is depicted as *already* sexual and aroused, even *before* their encounter. She is ready, without any overture from him. As their 'love' develops, the motif of self-willed abandonment to sexual ecstasy deepens. Part II of the poem opens with the narrator addressing her. He notes:

> When your friend in nocturnal darkness
> Kissed you with a mute kiss,
> Burning with languor and desire,
> You forgot the earthly world . . . .

(ll.419–22)[31]

Now, as their passion is (or already has been) fulfilled, her sexual energy becomes her predominant (although still not only) characteristic: she forgets the 'earthly world' for her 'desire'.

In this she can be seen as Byronic, in two rather different ways. On the one hand, as already noted, she conforms to the convention of the 'Southern/Eastern' beauty of Byron's works, and anticipates Zarema and Zemfira. Equally, this links her, at least by implication, to the 'black-eyed women captives' and, by further implication, her 'caresses' have the same status. Later she is to develop features more normally associated with the Byronic male.[32] John Bayley has noted, in connection with *The Gipsies*, that 'It is Zemfira and not Aleko who has the qualities of will, determination and ruthless style'.[33] Similar comments could be made about the Circassian woman. It is she who initiates the action, both in coming to the Prisoner in the first place, and offering him her desire, and later she is the agent of his liberation. We see her as self-uttering and, for a moment at least, as self-determining, primarily in the conversation between the two at the opening of Part II. Once more she comes to him and declares herself:

> Love me; til now no-one
> Has kissed my eyes; . . .
> . . . .
> I am renowned as a cruel maid,
> As a pitiless beauty.
>
> (ll.429–35)

For a brief time, then, she is able to speak of herself, with 'will' and 'determination' and indeed with pride. But several caveats need to be made. She is, of course, rejected and this leads to her suicide. Even now (l.441) she talks of suicide, because she is fully aware that there can be no place for female desire in her patriarchal milieu: her father and brother are preparing to sell her.[34] Her desire must either submit to men's desire, or else she must kill herself. So, the fact that she does make all the running and utter her own desire is, in the end, irrelevant and futile. Furthermore, on a more general level, this desire can be seen as a mere projection of male desire, the European male fantasy of the willing 'black-eyed' maiden of exotic climes. In this sense, her words and behaviour do not exceed the boundaries of another stereotype – the willing whore.

The paradoxical imbrication of diametrically opposed stereotypes in her portrait are especially apparent in the area of her sexuality. Not only is the Circassian woman 'mother' and 'whore' she is also, and simultaneously, 'virgin'[35] and 'child'. On her first appearance (and persistently thereafter) she is referred to as 'deva' (maid) (l.160); and then as *'young maid'* (l.171). Later the narrator makes explicit these themes:

> For the first time with her *virginal* soul
> She loved. . . .
>
> (ll.211–12)

The Prisoner, however, is unable to respond to her *'Infantile* love' (l.216). An address from the narrator to 'maid of the mountains' (l.415) opens Part II. A further initial motif adds another level to the powerlessness and vulnerability suggested by her *'childish virginity'*. When they first meet the narrative draws attention to her mutism.[36] She stands before him 'With a tender and mute welcome' (l.158); then, she offers him the cup 'with a quiet hand' (l.167). Her silence (later to be replaced, as Sandler has noted,[37] by a rather miraculous fluency in emotionally expressive Russian) emphasises both her function as an emblematic symbol (to which I shall return) and her *powerlessness*. All these motifs – her youth, her virginity, her initial speechlessness – can be conflated into the stereotype of 'victim'. Certainly, her submissiveness, already noted by Sandler,[38] is a constant refrain in her character and in her behaviour. This is apparent even when she appears at her most self-determined and self-defining. As she tells him of her virginity and of her reputation as a 'cruel beauty' she addresses him as 'tsar of my soul' (l.428). Even when she performs her act of 'heroism' in freeing him, she, for the third time, is at his feet (see ll.165, 551 and 656). This is characteristic of the work's whole approach to her. Not only does the narrative pile one incompatible stereotype on another; it is also duplicitous in that it seemingly portrays her as strong and noble, while simultaneously undercutting this impression, by providing an exactly opposing value, either explicitly or by implication. She is a whore while she is a virgin, a mother while a child, speechless and then fluent, heroic while on her knees. Consequently, the overall impression is of profound instability.

This impression is exacerbated by other motifs. The nocturnal visit was one of the topoi that Pushkin borrowed from Byron and was to use in all his Southern Poems.[39] That the Circassian woman visits the Prisoner at night is also conditioned by questions of realism and verisimilitude. (She could hardly have sawn off his chains in broad daylight.) Yet the fact that we see her exclusively as a 'creature of the night' inevitably shapes our perception of her. She is associated with 'dark' forces – dangerous sexuality and the irrational. This latter motif is drawn out by the Circassian woman herself in terms that anticipate Tatyana's letter and Tamara's enthralment by Lermontov's Demon.[40] She concludes her first speech to him (ll.423–45) with the words:

> By an incomprehensible, wonderful force
> I am completely drawn to you;
> I love you, dear captive,
> My soul is intoxicated with you. . . .

(ll.442–5)

Her 'love' for him is, then, *not* a feature of her will or desire: she is the passive recipient, or victim of seemingly supernatural forces beyond her control.

Thus far I have considered the Circassian woman as conforming to fairly universal stereotypes, as well as noting the more immediate Byronic antecedents. There are other literary forces at work, however, in the mélange of her characterisation. John Bayley notes:

> Though the Circassian maid is outwardly the sloe-eyed beauty of modern romance, she is really a sister of the white muslined ladies who haunt the eighteenth-century novel of sentiment.[41]

Indeed, almost from the outset many of the motifs attached to the Circassian woman conform to the sentimentalist iconography which runs through Russian literature from Karamzin to Turgenev.[42] At the first, mute encounter, she sits 'pensive' (l.185); she tries to speak but fails and rather:

> She was *sighing*, and more than once
> Her eyes filled with *tears*.

(ll.190–1)

This iconographic, paradigmatic behaviour of pensive sitting (or kneeling), sighs and tears is especially apparent in Part II where the woman adopts the same mechanistic (and, in the end, rather comical) poses of the typical abandoned or rejected heroine. This emotionalism is, indeed, particularly marked when the Prisoner rejects her. She sits 'sobbing without tears' (l.516); 'Pale as a shadow, she trembled' (l.520); her hand is cold. She now manages to speak, but then collapses, swooning:

> Tears and groans
> Restricted the poor maid's breast.
> Her lips without words murmured reproaches.
> Without feeling, embracing his knees,
> She could barely breathe.
>
> (ll.548–52)

Similar motifs are picked up when she returns to liberate him, by which time her image has crystallised more or less completely into that of the typical sentimental heroine. She is 'sad and pale' (l.639) – for all her military accoutrements. Even as she saws away at his chains (with a 'shaking hand' (l.655), she sheds 'An involuntary tear' (l.658) and sets him free with 'an insane look' (l.661).

What, then, are we to make of all this image-making? Perhaps that is, indeed, the central point. Stephanie Sandler has suggested that this is 'perhaps [Pushkin's] only poem in which a woman of passion, rather than of character, appears'.[43] Yet, 'passion' is insufficient, even if 'character' is too much. The Circassian woman cannot be termed a 'character', but 'passion' is only one of half a dozen motifs which do not blend but contradict each other. As a result, her image is constantly shifting and unstable. Earlier Sandler had spoken of 'a massive externalisation of the Captive's values'[44] in the poem. I would suggest that the Circassian woman is a product of his values only rather partially. Rather she should be seen as an instance of male wish-fulfilment. The various males implicated – Pushkin, Raevsky (to whom the poem is dedicated), the narrator, the Prisoner and the implied male reader – all five male gazes penetrate the image of the Circassian woman. Indirectly, at least, all ask of her image 'what is femininity?' And the answer seems to be 'everything', but, really this 'everything' amounts to 'nothing'.[45] She is Mother, child, virgin, whore, victim and so on. But, in the end, she is rarely herself, and remains at the level of a projection of male fantasy, a blank screen onto which anything may be projected.

1.2 Images of Men

If female gender is depicted as contradictory, unstable and impossible to pin down, then in *The Prisoner of the Caucasus* male images are much more unitary and, in more than one sense as a result, phallic. This can immediately be seen in considering the work's point of view.[46] As Sandler has noted, Pushkin's narrative poems 'ask[ing] us to reflect on who controls the plot, who speaks with authority, who listens in silence and rage'.[47] For the most part, in the present work, the woman's voice, while not actually silenced (as is Mariya's in *The Fountain of Bakhchisaray*), struggles to be heard within an extremely androcentric discourse and narrative world. The work begins, of course, with a dedication to Nikolai Raevsky and these first 43 lines have a powerful determining effect on the themes and values of the rest of the poem. It becomes a kind of gift to Pushkin's friend, so that the tale of the Circassian woman is 'positioned so as to facilitate an exchange between men'.[48] Pushkin addresses his (now distant) friend in terms of quasi-erotic intimacy: 'I rested in my heart – we loved one another' (l.11),[49] while thanking him for the 'peace' he had found with Raevsky during times of 'the heavy dream of love' (ll.8–10).

Consequently, male bonding is immediately established as the norm, the *given*.[50] However, it is not only the love of two close male friends that is celebrated in the work: male-bonding is seen as the norm on a more general level. The Dedication ends with the lines:

> I waited light-heartedly for better days;
> And the happiness of *my friends*
> Was a consolation for me.
>
> (ll.41–3, my italics).

By implication, Raevsky is only one of such men. Equally these lines suggest that the work has implied *male* addresses. Consequently, we the readers are positioned in a certain discourse – of phallic desire. Moreover, we are overlooked in the act of looking[51] and the ensuing narrative has to be read against this androcentric and phallic positionality.

The opening lines of Part I immediately reinforce these emphases as we are introduced to the Circassian warriors at rest: the first thirteen lines concern themselves with men at leisure discussing their exploits with other men. The first six lines read:

> In the *aul*, on their doorsteps,
> The idle Circassians sit.
> The sons of the Caucasus speak
> Of military, fateful alarms,
> Of the beauty of their steeds,
> Of the pleasures of wild languor.
>
> (ll.44–9)

The Homerically entitled men (Sons of the Caucasus) recall their military exploits, the beauty of their horses, and then the pleasures of 'wild languor' (force implied again). It is significant that it is in *that* order, because these lines establish exactly the hierarchy of their values. First comes killing other men, then their love for their horses, and only then women, who as already discussed, are forced into sexual pleasure. As we already know, almost all the Circassians in this particular locale are men and 'battle is practically the only activity that engages these men'.[52]

This is especially apparent in the long digression which occupies the latter stages of Part I. Running from l.267 to the end of the Part (l.414), it occupies almost 150 lines, that is, about one fifth of the entire work, and concerns itself with various aspects of war. It acts as (literally) the centre-piece of the poem, and so the values of this military (or, rather, militaristic) patriarchy are placed at the very centre of the work. Given Pushkin's celebrated care over formal matters, this cannot be an accident. Indeed, the structural significance and centrality of this section is emphasised by the fact that the narrative begins and ends with military motifs, which are echoed in the Epilogue. The beginning, middle and end of the work, then, do not merely focus on a world almost exclusively of men, but on men who find pleasure in killing other men and in forcing 'captive women' into 'wild languor'. In both these activities they are, of course, engaged in 'forcing a change in another'.

Certain motifs in this digression need particular emphasis. While eschewing the company of women, these soldiers do have valued companions, namely, animals[53] and weapons. The 'beauty of horses' had already been noted: this value is taken up in the description of the activities of the lone Circassian:

> His wealth is his ardent steed,
> The scion of mountain herds,
> His *faithful, patient comrade*.
>
> (ll.296–8 my italics)

Indeed, a four-legged friend will never let you down.[54] Even more striking, however, is the loving, detailed attention paid to his weaponry:

> He has armour, arquebus, quiver,
> A Kuban bow, knife, lasso
> And a sabre, the eternal [female] friend
> Of his labours, of his leisure.
>
> (ll.287–90)

Seven different accoutrements, most of them lethal, are itemised. Most significant is the 'sabre' which is his 'eternal female friend'.[55] Once more women are set aside, but here with an added irony in that the phallic sword is the true [female] companion for this man. Death, or sadism, is thus the *dominanta* of the setting as well as the narrative proper. Indeed, military activity permeates almost everything in the poem. After the brief domestic interior to which I have already referred, the narrator announces

> But monotonous peace is tedious
> For hearts, born for war.
>
> (ll.380–1)

Peace is monotonous, the military ethos is innate and the games of the young men which are now described degenerate into violence,[56] culminating in the gruesome lines:

> And the heads of slaves fly in the dust,
> And the boys clap with joy.
>
> (ll.386–7)

Severed heads bring joy to the (*male*) children. Thus, indeed, sadistic violence is the mark of masculinity and it is all-encompassing. The death of the Circassian woman can be seen as being pre-determined in this world where women, and still more their desire, have no place.

By virtue of the plot, and, of course, his nationality, the Russian Prisoner would seem to be set apart from this world. 'The Circassians find him incomprehensible', as Sandler notes.[57] His flight from society, his egoism, his alienation, his 'premature senility'[58] and other Byronic qualities all seem to differentiate him from the stereotypical men of war. Equally, he is clearly differentiated from the Circassian woman, in characterological terms, in that we enter his inner life much more than hers and he is clearly the centre of the narrative focus: the work is androcentric in this as well. However, later developments reveal that we should also regard the Prisoner as very much akin to the men of the Circassian village.[59] As he observes the lone Circassian, and the gruesome games of decapitation, we are told that he watches indifferently. However, in the past things had been different:

> Formerly he had loved the games of glory
> And had burned with a fateful thirst.
> . . . .
> *Hard, cold* at duels,
> Facing the fateful lead.
>
> (ll.390–5, my italics)

He had been, and perhaps still is, as much in love with death and killing as the other men. He is, at least as regards his past, engendered as male by his hardness and coldness. For him, too, women are to be eschewed and this, of course, is to have lethal consequences for the Circassian virgin. We should also note that the Circassians admire his 'boldness', even if they do not understand him:

> The awesome Circassians wondered at
> His carefree bravery.
>
> (ll.410–11)

They recognise him as a man like themselves, it would seem.

As the narrative ends the Prisoner leaves this cruel world and recalls what he has experienced there. No mention is made of the woman,[60] but he does recall the 'stern Circassian' (1.708). Just as the poem had begun with one man (Pushkin) recalling another now distant male, it is fitting and significant that the narrative should end in similar terms, emphasising the clear parallels drawn between the Prisoner and the Circassian man. Moreover, the final lines of Part II add a reworking of the military theme, linking it yet again to death:

> And already before him in the mists
> The Russian *bayonets* glinted,
> And on the *funeral mounds*[61] called to each other
> The Cossacks on watch.
>
> (ll.714–17, my italics)

The Epilogue sets the seal on the theme of men at war, death and violation.[62] This final section opens with a seemingly innocuous, rather laboured set of poetic clichés:

> So the Muse, the light friend of Dream,
> Flew to the limits of Asia
> And to make a crown for herself ripped off
> The wild flowers of the Caucasus.
>
> (ll.718–21)

The implications of these lines, however, add yet another echo of the poem's themes. We should note the violence of the verb 'ripped off'[63] and the euphemism of 'flowers'. The Muse itself, or rather the poetic project, acts violently, destroying innocence for its [her?] own pleasure. Flowers stand not only for innocence of Nature, I would argue, but for women.[64] Their death echoes that of the Circassian woman.

Throughout the Epilogue the emphasis is once more on military motifs and also on the harshness of the maiden's lot in this milieu. Having herself torn up the Caucasian flowers the Muse:

> And to the songs of *orphaned maids*
> She listened there.
>
> (ll.728–9, my italics)

The Epilogue ends with the seemingly inevitable subjugation of the Caucasus. History, like any story, 'demands sadism, depends on making something happen, forcing a change in another'. From first to last, men are valorised and men are engendered as violent killers of other men, and of violent aggressors towards 'captive women', or 'wild flowers'.

This harsh differentiation of the genders is a central feature of the work's discourse. Even more centrally, however, it is the essence of the narrative. I now return to my initial theoretical remarks to argue that the plot of *The Prisoner of the Caucasus* matches very closely those typological models, according to which 'the hero must be male . . . because the obstacle . . . is morphologically female'.

1.3 Plot

That the narrative will be androcentric is at least implied in the work's title, while the second word, 'Prisoner' suggests the basic plot typology of a man's entry into enclosed space, to be followed by his emergence from it, reborn. Indeed, as we shall see, the narrative does involve precisely his symbolic death, entry into the grave and his rebirth, while the woman is identified with the space. He is to be the active, mobile actant-subject, she the immobile actant-object.

The plot commences with his arrival in the Circassian village as a prisoner. Both protagonists are to remain nameless, which universalises the situation, suggesting the very folk-tale/mythic world with which Lotman is concerned. Accordingly, the plot and the functions of the two protagonists are rendered abstract. The opening sections of the narrative are also very evocative of the sadistic nature of narrative which Mulvey and de Lauretis have indicated. The pleasures of 'the caresses of black-eyed captive women' (l.56) and 'wild languor' (l.49) have already been noted. These motifs are taken up and reworked in the introduction of the Prisoner to the village:

> He *dragged in the prisoner*.
> 'Here's a Russian!' *the plunderer yelled*.
> The aul ran round at his cry
> In an *embittered* crowd.
>
> (ll.61–4, my italics)

The scene is thus set as a battle-ground of wills. The Prisoner is initially both the victim of this narrative sadism, and the hero whose 'death' acts as the starting-point of the typological plot. The first forty or so lines (of Part I) are peppered with motifs of harshness and cruelty, enacted by men, against both 'captive women' and the captive man.

As the half-dead Russian begins to revive, much attention is paid to the setting in which he finds himself and, significantly, this is frequently described in feminine terms. Even before the Circassian woman appears the 'space' which he has entered, and with which she will be identified, *of* which she is, is seen as female space. He looks around

> He sees: above him rose
> The massif [*gromada*] of the inaccessible mountains [*gor*].

(ll.181–2, my italics)

Shortly afterwards further feminine nouns are enumerated to describe the space: *ograda* [boundary] (l.83) and *priroda* [nature] (l.90), and then others. Female spaces thus act as markers of his destiny. He has left one female space (*Rossiya*), which has led to his death; he now enters another to begin the process of resurrection/rebirth. Given the typological identification of 'cave', 'house', and 'woman', it is clearly important that the setting be marked primarily as female. Space is female and the female character will be merely (in typological terms) a function of this space.

In the flash-back to the Prisoner's past which now follows (the pre-prologue) we are told that he had fled home

> And had flown to a distant land
> With the happy spectre of freedom.

(ll.124–5)

He had left his original space specifically to enter on a *quest* (significantly, for a feminine value (*svoboda* [freedom]), but, as yet, his quest remains a failure. 'He is a slave' of l.138 repeats the same sentence of l.92. His capture thus represents a 'descent into the world beyond the grave',[65] while the repetition also can be seen as an early plot rhyme, suggesting once more the ritualistic nature of the narrative. That is, to use Lotman's terminology, his leaving his own world signifies his death to that world 'the end of the *first* life':[66] now he has died a second time. The thanatognomic implications of his plot are made explicit:

> He waits, with the gloomy dusk,
> For the flame of sad life to go out,
> And thirsts for the canopy of the grave.
>
> (ll.139–41)

As Lotman puts it: 'the end of childhood . . . is marked by a constantly increasing attraction to death, a conscious breaking of the ties linking the hero to the world'.[67]

Once more the setting echoes the plot: the Prisoner's spiritual death is noted by the narrator, and now the sun sets. Night equals death, and as he enters the underworld he encounters the spirit who will save him and in this context too it is highly significant that the Circassian woman now comes to him at night. Her first actions immediately, in plot terms, establish her as a Donor, bringing her maternal gift of mare's milk. But other motifs also emerge in this initial encounter, symbols that are deeply rooted in the Christian tradition (although, presumably, she is a Moslem!) and which are difficult to decode fully. At this stage they cannot understand each other's language:

> But her sweet gaze, the fire of her cheeks,
> But the tender voice says:
> Live! and the prisoner comes to life.
>
> (ll.173–5)

These lines confirm her symbolically revivifying function, but also suggest a Christian miracle. Like Lazarus, the prisoner rises from the dead: he is reborn by the agency of the Virgin Mother and, at least indirectly, her milk. The Christian connotation is taken up when he finally sups of the milk:

> He half gets up – and with the *beneficent cup*
> He slaked his parching thirst.
>
> (ll.178–9, my italics)

The clear allusion in these lines is to the Christian Eucharist. Taking all these inferences together we have a rather bizarre collocation of images. The virgin, who is also a nurturing mother, kneels before her 'son' (a kind of pietà), offers him her milk, which is also the Eucharist, and in the process he is 'miraculously' reborn. Moreover, bearing in mind what is later to happen, the Mother has to die so that he may rise again. In the end, I find it impossible to discern any logic to this imagery: it is as paradoxical as much else to do with the engendering processes of the work. What does emerge, however, is the *functionality* of the Circassian woman and also the fact that her function is polyvalent, although not consistent.

The Prisoner's rebirth is not yet accomplished, however, and he remains in the grave:

> The moist coolness of the *cave*
> Hides him during the summer heat.
>
> (ll.195–6, my italics)

The Circassian woman's role as (Christian) Donor is also repeated: she brings him

> Kumys, and the fragrant honeycomb
> And the snow-white millet.
>
> (ll.200–2)

Bread and wine, milk and honey: the references could not really be any clearer.

Having established their functions in the plot, however, the narrative as such now breaks off, as much of the rest of Part I is taken up by the extended digression on local life already referred to. This has a double function. In narrative terms it is a 'retardation device'. That is, once the complication has been entered into, the peripeteia is postponed, the delay having the same titillating effect that Lermontov was to offer his male readers of *Bela*.[68] Equally, given the subject-matter of this digression (militarism), the love-plot, which concerns a woman, is down-graded. By implication, at least, in the narrative structure as well as in the actual milieu, women have little importance.

Part II provides the dénouement and resolution and the eventual resurrection of the 'dead' hero. After the initial address by the narrator to the 'maid of the mountains', this Part opens with her speech to the Prisoner, offering herself to him. In so doing, and in recognising the risks she takes she 'resist[s] confinement in that symbolic space by disturbing it, perverting it, making trouble, seeking to exceed the boundary'.[69] The Prisoner, however, refuses her offer and his refusal, in plot terms, can be seen as pre-determined.[70] She, as the 'personified obstacle' *must* be slain and/or defeated so that he can accomplish his destiny. That is, given the mythic typology which is, in my view, so central to this particular plot, the Prisoner *must be reborn*. In other words, her self-uttering desire is a test, to qualify him as a hero.[71] If he had accepted her passion he would have become part of her story, remained within her space, would not have re-emerged from the enclosed space, would not have left the grave to be reborn. In reverse, her story 'like any other story, is a question of his desire'.[72] She is awakened to desire in encountering him, but, as for many other heroines, to awaken to sexuality is to begin to die. As Elaine Showalter puts it, in words which could have been written for this story:

> To waken from the drugged pleasant sleep of Victorian womanhood was agonising; in fiction it is much more likely *to end in drowning than in discovery* . . . [heroines] wake to worlds which offer no places for the women they wish to become; and rather than struggling they die. Female suffering thus becomes a kind of literary commodity which both men and women consume.[73] (My italics)

In his reply to the Circassian woman, the Prisoner signals his own basic plot typology: 'I have died for happiness' (l.478), while adding a modish necrophiliac frisson to this:

> How grievous it is with dead lips
> To respond to living kisses.
>
> (ll.482–3)

In this speech, he claims that he will die far from home, forgotten by the world, but he has not yet given up hope of returning to life: 'he thirsts for freedom' (l.575). On some level he is aware that to live he must escape, that is, emerge from the space and be reborn.

In terms of the overall value system of the work it is significant and fitting that the dénouement is occasioned by the onset of renewed military action which allows the Circassian woman the opportunity to set him free. She returns for her final nocturnal visit as if dressed for war.[74] Indeed, it is arguable that she could just have easily killed him, with 'her steel dagger' (1.646). Such an action would, however, have thwarted two different plot expectations. He would not have been reborn, and, in more Sentimentalist terms, the suffering heroine might not have slain herself. Indeed, her death is, in typological terms, a pre-condition of his rebirth.[75] This implication is finally made explicit in their passionate farewell. She refuses his offer to flee with him and:

> He stretched out his arms to the Circassian
> He flew to her with his *resurrected* heart,
> And a long kiss of parting
> Sealed the union of love.
>
> (ll.681–4, my italics)

And so, he swims back across the river, to be reborn, while the Sentimental maiden, echoing Poor Liza amongst many others, accomplishes her own destiny.

As Sandler has put it, 'Pushkin's narrative poems from the years of exile explore sexual themes, but always within a vocabulary of domination and defeat'.[76] For Sandler, the Circassian woman's 'fate has all along been determined by his [the Prisoner's] egoism'.[77] I would see it rather differently. Her fate is, indeed, determined, or rather pre-determined, on the one hand, by the harsh exclusion of women from a thoroughly masculinised world, and, on the other, by the underlying plot typology, according to which the 'hero must be male' and where this particular 'story demands sadism'. His victory demands her defeat, her death is a pre-condition of his re-birth.

2. THE FOUNTAIN OF BAKHCHISARAY[78]

2.1 Plot

Fountain can be seen to be comprised of four separate plot-lines: all four involve sadism, in line with de Lauretis's formulation. In the pre-prologue (which is recounted in the main body of the text by Zarema) Girey had abducted the then Christian princess Zarema, who had turned both to Islam and to 'love'. In the prologue, Girey had abducted a second Christian Princess, Mariya, who proves less willing to make the transition from emblematic virginity. The peripeteia is formed by Zarema's murder of Mariya, while the dénouement is the death of Zarema, at the behest of Girey. These four plots form a ritualistic symmetrical pattern, framed by Girey's violation of Zarema, with Mariya the recipient of violence in the intervening pair of plots. In all four the actant-subject is either actually male (Girey) or morphologically so (Zarema),[79] while the actant-object is always female. This symmetry and parallelism endows the basic plots and their narrative structure with a ritualistic, almost mythical paradigm, which can be, seemingly, endlessly repeated.[80] *Fountain*, then, can be seen to operate on the boundaries of Lotman's two basic typologies, of myth-narration and plot narration, each of which, in this instance at least, demands sadism. The universality of the *poema's* plots is suggested by other mechanisms as well. For example, we are told that the ubiquitous Eunuch, acting like Argus or Foucault's panopticon[81] establishes

> An *eternal* order. The Khan's will
> Is his only law;
> The holy precept of The Koran
> He observes on watch.
>
> (ll.64–7, my italics)

The pattern of the story becomes universalised: the basic, universalised paradigm is of sadism against the actant-object, which is, paradigmatically, female. The 'eternal order', ratified by Islamic Holy Writ, is that women shall be enslaved to 'love', killed and, more generally dehumanised.

These paradigms ensure also that female desire in the narrative is suppressed. If women do dare to desire, as the collectivity of the harem does not,

> No, Girey's timid wives
> Not daring to desire, nor to think,
> Bloom in despondent silence [.]
>
> (ll.33–5)

they are punished for it. Mariya desires to remain Christian and Virgin; Zarema desires to be a slave to love, but both die as a direct consequence of these opposite desires. Against the background of the wives' perfect thraldom two rebellions occur, one passive, one active, but both lead to death. The only role allowed female actants is to enact male narrative desire: if this is thwarted they are physically removed from the text. In short, whether women listen to male narrative demands and determination or not, they end up dead.

That female desire will be punished by the narrative strategies of the *poema* is clear from the exposition. The first ten lines contain an emphatic demonstration of female servitude and potential male violence and ultimate vengeance:

> The *servile* court *silently*
> Crowded around the *terrible* Khan.
> All was *quiet* in the palace;
> *In reverence*, everyone read
> The signs of *anger* and *sorrow*
> On his *gloomy* face.
> But the *haughty sovereign*
> *Waved his impatient hand:*
> And all, *bowing, go forth*.
>
> (ll.3–11, my italics)

The reader realises that such an opening allows for no happy endings: that is, what befalls Mariya and Zarema is predetermined, indeed, overdetermined. The rest of the exposition, which occupies about one quarter of the *poema*, reinforces this impression. The scenes of harem life emphasise the enforced idleness of the young wives, their slavery. Force, or sadism, is the *dominanta* in their lot. The Eunch watches all: even their dreams are not free:

> And woe to her whose sleepy whisper
> Called another's name.
>
> (ll.98–9)

As we later see, the euphemistic 'woe' is synonymous with the ultimate sadism, death. Women cannot escape male violence, even in sleep.

The 'eternal order' of the harem has, however, been disrupted, as we finally move into the diegetic present. A 'Polish princess' has been introduced to the harem: from the outset, her plot-line follows the pre-established pattern of abduction and eventual 'seduction' or 'consent' to femininity. Moreover, she has been propelled into this enslavement by yet another instance of male violence, in that her capture had been in time of war, which in turn had deprived her of her patriarch's protection:

> The father is in the grave, the daughter in captivity.
>
> (l.208)[82]

Her pre-prologue had already been detailed and, significantly, it is almost entirely in terms of her Oedipal preparation for her eventual submission to a feminine destiny:[83]

> Only one care he knew:
> . . . .
> That even when married she
> Would remember with tender emotion
> Her time as a maid.
>
> (ll.169–76)

Once in the diegetic present of the harem Mariya disrupts the 'eternal order': she is treated with special fastidiousness because, in terms of male narrative desire, she *is* special. She, as her name betokens, is a, or one might say, *the* Virgin. Her depiction certainly lays great stress on this attribute and it is to have dramatic, indeed, tragic consequences. The Virgin will be killed, admittedly by another woman, no longer a virgin, who not only acts as morphologically male, but is also propelled by male desire.

Before the peripeteia and dénouement, however, Mariya's special qualities are such that all the usual 'strict laws' are suspended. Stern Girey fears to trouble her, while the Eunch does not watch over her. Her virginity, therefore, is not only highlighted, but valorised. In the end, however, even this supreme value will prove insufficient to save her from the narrative's sadism. Indeed, the violent death of the Virgin, which is commemorated in the monument which provides the *poema's* title, is to be the supreme narrative moment.

The agent of her death is merely *morphologically* male. Zarema, in terms of the Romantic duality of the *poema* is a contrastive type,[84] yet their plots have several significant similarities. This in turn tends to universalise the narrative yet further. Although Zarema appears relatively early in the *poema's* diegetic present (ll.131ff.) her real entry into the plot is on the fateful night that she and Mariya are to die:[85] in terms of the chronotope of the work her presence, while dramatic, is short-lived. Just as she had been initially chosen from a crowd of women by Girey (ll.373ff.) her brief participation as an actant-subject is clearly marked: 'All the wives sleep. One does not sleep' (l.297). She is set apart from the other women not only by having been chosen as a favourite by Girey, but by her desire to remain such. Her desire is to generate the remaining, climactic part of the narrative, but her desire is clearly constituted by Girey, that is by her desire to be his love object.

It is interesting that her unbroken monologue to Mariya is the only significant utterance by any character in the work, yet it is largely in terms of how she had first been 'seduced' and then 'consented' to male desire and hence, male definitions of femininity. She, like Mariya, is afforded an Oedipal past.[86] Also like Mariya, she had been a Christian princess and had been abducted to the harem. But unlike Mariya she had willingly, obediently anticipated her 'seduction':

> I in peaceful silence
> In the shade of the harem blossomed
> And the first experience of *love*
> I waited with an *obedient* heart.
> My secret *desires*
> Came true.
>
> (ll.364–9, my italics)

There are a number of significant details. She had awaited 'love' (a euphemism in the context of enslavement) with an 'obedient heart'. Not only had she consented to male desire, but she herself had desired this. Since her 'desires came true' she had remained happy, before Mariya's arrival, of course. In short, her plot and especially this Oedipal past, can be seen as a male fantasy: she had been a virgin who had not only consented but had desired to be a whore.

Zarema speaks on for 79 lines. She is clearly a self-uttering subject at this point. Equally clearly, she is not self-determining as her desires and actions are located within the discourse of male desire. In the end she *becomes*, at least morphologically, male in her murder of the less compliant virgin, significantly with the phallic knife. However, in the context of this narrative, to act as male is insufficient as Zarema also pays with her life.

It is also of interest that the central, indeed, the only dramatic interchange in the work is between two women. Yet, although Zarema recognises that 'it is not your fault' (l.391) there can be no question of 'sisterly' feelings between the two women.[87] In an economy of male desire women tend to be deadly rivals. That the *poema* is, indeed, constructed primarily in terms of male desire is echoed in the epilogue to the work. Here the narrator visits the now-abandoned harem and evokes the twin female ghosts, the 'pure soul' (l.543) of Mariya and Zarema, 'breathing jealousy' (l.545). Even after death the two women are defined in terms of their polarised sexuality.

Given that the four plots, the prologues, the main action and the epilogue are all constituted by male desire (whether of the character of Girey, the narrator, or, indeed, the reader) it is hardly surprising that, by contrast, female desire is both disruptive and, ultimately, destructive.[88] Mariya, by withholding her consent to femininity (though remaining archetypally feminine in another way) disrupts the mutuality of Girey and Zarema, while Zarema's dramatic intervention leads to two deaths, the closure of the harem (with unknown cost to the other wives) and to Girey's bathetic return to war, that is, to the perpetuation of the scenes of devastation which had surrounded Mariya's abduction. In the broader context of the *poema*, female desire not only causes the peripeteia, but is genuinely catastrophic. Mariya and Zarema together threaten to disturb the patriarchal order of the text, and, by implication, the narrative order. Indeed, one may take this a stage further, to suggest that *to disturb the patriarchal order is to disturb narrative*, and *vice versa*.

Perhaps the most remarkable aspect of *The Fountain of Bakhchisaray* in the present context is that the work appears to be concerned with *female* sexuality, desire and destiny, while it is actually constructed by *male* desire and presence. Girey himself may cut a pathetic and bathetic figure, but his desire, coupled with that of the narrator and reader, as well as the omnipresence of the eunuch, control all aspects of the narrative. He begins and ends all narrative lines, both within and beyond the diegetic frame. It can be argued, then, that the work creates two polarised female types, the Virgin and the whore, suppresses the desire of both, thereby valorising the desire of the male, even though the male character, Girey, remains at a bathetically emblematic level.

In these terms, it is important to return to the four *dramatis personae* of the *poema*, Girey, the eunuch and the two women, to assess their respective roles in the narrative process.

2.2 Images of Men

That Girey is to control all narrative processes and all desire is signalled by the opening of the *poema*. His name is the first word and 'Alone', referring to him, stands at the head of line 12. This famous, iconic opening description is reprised later (ll.102ff.) to emphasise his lowering presence. His plot partially re-enacts Lotman's typology of 'death – sexual relations – rebirth'.[89] When he does return to war his drooping phallic sabre strikes another note: the Stern Father has been unmanned by 'love'. In this rebirth, Girey fulfils yet another typological narrative function in that women are encountered by the questing male hero as obstacles, who 'must be slain or defeated so that he can go forward to fulfil his destiny – and his story'.[90] In the end, Mariya and Zarema are, indeed, merely obstacles in Girey's story and both are slain.

The unnamed Eunuch plays an equally important part in the text's extirpation of female desire. He is perfectly suited for this role in the sense that he himself is deprived of all desire, and so is free of 'temptation' and can resist the 'dangerous' wiles of the 'deceitful' wives. Moreover, because he intermittently reappears, including on the fateful night, he becomes the embodiment of the 'eternal order' which controls women. Indeed, the text makes explicit this function:

> Women's nature is known to him;
> He has experienced how cunning it is
> Both in freedom and captivity:
> The tender gaze, the mute reproach of tears
> Have no power over his soul;
> He no longer trusts them.
>
> (ll.74–9)

Because he cannot be deceived, female sexuality, which like the unconscious (and the two are closely connected), threatens constantly to return to disturb the 'eternal [patriarchal] order', can be suppressed by him. As we have noted, the women cannot escape his watchful gaze even when asleep. At *no time* can women be free as

> His jealous gaze and ear
> Follow them *at all hours*.
>
> (ll.61–2, my italics)

The Eunuch's is not the only male gaze which surveys the women. Behind him stands Girey and the 'eternal order' of Islam, and patriarchy more generally. But the narrator and reader are also implicated in this process. The opening quarter of the *poema* details the wives' daily round in the harem and we are invited to gaze on 'seductive', quasi-pornographic scenes of the 'young captive women' (l.81) bathing as a 'Naked swarm of charmers' (l.87). As is often the case in the literature of the period, women's bodies are displayed to the admiring male gaze.

The point of view (in the literal as well as literary sense) is clearly male throughout the text. Furthermore, this voice often speaks duplicitously. This duplicity is perhaps most evident in the 'Tartar Song', sung by 'the *entire* harem (l.122, my italics), which acclaims Girey more blessed than a Hadji, because he loves Zarema. The women sing to praise 'love' in the harem, although this 'love' is merely yet another instance of the sadism of the narrative. Women are slaves, yet they sing joyfully of this enslavement. Indeed, as we have already seen, Zarema recalls her own violation fondly.

Women, then, in the harem are usually silenced. When they do speak, as in their song or in Zarema's monologue, the female utterance is a form of ventriloquism. In reverse, Mariya utters only one and a half lines (ll.342–3), so that her inner life[91] is mediated through the desire and voice of the male narrator. The narrator is specifically male and he not only tells us the tale, but enters it twice. He seems to be present on the fateful night ('I hear' – l.255) and so his account of these events has the frisson of immediacy and voyeurism.[92] When he returns to visit the now deserted harem he identifies himself with the view of women expressed in the main body of the text, recalling 'a just as sweet glance' (l.547) and the torments his former love had caused him. Finally, the addressee of the *poema* is also explicitly male, as well as implicitly so: 'Whose shade, O friends, did I see?' (l.539). In sum, then, it can be argued that on every level the narrative is constructed by and for the male perspective, despite the fact that the two central actants are female.

2.3 Images of Women

Indeed in turning to the representation of the female character in the *poema*, the first point to be reiterated is the extent to which the text seeks to silence women. As we have already seen, the opening lines emphasise, *inter alia* the absence of the female voice ('silently' 'quietly'). This note is taken up again in the general description of life in the harem (ll.33ff.) – 'They bloom in despondent silence' (l.35). Moreover, by virtue of their situation, the women of the harem are persistently characterised by their enslavement. In this, as in other respects, the harem can be seen as the perfect paradigm of patriarchy. From the 'servile court' of line 3, the submissiveness and actual imprisonment of the women is reiterated, in such recurrent terms as 'female captives' (l.119). Another *topos* of the characterisation of this female collective is their youth: all the women of the *poema* are referred to as 'young wives' (l.51), or as the doubly subordinated 'young captive women' (l.81). They are observed at their leisure, watching the fish swimming with 'childish joy'.[93] By their age, by their captivity and by their functionality all women are subordinated to and defined by the male desire which permeates the work. This is seen at the very end of the work as well as in the exposition. After Girey has returned to war, 'the wives grow old'. Without his desire, women cease to have any meaning and the Sleeping Beauty theme becomes inverted.

The two principal female *dramatis personae* Zarema and Mariya first emerge as contrastive types, both physically and characterologically,[94] although they have at least as much in common: for Bayley they are 'twin foci of nostalgic and erotic reverie'.[95] It should be noted, as Zhirmunsky has done, that they are more realistic portraits than their Byronic prototypes,[96] and a large part of this greater realism is occasioned by the attention given to their past lives. However, as Bayley notes, they both exist *only* in terms of the past (which is specifically Oedipal in both cases, as noted earlier). In the diegetic present their only function is to exist for, and to excite male desire.

Zarema emerges from the collective background first. In many respects she can also be traced to the Byronic prototype of the dark Eastern (in this case Southern) beauty.[97] Yet, as we have seen, this beauty is also purely functional, once more in terms of the demands of male desire – that of Girey, but also the narrator and reader. She is the 'star of love, the adornment of the harem' (l.136). As she herself puts it 'But I was born for passion' (l.395). That is, she is a focus of 'erotic reverie' precisely because she is the self-uttering, compliant slave to male desire, the Whore incarnate, with an 'enterprising animal nature'.[98] Moreover, although she stands out from the other wives, she shares the *topoi* of their characterisation, in that she is young and a slave. Onto these common characteristics is imbricated another stereotype of post-Sentimentalist literature, in that Zarema is also a suffering victim: indeed, this is the first iconic image we receive of her:

> Alas, sad and pale,
> She does not hear the praises.
> Like a palm, crushed by the storm,
> She bowed her young head.
>
> (ll.137–40)

Mariya shares many of these features, which, in her case, make her the perfect, almost entirely mute victim. She too is young, a slave and defined by male desire: the only major contrast with Zarema is the classic one of hair colour in that Mariya is fair. Like Zarema, she is further presented as a Sentimentalist icon of vulnerability and suffering:

> Fading in *quiet captivity*,
> Mariya *weeps* and *is sad*.
> Girey spares the *unhappy one:*
> Her *despondency, tears, groans*
> Alarm the Khan's brief sleep.
>
> (ll.214–18, my italics)

Zarema had once been a Christian Virgin. As we know, she had willingly forsaken both these values for 'love'. Mariya, however, refuses so to do and in her brief narrative life great stress is put on her holiness and purity. Her virginity is valorised within the narrative, as we have seen, and it is remarked upon incessantly by the narrator. Her very name, of course, suggests that she may be a reincarnation of *the* Virgin and this resonance echoes throughout the rest of the text. After the 'strict laws' (1.220) of the harem have been softened for her, it is thought that 'someone unearthly' (1.234) has descended to inhabit this world of luxuriant sensuousness:

> There day and night the icon-lamp burns
> Before the visage of the *most holy maiden.*
>
> (ll.235–6, my italics)

Explicitly, then, she is 'the most holy maiden', and later, this holiness is reiterated in the formulae 'strict holy object' (1.246) and 'divine feeling' (1.251). Her identification with all that is pure and holy (and the two are virtually synonymous) is complete when Zarema enters Mariya's cell:

> The lonely light of the *icon lamp,*
> *The icon case,* sadly illuminated,
> *The meek visage of the most pure maiden*
> And *the cross, the sacred symbol of love.*
>
> (ll.312–15, my italics)

This repeated, even repetitive and tautological emphasis on Mariya's holy purity, that is, her Virginity is not accidental. Mariya is fair, young, enslaved, suffering and supremely pure, the very essence of untouched, intact female sexuality. Moreover, it is her death which forms the climactic peripeteia of the narrative, leading to Zarema's death, Girey's 'rebirth' in war and the abandonment of all the other wives. Her death is immortalised in the fountain which provides the work with its title. Although the text decorously refuses to depict her actual slaying, its central event can be seen as a reenactment of Edgar Allan Poe's dictum 'The death of a beautiful woman is the most poetical topic'.

Indeed, it can be further suggested that *The Fountain of Bakhchisaray* is a perfect exemplar of narrative sadism. The death of the Virgin is the fulfilment of male narrative desire. Returning to the narrative typologies developed by de Lauretis we can conclude by proposing that not only does a story demand sadism, but that this sadism involves the violation of the woman and that the typological paradigm of this is the death of the Virgin.

3. THE GIPSIES[99]

Like the other two Southern Poems *The Gipsies* concerns itself centrally with issues of personal freedom, sexual identity, or gender, and the relative roles and narrative expectations of male and female characters. Indeed, 'what is femininity – for men?' forms the kernel questions of the extended debate between the two principal male *dramatis personae*, the Old Man and Aleko, and so it is appropriate to begin an analysis of the work with a discussion of the female type within the work, as embodied in the heroine Zemfira.

3.1 Images of Women

Critical discussions of the poem have had little to say about Zemfira. Fennell speaks of her 'highly-strung, passionate nature', and sums her up as a 'primitive, instinctive child of nature'.[100] Instructively, he also notes that, implicitly at least, he follows Pushkin in his reticence to comment on Zemfira in that the author 'seems to have given it [Zemfira's language] as little thought as he gave the delineation of her physical appearance or character'.[101] As is well known, Pushkin's 'Southern Poems' were modelled on Byron's 'Eastern Poems' and Zhirmunsky's seminal work on the subject draws our attention to Zemfira's ancestors among the Lord's 'eastern beauties' with their sloe-eyes and dark curls, while noting that Zemfira is of more independent dramatic interest than her predecessors.[102] John Bayley takes up this point and adds an interesting development: 'In *The Gipsies* the Byronic male becomes the female . . . It is Zemfira and not Aleko who has the qualities of will, determination and ruthless style'.[103] In other terms, his argument is that Zemfira should be construed as *morphologically* male: as we will see, this is true, but only up to a point.

In the poem itself Zemfira is introduced specifically within a patriarchal context: she is first mentioned as the 'young daughter' (1.31) of the Old Man. Immediately, that is, she is placed in an Oedipal context, which is soon emphasised by the first interchange of the drama: '"My father", the maiden says', (1.42). Simultaneously, ('maiden') she is en-gendered in terms of male desire, as the available virgin. The narrative discourse concentrates on her sexualisation throughout this introductory section. As the Old Man awaits her return, the narrator notes that 'She has grown accustomed to playful freedom' (1.33) which implies sexual availability, certainly so in terms of the work's frame of reference. Indeed, Zemfira, however 'independent', or 'male' she may seem to some critics is persistently sexualised. On the morning after she has introduced Aleko to the Gipsy community they are awoken by her father with words 'Leave, children, your couch of bliss' (1.72):[104] Zemfira has initiated the sexual liaison, as the Byronic hero, as morphologically male, but, equally, her sexuality is and remains her *only* commodity: her sexual freedom *is* her gender. As noted in the critical literature, the only physical description of her is the cliché 'black-eyed Zemfira' (1.98).[105] In the Byronic context, of course, this is not a neutral epithet. Zemfira is instantly categorised as the *type* of Eastern/Southern beauty, that is, the woman of passion, that is the woman who is defined by male desire – that of the male narrator and (male) reader. That Zemfira and her engendering have little significance beyond her sexuality is further emphasised by the 'little attention' paid to her language and, indeed, by the little she has to say. Her only significant dialogue (with Aleko) comes in their discussion of what he has left behind in the 'civilised' world to join the 'poor sons of nature'. Her commentary on urban life denotes merely vain materialism, vacuous consumerism (see ll.164–7).

By contrast, it is the male characters, The Old Man and Aleko, whose voices are privileged in the text. They are hardly characterised physically at all, but their speech dominates the text, while Aleko's alienation (eventually double alienation) forms the work's apparent central concern, at least in terms of the traditional critical view.[106] It is in a discussion of the poem's point of view that we see the contrastive discursive engendering particularly clearly.

3.2 Point of View

As Fennell notes 'Four basic "voices" can be heard: those of the "objective [male] narrator", the Old Man, Aleko and Zemfira'.[107] Of these, the two dominant ones are the first two: indeed they are the closest to each other, in the sense that the Old Man is virtually the 'mouthpiece' for the narrator.[108] As the work progresses these three male voices contend for centre-stage, while Zemfira is rarely heard. After the introductory section we are led into Aleko's inner world in the 'Little Bird of God' digression (ll.104–19). This passage along with the ensuing interpretation of it (ll.120–45) may contain much melodramatic cliché and artificial rhetoric, but at least an attempt is made to understand the alienated hero's psyche.[109] That is, the male is engendered by complex language, metaphysical anguish and poetic tropes. Zemfira immediately re-appears but, as we have already noted, she has little to say beyond acting as an interlocutor and her views are banal. Her voice is engendered by its 'uncomplicated sentence structure' and general lack of sophistication.[110] Throughout the woman struggles to be heard within and against the prevailing male discourse: the narrator and his text effectively silence her, before Aleko's narrative sadism will silence her forever. Significantly, her most famous utterance, the song announcing her infidelity is not even her own, but a quotation. Equally, the most important discussion of the poem, on how to deal with sexual love and infidelity, which occupies over one sixth of the text (ll.339–432), is conducted exclusively by the two men: indeed, Zemfira is not even present. The narrator's epilogue chooses to mention Mariula (Zemfira's mother) but Zemfira is excluded here as well. Aleko in his debate with the Old Man refers to her 'sweet babble' (l.366).[111] In terms of the work's discourse it should be said that the three male voices contain and control female desire (as it is expressed in language), which only spasmodically irrupts when the narrator condescends to her (childish) babble. In *The Gipsies* language and discourse are deeply gender specific. This proposition applies *a fortiori* to the work's plot and narrative, to which I now turn.

3.3 Plot

As I have already noted, following Bayley, the narrative of the poem opens with Zemfira initiating the action. Immediately the question arises as to whether she can be considered the actant-subject (rather than actant-object[112]): is she morphologically male, does she 'force a change' in others (Aleko, the Old Man, the Young Gipsy) in the same way as her mother, Mariula had caused a change in the Old Man? Does her desire generate the plot? The opening section suggests that she should be so considered, although it should be equally remembered that the eventual effect of her desire will be to excite male narrative sadism, culminating in two deaths (her own and that of her lover) and the second alienation of Aleko. Indeed, there is another typology immediately at work. Although Zemfira introduces him to the Gipsy space, it is Aleko who enters this space, enters into sexual relations and eventually leaves this space (however unwillingly). The principal plot-line will be his and the story will tell of his human becoming.[113] Because he is the intruder, the stranger, he will be narratively constructed as the subject, while Zemfira will ultimately remain, explicitly so, part of the space he enters, and will be slain as an obstacle in Aleko's path to fulfilment.

Initially, however, Zemfira proudly engenders herself as the subject. Her opening speech features 'I' three times as she lays down the terms of her relationship. 'I bring a guest . . . I found him . . . I will be a friend to him' (ll.43–8). That is, she organises the plot and 'He will be mine' (l.63) reinforces his role as actant-object. But almost immediately he has been introduced to the space inhabited by Zemfira, Aleko becomes the central narrative focus for the narrator. As we know, one of the central questions of the work's discourse will be 'what is femininity – for men?': in narrative terms, the question is much more, 'what kind of man will Aleko become?' In the dysphoric tradition of much patriarchal literature, masculinity and femininity will prove to be incompatible. This is immediately emphasised by the increasing narrative silence surrounding Zemfira. In ll.94–145 the narrator, admittedly somewhat tortuously and rhetorically, investigates the new and old worlds cohabiting within Aleko: no mention is made of Zemfira. This passage does, however, strike important notes about narrative and desire. 'But, oh God! how the passions played/With his obedient soul' (ll.140–1): 'they will awake'; the narrator tells us a few lines later. In other words, the violent dénouement is effectively predetermined. The clear indication, moreover, is that it will be his desire ('passions') which will speak.

Now Zemfira re-appears for her first, and last, important discussion. Her views on city life are rejected by Aleko:

> And the maids . . . How you are better than them
> Even without expensive clothes
> Without pearls, without necklaces!
>
> (ll.170–2)

His desire, that is, seeks to define her femininity, as the unspoiled 'child of nature'. Moreover, he continues, his 'one wish' (l.174) is to share with her 'love, leisure/And voluntary exile'. Clearly he expects his desire to be observed. Moreover, when Zemfira expresses *her* desire to share his life no longer, his desire changes to narrative sadism.

The narrative now gathers pace as two years pass. 'Aleko is as free as they' (l.231) we learn. What freedom means in terms of masculinity becomes clear when Zemfira next appears, to sing her celebrated song. Significantly, her words locate her once more within the patriarchal tradition, in the sense that they are addressed to the 'Stern Father': 'Old husband, awesome husband' (1.260). In these terms Zemfira refuses to be the dutiful daughter. Her desire is to be free of the Oedipal context, to reject the patriarchs. For her attempt to 'violate the primordial order', she will be killed.

Zemfira, in her song, states quite unequivocally her desire to be free, her lack of fear: 'I am strong: I fear/Neither knife, nor fire' (ll.262–3). This eruption of female strength, the denial of dutiful daughterhood within patriarchy, the refusal to 'consent or [to] be seduced into consenting to femininity'[114] has a precedent in that Zemfira's song had been sung by her mother, Mariula, when she had rejected her 'old husband'. Quite explicitly both women reject the Father and this is why their desire is so threatening. The song does not merely reject, however: it taunts. Zemfira eulogises the youthfulness of her lover (later significantly called the Young Gipsy) and laughs at Aleko's 'grey hair' (1.283). Aleko's apparent agedness breaches realism (two years earlier he had been 'youth' – 1.40) but this solecism is required both to underscore the parallels with the Old Man and to emphasise the threat that female desire represents to the two fathers. Women's sexuality if expressed is so worrying because it cannot be controlled.

These implications are soon made explicit by the Old Man's commentary on the song and by his tale of Mariula's infidelity and departure. And, of course, we are to believe his reading of this interpolated text because his voice is valorised by its proximity to that of the omniscient narrator. Moreover, his commentary and his broader discussion with Aleko around the issues the song raises are clearly foregrounded narratively, as we have seen, by the dominant place it occupies, if only by its very length.

The discussion had been preceded by Zemfira declaring that Aleko's love had 'grown cold': 'I'm bored; my heart begs freedom' (ll.316–17). The nature of female freedom now receives a masculinist, and misogynist gloss. The Old Man attempts to console Aleko: 'Console yourself, friend: she is a child'. Aleko, the man, loves 'heavily', 'but the female heart [loves] jokingly'. The rhyme *ditya/shutya* (child/jokingly) emphasises the male definition of female desire. Zemfira is, as I have noted, absent from the text at this point. Nonetheless her desire is talked of only to be dismissed. Women, in the view of the privileged male voice, love almost at random. Freedom for them is irrational, irresponsible self-will: they are children who mouth 'sweet babbling' and they cannot be trusted. Their desire is therefore doubly dangerous and disruptive. Not only do they reject the 'old' Fathers, the Patriarchs; their desire is wild, random and uncontrollable like the moon,[115] pure id which must be repressed and extirpated by the representatives of the symbolic order.[116] Indeed, this is precisely what Aleko and the Old Man are about at this stage – attempting to wield and manipulate the symbolic code to control the irruption of the semiotic. But, of course, like the unconscious, female desire cannot be ultimately controlled: it will always return and this is why it is so disturbing and threatening.

Mariula's tale represents another variation on the same theme. The Old Man's introduction to it lends it the validity of ancient myth. We are not sure exactly how long ago this had happened. Zemfira is still his 'young daughter' at the opening of the story (fifteen or so?). She had been abandoned by her mother as a 'little daughter' (l.400), so we assume Mariula had left no more than a dozen or so years before. Realism is breached once more as the Old Man intones 'long, long ago' (l.374), but this second solecism has the effect of universalising the tale. In other words, by implication, throughout recorded history – or even before – women have been abandoning their 'old husbands' for younger men and leaving behind motherless children. The work does not discuss motherhood as such, but, given that both women abandon their offspring, women's desire is shown to be dangerous in yet another way. In seeking 'freedom' they reject not only their duty as daughters but equally as mothers. Desire disturbs ('violates') the most fundamental of 'natural' orders.

The Old Man (the Father) had since these distant days sought out no other woman. In so doing he rejects desire and his decision is clearly valorised. If 'youth is freer than a bird' (l.416) why try to control it? Aleko rejects this view and his chillingly vengeful speech (ll.420–32) makes explicit the nature of desire in the man who is not yet fully the Father. Aleko should, in this context, be seen as the more typical of the two male characters. In him the theme of narrative sadism receives full expression. He cannot control female desire, so he will kill the one who expresses this desire. He too universalises his story: 'I will not renounce my *rights*' (l.421 – my italics). The rights of man are to control female desire. Failing that, he will 'slay/defeat' the 'obstacle' in his path to becoming man.

We now encounter the Young Gipsy as the poem reaches its fatal conclusion. Like the Old Man and Aleko he too does not trust the woman, and joins those who 'throughout history . . . have knocked their heads against the riddle of femininity'.[117] 'She will deceive! She will not come!' (1.440) he exclaims. Thereby he shares the disturbing confusion that has beset the two 'old husbands': what *do* women want? The text has suggested an answer: they want to be as free as the moon, 'freer than a bird'. But this particular engendering of femininity leads to a cul-de-sac for both men and women. Lurking in this cul-de-sac is death, either literal mortality or death of love. The end-point of the plot is reached in the double murder committed by Aleko and the morbidity surrounding sexual love is heavily underscored by the other privileged male voice, the narrator. Zemfira had first met Aleko 'beyond a funeral mound' (1.43) and it is in the same grisly locale that she arranges her final tryst. The plot rhyme is insufficient for the narrator: to bring out the meaning of Zemfira's words in her (and Mariula's) song ('I die loving' (1.267)) he peppers the last 100 lines of the poem proper with the lexicon of death: 'funeral mound' (1.458), 'grave' (1.461), 'grave' (1.469), 'you will destroy' (1.473), 'by the grave' (1.477), 'I die' (1.480), 'you will kill' (1.481), 'murder' (1.487), 'die' (1.488), 'I will die loving' (1.488), and so on. (Eight more such terms in lines 492–504). This concentration of thanatognomic words leads to an inexorable conclusion. Love and death are intimately connected. The woman seeks to define herself in freedom: instead her desire leads to the grave. Men cannot understand female desire: they either avoid it (the Old Man) or kill it (Aleko). The primordial order of patriarchy cannot accommodate self-engendering female desire.

In some sense, *The Gipsies* is rightly considered the first major piece of Russian realism. As Fennell notes, it is the first 'problem piece' in Russian literature,[118] Pushkin's 'first truly polyphonic work'.[119] As Briggs observes, freedom is the main theme.[120] However, certainly within the framework of the present analysis, other issues appear rather more significant. Although, as Briggs again notes, the words for freedom occur with 'tedious regularity',[121] other themes are also emphasised. Indeed, contrary to the traditional view that the poem deals with the 'wild', 'exotic' gipsy life, there is a remarkable concentration on the prosaically familial, particularly in the prologue. Words like 'family', 'children' are repeated throughout this section, emphasising not so much the wildness of the gipsies, but rather their domesticity. This emphasis is important, as in the celebrated, lapidary opening sentence of *Anna Karenina*: 'All happy families are like one another, each unhappy family is unhappy in its own way'. The family is the opening theme of *The Gipsies* and the work provides an extended consideration of family relationships. More particularly, it seems to me, the poem discusses not freedom in a somewhat abstract, still less political, sense, but rather sexual freedom, and thereby sexual identity, or gender. From this discussion we derive two versions of masculinity and a more unitary view of femininity. The wise Father eschews desire and achieves tranquility; the immature son, not yet the Father, is subject to desire and refuses the free expression of female desire. We learn what women want – to be free to express desire, but their freedom is immature, irrational and irresponsible. Moreover, it is deeply threatening to patriarchy and so, ultimately, is rejected as beyond the bounds of civilisation.

3

V.F. Odoevsky and the Two Princesses

Ivan Turgenev's works, both at the time and since, have been regarded as amongst the first in Russian literature to present positive portraits of the 'strong heroine' or 'new woman'.[1] Closer examination, however, especially of the shorter works like *Asya*, *First Love* and *Spring Torrents*, particularly from a feminist perspective, reveals that much traditional misogyny remains in his writing and that, ultimately, his depiction of women is fundamentally ambivalent.[2] The Work of V.F. Odoevsky is a similar instance. Although he began publishing in the 1820s,[3] Odoevsky published his most significant works in the 1830s and early 1840s, that is, precisely at the same time as the first real emergence of women prose writers in any numbers, including Elen Gan and Mariya Zhukova.[4] Gan, Zhukova and other writers of the period began to formulate what later became known as the 'woman question',[5] a somewhat portmanteau term which covered in particular the lack of opportunities for women to find any sort of career and the problems of the 'marriage market', especially the arranged marriage. One issue which received an especially high prominence was that of women's education (or rather, the lack of it).

At first sight (or rather reading) V.F. Odoevsky would seem to be what we might call a sympathetic fellow traveller to writers like Gan and Zhukova. Many of his works offer considerations of the nature of gender definitions (*Tale of How it is Dangerous for Girls to Walk in a Crowd along Nevksy Prospekt* (1833), *The Salamander* (1841), *Katya, or The Story of a Young Ward* (1834) and others), and the works I will mainly be considering here, *Princess Mimi* (1834) and *Princess Zizi* (1836/9),[6] place, as their titles suggest,[7] female characters at the very centre of his fiction. As I will argue, however, the narratives concerning these two princesses, while dealing very directly and centrally with questions of gender and desire, ultimately reflect an androcentric ambivalence about the nature of womanhood. To throw this contention in sharper relief I will, in fact, begin my consideration of

Odoevsky's work with a discussion of *New Year* (1837), a tale in which, significantly, women play virtually no part whatsoever.

1. NEW YEAR

In the view of the foremost Western commentator on Odoevsky, Neil Cornwell, *New Year* is one of the writer's finest short works: 'This poignant story of lost ideals, wasted talent and the erosion of camaraderie is one of Odoevsky's best-executed short works.'[8] The story (or rather, series of scenes) is narrated by a proto-Turgenevan 'superfluous man' ('the notes of an idler' [35]). Although he plays no real role in the three New Year's Eves he depicts, it is he who organises and directs the text. In this sense, *New Year* can be viewed as a classic text of the school of lost illusions, the topos of a middle-aged man reflecting on the cherished *temps perdu* of his youth, thereby anticipating the narrators of *Asya* and *First Love*. Significantly, however, the present work differs from Turgenev's tales by the absence of erotic intrigue and of women more generally.

The work (which recounts first a lively New Year's Eve and then two much more down-beat gatherings) depicts a world where only men have any significant role. On the first occasion ('Act One'), we encounter a gathering of friends on the verge of manhood. All those present are male. Moreover, we are told, 'there were about twelve of us' (36), a clear reference to the Apostles, and the implications of this theme of discipleship, of going out into the world on a zealous mission will become clearer and grow in significance, albeit in an ironic key. As noted, no women are present at this first gathering: moreover, there is not even any reference to them, nor even to love. That is, by inference, women are not only of no importance, but also, in terms of the symbolic code, *non-existent*.

This first evening is deeply valorised, and so too is male camaraderie. The young men, who have just left university, are full of enthusiasm, joy and expectancy as they drink their wine, smoke their emblematic pipes[9] and shout their hurrahs at the midnight hour. All have bright hopes for their glorious futures, unsullied as yet by disappointments or worldly cares – or women. The first note that is struck is the intimacy that exists amongst these friends.[10] Act One opens with directly quoted conversation, conveying the light-hearted banter between the youths. Physical proximity and intimacy are also stressed ('on the Voltairean armchair alone, I think, three people were sitting!' (36) It is also a haven, a place of refuge for men before going out into the world, to encounter the inevitable disappointments – and women. Their discussions 'brought the comrades closer together in our small circle' (38), and this degree of affection, solidarity and intimacy will never be repeated. This is the finest of times, when men could be close to other men.

Although *New Year* may seem to be plot-less, merely a series of tableaux (or 'Acts'), certain structural motifs are important and lend the story a clear folkloric resonance. As already noted, there are twelve young men (Camelot as well as the New Testament), and 'we had all just left university' (36). That is, in Proppian terms, these heroes are about 'to leave home'. Symbolic birth, leaving 'an enclosed space'[11] is also hinted at: 'We had only just torn ourselves from our incarceration at school, we were just stepping out into the world: a wide road was opening before us' (37). This motif is later modulated in the discussion of the innocence (virginity) of these Camelotish young men: 'We trusted ourselves and others, for our thoughts were pure and our hearts knew no calculation' (39). Also important in terms of the work's structure is the space accorded to each of the three New Years: about four pages are devoted to the first, two to the second, and only one to the third, which exactly mirrors the diminishing *joie de vivre* of the story. By implication at least, to leave home, to leave the haven of all-male camaraderie, to enter the world and to encounter women is to slowly die.

Another important dimension of the first New Year is the emphasis given to literary matters: nearly two of the four pages in this section are given over to discussions about their aspirations towards this field, to literary quarrels and polemics. In Lacanian terms this world of the Word is engendered as male,[12] and for Odoevsky, too, the literary, the symbolic code is exclusively male (as I will argue with reference to *Princess Mimi*). A sub-theme within this literary section is that of artistic *squabbles*: in other words, then, to enter phallogocentric[13] culture is to leave the haven of male camaraderie to engage in competition with other men.

Certainly, there is some emphasis in all this on the naivety (as well as purity) of these young braves, on their silliness, but, overall, these first four pages ring with idealism, which is accorded an almost high-style rhetoric:

> Our conversation on New Year's Eve was full of this fiery, this animated, youthful life. – How many fine hopes! How many plans, intermingled with astute, attic epigrams against our persecutors! . . . (38)

Their flights of fancy soar away in majestic, rhetorical, ringing prose.

In nearly every respect, then, Act One can be considered an almost perfectly androcentric text, and one which, I believe, sheds an important light on Odoevsky's orientation in his other works. The first section ends with a brief coda, relating how the brotherhood remained intact over a number of years: 'For several years we were inseparable' (39). Their provisions and environment gradually improve but they deliberately seek to retain and preserve the innocence of this first night: 'but we, in honour of the old student life, got together in a simple fashion, in jackets, and in the old way shared our frank thoughts and feelings' (ibid.). Even though some have already embarked on their careers, and other have moved far away, there is still no mention of women, of love, of marriage. These will only appear in Act Two and will be equated with the collapse of the Ideal into the banal world of materiality.

There is, I think, a very revealing parallel to be drawn here with an almost exactly contemporary works, Gogol's *Mirgorod* of 1835, and especially with the longest tale from this cycle, *Taras Bulba*. The themes, although presented very differently by Gogol, are exactly the same – a nostalgic pæan to brotherhood; and a lament over the collapse of *tovarischchestvo* through the agency of women.[14] It is also interesting to note that Gan and Zhukova published their first works in the same year (1837) that Odoevsky's tale appeared: perhaps this lament for the passing of an exclusively male world should be read as a coded (or at least unconscious) reaction from this literary Prince to the incursion of somewhat plebeian authoresses.[15]

But to move to Act Two. Several more years have gone by when the narrator returns to Moscow, where he seeks out the centre of the brotherhood, Vyacheslav (in whose flat the earlier gatherings took place). Immediately, the change is marked, in that Vyacheslav now lives in the suburbs: the centre has collapsed, King Arthur has moved from his court to the chronotope of the quotidian. Here he is apprehended in a scene of complete domesticity, '*on his knees* before the cradle of a sleeping boy' (39 – my italics), and with a splendid wife. As we shall see, Vyacheslav is happy in his new milieu, but it is a lowering by comparison with the boisterous, gay scenes of Act One. Indeed, the narrowness of this new chronotope is immediately emphasised: the narrator is asked to talk in hushed tones (no hurrahs!) so as not awaken the sleeping boy. Another marked contrast is, of course, the presence of a woman, as well as the absence of any other 'comrades'. *Tovarischchestvo* has collapsed. The very first reference to a woman and child and, therefore, to sexual relations, signals not a rebirth but a decline, the end of the dream. Woman, therefore, is equated with loss.

To be sure, there is no overt (misogynistic) denigration of the domestic or familial, but the 'idler' continues to damn with faint praise: 'everything was thought of with English insight for *family, everyday life*' (40 – my italics). Thus, the collocation of 'family/everyday' invokes the absence of the exceptional, the Homeric. Finally, the boy sleeps soundly, Vyacheslav embraces the narrator and declares that they must celebrate New Year 'in the old way' (ibid.). But the ensuing scene only emphasises how much has changed, how much has been lost. Only three people are present (and only two 'comrades', of course), while, as they recall, in terms which evoke Pushkin's 'There Was a Time',[16] many of their comrades are already dead. And they talk in whispers, lest the child awake. Vyacheslav, the quasi-Homeric poet of Act One himself declares 'My time has passed': he has burned his poetry.

In the end, the narrator leaves early and between them they have drunk less than a quarter of a bottle of champagne: Vyacheslav 'as a family man, did not like to turn night into day' (41). Quite unequivocally, it seems to me, marriage (that is, sexual relations with a woman) is a kind of symbolic death. The role of the unnamed wife is, indeed, purely symbolic. Apart from the opening reference to her, no further mention is made, and she does not speak, but her silence, and the textual silence around her only go to highlight her functionality.

Act Three moves us from the elegiac to the bathetic, and there is now no trace whatsoever of *tovarishchestvo*. Vyacheslav no longer lives in Moscow but in P., a dull provincial town, which was fast becoming one of the key chrontopes of early Russian realism.[17] In one sense, Vyacheslav has clearly gone up in the world, but in terms of the ethos of *New Year*, brotherhood has not been so much lost, as banalised. He has only the most cursory of conversations with the narrator before dashing off to a bastardised form of *tovarishchestvo*, a game of whist. The final New Year gathering, then, is no gathering at all, as the narrator sits alone in his hotel room drinking seltzer water rather than champagne.

It would be an exaggeration to reduce the dynamics of the story to a simplistic equation of 'woman equals death'. The tale also touches upon the loss of ideals and of youth more generally, and the banalisation of ideals in everyday life. This said, however, it does remain the case that women and sexual relations do play a lapidary symbolic role in these processes and that the world that is valorised in Act One is one that is perfectly and hermetically androcentric.

2. PRINCESS MIMI

'*Princess Mimi* has claims to be considered Odoevsky's society tale *par excellence:* it is Odoevsky's most outspoken attack on the destructive, hypocritical and sterile aspects of *svetskaya zhizn'* . . .; furthermore it constitutes, in the person of its eponymous protagonist, Odoevsky's most serious attempt at psychological characterization.'[18] Given the centrality of the 'society tale' for an understanding of Russian fiction in the 1830s, *Princess Mimi* is clearly a work of some significance. Certainly, it can be read as an attack on the straitjackets in which women were placed (particularly by their education), but, at the same time it goes little further than stating the problems, while, in the central character, it offers the portrait of one of the most actively destructive female characters of the period.

2.1 Setting

Unlike his female contemporary, Gan, Odoevsky pays little attention to externals, but rather, like Zhukova, concentrates on the inner dimensions of his characters. Given this tendency, there is little actual description of the milieu in which his protagonists play out their limited lives. What there is, however, is highly emblematic.

Like most society tales, *Princess Mimi* makes prominent use of the chronotope of the society ball and, indeed, like a number of others, opens with this characteristic locus. This setting not merely introduces the reader to a particular place and time and to a given social stratum (the aristocracy), but also plays a determining function for the remainder of the story. If it can be argued that women are 'an equivalent more universal than money',[19] then the society ball is the chronotope of the period where this phenomenon is most clearly manifested. Women come here to be displayed, to be prepared for marriage ('exchange'). Indeed, one of Princess Mimi's problems as an older but unmarried woman is that she does not know where to stand at a ball. That is, as no longer deemed marriageable, and without the power a husband lends a woman she is, in terms of this literary sociolect, invisible.

As Cornwell has argued, *Princess Mimi* allows 'Odoevsky's ... ire [to] fall upon the usual social frivolities'[20] and this satirical purpose is also evident in his choice of opening setting, as it is throughout his handling of this structural dimension. What little we see of the externals of this society emphasises both the triviality of their occupations as well as the very *confined* spaces in which women lead their lives. During the opening ball scene we move to the 'gynocæum', a parodic 'women's room' where women go not to find a symbolic refuge but merely to check that they are still fit to be looked at. After the ball, Chapter Two is entitled 'The Round Table'. The irony of the Arthurian reference soon becomes apparent. Instead of a band of brave young knights (as in *New Year*), we encounter three women (Mimi, her widowed sister and mother) sitting at needlepoint, engaged in petty nastiness at each other's expense, as well as that of their acquaintance. Their extremely limited interaction is interrupted by the arrival of guests for another topos designed to emphasise both the constriction and triviality of society, the game of whist. And so it goes on. Apart from some brief digressions (to Italy, for instance) the entire action takes place inside the spacious yet confined residences and assemblies of the idle rich.

2.2 Images of Men

As in the work of Zhukova, male characters play a very paradoxical role in *Princess Mimi*. They are of little narrative interest and nearly all the action centres on the lives of women. At the same time, men's power is seen to be ubiquitous, particularly in the area of language and culture. Indeed, one of the main themes of the tale, as already noted, is the power of education to delimit and distort the lives of women and, in the latter parts of the story, the same motif is applied to men. That is, the dominant value in the society which Odoevsky depicts is *prilichiye* ('decorum') and it is seen to have tragic, indeed fatal consequences.

Although, as we shall see, Granitsky has been implicated in the vicious whispering campaign orchestrated by Mimi, no male character plays any significant role in the plot until the introduction of the younger Baron Dauertal towards the end. He is introduced in Oneginesque terms, conceived in the spirit of social typification, as the model product of a traditional aristocratic upbringing, in whose system 'were placed an epigram from Voltaire, an anecdote related by grandmother, a line from Parny, a morally-arithmetic phrase from Bentham' (248) and so on. It is precisely the same sort of smattering of knowledge that we find in Chapter One of *Evgeny Onegin*, and which was characteristic of Pushkin's own education.[21] Following the themes of Pushkin's novel, Odoevsky goes on to show how this liberal gentleman's upbringing, and, in particular, the gentleman's adherence to his honorific code, lead to death.

At first, the young Baron refuses to believe the gossip surrounding Granitsky and his sister-in-law, and staunchly defends the honour of his 'brother'. Eventually, however, his aunt is able to persuade him that the tale must be true (because everyone is repeating it) and the Baron reassures her: 'Be sure that everything will be done, auntie. I thank you for the news. My brother is old, weak; this is my affair, my duty' (251). His 'duty' is to preserve the good name of his noble family, even though this will mean killing a friend (of whose innocence he was convinced a moment before!). This concept of honour, as for Onegin (and indeed, his creator) is central to the Baron's sense of masculinity. This becomes even clearer when he goes to see Granitsky to discuss the matter. As he awaits his friend's arrival, Odoevsky shows the 'extreme agitation' (254) in his mind as he reflects upon what is at stake, in terms which show very precisely that the young Baron feels the need not only to do his 'duty', to satisfy family honour, but also to prove that he is *man* enough to do this:

> There presented themselves to him, as if in a dream, the rumours going round the city; his grey-haired brother, insulted and weak; his desire to show his love and gratitude to the *old man*; his colleagues, epaulettes, sabre, *childish* annoyance; the wish to show that *he was no longer a child*. (ibid. – my italics)

In other words, the young Baron, to please the 'father' ('old man') (and to escape the ridicule of his 'colleagues') will put childish things behind him. And, again like Onegin, he will prove obedient to the sociolect by killing a friend.[22] The link between these values and education is now made explicit. In his confusion, 'he was not able to ask of that court which does not depend on temporal prejudices and opinions . . . his education had forgotten to tell him of that court' (ibid.).

Soon the duel is arranged, on the flimsiest of grounds and the satire becomes even more obvious, especially when Granitsky remarks 'Before we send one another to the next world, I am very curious to find out why we're having the duel' (255). But the satire is meant to be rather heavy-handed, in order to show that men in this society are prepared to kill each other for no reason at all. Masculinity may be a rather secondary theme in the plot dynamics of *Princess Mimi* but the fateful consequences of it are plain enough. As the title of this chapter puts it, 'This Could Be Foreseen' (254).

2.3 Plot

Just as the opening chapter ('The Ball') can be seen as a determining chronotope, so too the main lines of the plot and which forces will shape it are immediately made apparent. The title in itself is significant. *Princess Mimi* is evocative of a number of things. Firstly the Russian word *knyazhna* ('princess') denotes an unmarried woman, so we are led to expect the tale of a young woman who will be the centre of amorous intrigue, possibly culminating in marriage. In this sense, the very first word of the story serves to mock its heroine who remains *knyazhna* long after she wished to become *knyaginya* (a married princess). 'Mimi' is an affectionate nickname: this second appellation will also prove to be deeply ironic as affection is the very last thing she inspires. The story's second epigraph is lapidary: 'La femme de César ne doit pas être soupçonnée' (220). Immediately, women's sexual honour is placed at the very centre of the work's discourse.

Seeming to corroborate the implications of the title, Princess Mimi opens the narrative with her spoken words as the first lines (she is also to be the last named character and to have almost the last word). All this suggests that Mimi will control the narrative and to a certain extent this will be true, although, significantly, she will gradually disappear in the latter half and play no direct part in the story's dénouement. Even more importantly, her control will be seen to be both utterly destructive and, in the final analysis, illusory.

The nature of the society world we are entering is also quickly sketched in. On the surface the opening lines convey nothing more than idle social chit-chat, but a more sinister note is immediately struck. Mimi's interlocutress is Baroness Eliza Dauertal and Mimi's question as to whom Eliza had just been dancing with plunges her into thought 'and not in vain' (ibid.), the narrator remarks. The reason for her anxiety is soon made apparent. Although she is already married (for the second time), she remains young and attractive and, so, potentially may be 'soupçonnée'. The main plot line is to play around this word: Mimi goes out of her way to fabricate suspicions around the utterly innocent Baroness, but it remains the case that the sexual faux pas (even if fictitious) of the woman is the main engine of the plot.[23] Women's chastity, or sexuality more generally, is the main issue.

After a brief concentration on Eliza, the reader is informed of Princess Mimi's sorry life (which forms the pre-prologue). For a variety of reasons she had failed to find a husband and because in this society a woman has no value without a husband, she has turned to bitter revenge – against all other women, but especially against Eliza whose first husband had once admired, but not married, Mimi. Her power in society is seemingly enormous: certainly other women fear and avoid her.

A second plot line (which is to be intertwined disastrously with the first) soon emerges in the adulterous liaison between Countess Lidiya Rifeyskaya and Granitsky. (Again women's sexual behaviour is the central issue.) In another excursus into the pre-prologue, we learn that Lidiya and Granitsky had met in Italy where a genuine love had blossomed between them. This is the only instance of genuine amorous feeling in the story. It is significant both that it is located in that favourite chronotope of early Russian realism, 'the warm south', the very antithesis of false, northern St Petersburg,[24] and that Mimi's machinations, as well as the broader sociolet will crush this love. This sub-plot reveals another aspect of the destructive sociolect even in the pre-prologue stage, in that their love had initially been thwarted by Lidiya's being married off, in St Petersburg of course, to Count Rifeysky, against her own will, and by the intervention of her mother. (I shall return to the largely negative – and misogynistic – image of the mother in this story.)

After these digressions (and *Princess Mimi* is famous for the *fabula/syuzhet* disjunction, especially the intercalated *Foreword*[25]), the plot proper enters its complication as Mimi begins to spread her rumours about Eliza and Granitsky, purely out of vengeful spite. It is significant that a woman is the main mover of the plot (Mimi's desire speaks), but it is to terrible effect. It should also be noted that for most of the story (before the rather rushed dénouement[26]) the actual plot is rather sketchy. This is because the story is, in reality, like most fiction of the 1830s,[27] not really orientated towards plot, but is rather composed of a series of tableaux of women's lives (the ball, the round table, the social visit and so on). This has the effect of showing women to be largely static ('immobile'[28]) characters. Moreover, the 'stage-manager' (245), as the narrator terms himself, frequently feels free to manipulate the plot-line, to break it off for lengthy digressions. Thus, just when the plot *is* beginning to develop by means of Mimi gathering ammunition against Eliza, and, therefore, her narrative power is beginning to grow, the narrator interrupts it for the best part of ten pages (237–46), firstly by having two unnamed gentlemen (who play no part in the story) engage in a lengthy discussion on literature, history, philosophy and so on and then by the famous *Foreword* which also concerns itself with matters literary.

Given the presence of the two gentlemen and the fact that the Foreword is addressed to 'dear sirs'[29] (243), the manipulation of plot can be seen to have important implications for a consideration of gender. Much of the plot that precedes these erudite digressions concerns women's discourse which is here seen to be trivial in the extreme, and, moreover, deeply malicious ('gossip'). Equally, most of the plot, as we have seen, is centred on women's lives and concerns. That it can be interrupted in such a cavalier fashion reveals that, in the end, it is of little real concern to the author. That is, women's discourse is trivial, men's is sophisticated: women's lives are pushed aside for the rather weightier and more meaningful address to the 'dear sirs'.

Finally, we return to the plot. Mimi has done her work well in that the rumours about the 'liaison' between Eliza and Granitsky persist, despite all the evidence to the contrary. Indeed, in an anticipation of *Dead Souls*, lies take on greater validity than the truth. After the scene between the younger Baron and his aunt we have a rare moment of authenticity in what turns out to be the final meeting of the true lovers, Lidiya and Granitsky. Their tears and anguished declarations are delivered almost exclusively through dialogue. Once more the theme of discourse is foregrounded: for a rare moment the narrator lays side his cynicism, irony and manipulation to allow real feelings to be expressed in genuine language. But even here the sociolect reigns. Lidiya tries to reassure her lover: 'I believe, we will be happy;

I believe that that which the absolute rule of society has taken from us will be returned to us by Providence' (253). But she is wrong.

As the dénouement is rushed through the plot again reveals its gendered nature. Although Mimi is the *éminence grise* who has set all this in motion, she is largely absent from the final scenes. Indeed, the dénouement, however satirically it may be handled, is comprised of all-male scenes. Consequently, women are marginalised yet further.

As we know, Granitsky is killed and the reaction to this event is also gendered. The men assume the duel must have taken place because Granitsky had insulted 'the bravery of the young baron' (256–7), while the 'moral ladies' (257) see it merely as confirmation of the 'truth' of their lies. Eliza, whose honour has been ruined, rapidly declines to her death while Mimi and her cronies are given the final verdict. She declares 'people do not kill, but illicit passions do.' '"Oh, without doubt!" many remarked' (ibid.). In terms of the plot, then, we can see the ambivalent view of women: they appear to be in control, whereas in reality they are not. We also note the centrality of the themes of education and discourse: these are also vital for our understanding of the female characters of *Princess Mimi*, to a consideration of which I now turn.

2.4 Images of Women

Once more we should begin with the story's title and its mocking ambivalence: it also encapsulates the duality of the story's orientation. Familiarity with 'Mimi' is at once established, while the reader might expect the heroine to be presented as the subject of the narrative. Or will it turn out that she is merely the object of a male narrative voice and gaze? Certainly, it seems to me, the latter is much nearer the truth. After this fleeting glimpse of Mimi, the narrative in fact initially focuses on another woman, Baroness Eliza Dauertal who is presented as the quintessence of the society woman and we learn much about the role of women in this society from her portrayal. Although she is married, her appearance and manner attract a whole crowd of admirers and we learn that 'her languid, moist eyes offered hope' (220). But this is as much of a disadvantage as a benefit to her, given the predatory world she inhabits: that is, Eliza must not only emulate Cæsar's wife, but keep her own feelings unaroused, and, given that she is married to a much older man, this is not always easy. Her whole life is taken up by seeking to avoid the wrong sort of attention, and so we see in her the same kind of rather eerie refrigeration of feeling as in Pushkin's Tat'yana. She can allow herself 'nothing that might stir her soul into movement' (221). The life of society women, then, is equated with the death of the soul.

Eliza knows that she is constantly watched (to ensure that her sexual honour is never endangered), and this motif of women being looked at is generalised, especially when the reader follows Eliza into the 'woman's room', which acts as a microcosmic chronotope of women's place in society. The 'gynæceum' (225), as the narrator calls it, is introduced as an 'intimate room, inaccessible to men' (ibid.). At first, then, it may seem that this is a place of retreat, a safe haven where women may avoid the predatory gaze of men,[30] and be alone or show sisterly feeling. Instead, it turns out to be merely a place where they can prepare themselves yet further to be looked at. It is significant, then, that the first detail mentioned is the 'large mirror', a sign that conveys the narcissism of women (as the narrator sees it). We then proceed to a brief discussion of ladies' shoes, 'this remembrance of pretty little feet' before an enumeration of the various corsets the ladies wear. Both these items of attire are very evocative: quite apart from the explicit reference to Pushkin's fetishisation of 'little feet' in *Evgeny Onegin*, both the shoes and the corsets suggest precisely the nature of women's allotted role and, in particular, their upbringing. That is, like the bound feet of China,[31] women's bodies (and minds) are constrained in a crippling way, to satisfy the desires of men. Another orientalist resonance emphasises this nexus. The only man who is allowed entry to this room is 'Monsieur Ravi' who 'like the head of a sultan's harem'[32] (that is, a eunuch) is unaffected by 'the magnetic air of the women's toilet-room' (ibid.).

Thus, in this microcosmic space, and more generally, the women are constrained and, metaphorically at least, captive wives. As so often in androcentric, patriarchal literature it is women who are seen to do the policing of women.[33] This motif too is sketched in at the very outset, in the consideration of the Baroness's situation: 'In the city for a long time now the virtuous ladies had sought out the object of the Baroness's tenderness' (221). It is these 'female guardians of morality' (ibid.), as the narrator facetiously terms them, who stand vigilant to preserve the 'properties', that is, female sexual honour. And Princess Mimi, for her own reasons, is the *prima inter pares*. (A specific instance of women's collusion in the suppression of female desire is Lidiya Rifeyskaya's mother. As Granitsky will say to Lidiya in their farewell scene 'You are the victim of the proprieties; you were given in marriage against your will' (253).)

Women writers of the period also tackled this subject and were fully conscious of the processes by which women acted as 'guardians of morality', most notably in Gan's emblematically entitled *Society's Judgement*. At the same time, however, Gan and Zhukova strove to depict the solidarity (or 'sisterhood') which could survive such pressures. Odoevsky, on the other hand, follows the masculinist tradition which represents women as being utterly lacking in any fellow-feeling, as deadly rivals of each other in the game of attracting male desire, of acquiring the phallus[34] which patriarchal society denies them. Mimi's vicious campaign against the entirely blameless Eliza is the most obvious instance, but this antagonism between women is really all-pervasive. Even the generally positive Eliza indulges in this form of *schadenfreude:* she 'died laughing on hearing the details of Mimi's toilet' (228), while Mimi and her younger, widowed sister indulge in a bitter slanging-match, made all the more vivid by being presented as a dramatic dialogue (231-2).

The principal weaponry that women use to dishonour other women and achieve their own superiority are gossip and slander or, more simply, lies. This operates throughout the social spectrum: it is from her own maid, for example, who is the sister of Mimi's maid, that Eliza hears the disgusting details about Mimi's toilet, while, again, Mimi herself is the prime exponent of this black art. From time to time the narrator expresses his disgust at this (247), and it is no accident that the story concludes with Mimi and her allies trading false horror over the events they have brought about. And, as we already know, the effects of turning truth into lies, and of believing the veracity of the latter, is literally fatal.

More generally, the lives and interests of the women of *Princess Mimi* are depicted as utterly trivial. Balls, self-adornment, gossip, needlepoint, cards: these are their spheres. And, it would seem, there are no exceptions to this pattern. Mimi's mother is a typical instance. She is a model of propriety, can speak French perfectly but 'did not like abstract deliberations, but for days on end could sustain a conversation about this and that' (230). (This sharp distinction between male and female attitudes to the word will be extremely significant.) The narrator concludes his brief sketch of Mimi's mother by encapsulating well the ennervating, demoralising effect all this triviality has on a woman:

> But the only thing was that for some time everything had become tedious and annoying to the Princess; whist and people, people and whist still somehow animated her, but before the start of a party she could not . . . conceal her involuntary depression, and suddenly on the surface there appeared a kind of hardness of the heart, some slight hatred to everything around her, some absence of any kind of cordiality . . . even some kind of revulsion at life.
> (230)

On one level it could be said that the story articulates some kind of proto-feminist protest about the conditions which 'corset' women to such crippling, stultifying effect. We see this especially in the retrospective account of Mimi's so-called education. 'Account' is rather too grand a word, however, as the narrator dismisses her upbringing in half a dozen lines:

> You know what feeling, what thought may be developed by the upbringing women receive: embroidery, a drawing master, a little cunning, tenez vous droite, and three anecdotes told by grandma as a reliable guide in this and a future life, – that's all the upbringing.
> (222)

Everything is geared to becoming 'both a good wife and a good mother' (ibid.) and Mimi's tragedy is that she failed to do this. But the message is fundamentally mixed. Certainly, an explicit attack is directed against the socialisation of women, but there is no mention made of Mimi's individuality, nor of her aspirations beyond this narrow sphere, of female friends and so on. As we can see from a comparison with the contemporary accounts of Gan and Zhukova (and others), it is simply not true to say that *Princess Mimi* is merely a faithful reflection of reality.

Leaving this aside for the moment, it remains the case that the typical 'education' of the society woman prepares her for marriage and for nothing else and it is Mimi's tragedy that she failed to marry because without the meaning a husband gives his wife, Mimi's life has no meaning. Moreover, it is impossible for her to abandon this monomania: not only had her education offered no alternative path in life, but also this socialisation process continued unabated:

> . . . but to reject the idea of marrying was terrible for her. What! to reject the idea which her mother went on about at family

gatherings; about which her grandmother spoke on her deathbed? the thought which was the favourite topic of conversation with their friends, the thought with which she fell asleep and awoke? It was terrible. (223)

(Again, we should note, it is other women who act as the conduit for the inculcation of the sociolect. Equally, however, we should note the profoundly different set of aspirations inculcated in their daughters by Gan's valorised maternal figures.)

Even poor Mimi's dreams are haunted, in an inversion of Ivan Shponka's famous nightmare,[35] by fiancés who are snatched away from her (by Eliza). Her position becomes intolerable, simply because everyone else succeeds where Mimi has failed and much younger women (including her own sister) come to treat her with mocking condescension. Given the social realities (as the tale presents them), however, Mimi's distress has a real etiology because it is only men, in the form of husbands, who can introduce women into the world of language and power, into the phallogocentric[36] universe. As with the motif of education, the story makes this point explicitly: 'Respect passed from the husbands to the wives; through their husbands wives had a voice and power' (ibid.). Mimi is therefore stranded in a kind of semiotic void that is the woman without access to the phallus. And we are invited not to blame her for her plight and the terrible vengeance she will seek: 'What is to be done, if for a girl in society the only aim in life – is to get married! . . . This is the limit and origin of her life. This is her life itself' (229). Thus, in this text, to be a woman is to be a wife and, therefore, Mimi, on one level, does not really exist. Ostensibly, *Princess Mimi* warns and protests against this iniquitous state of affairs, but we should also be aware that all the women 'consent . . . to femininity'[37] (so construed), that the text offers no alternatives, and women, seemingly, have no other aspirations.

Mimi's response, then, is to punish those who have crippled her: it is the revenge of the marginalised woman, she who has been excluded from her 'natural' fulfilment. The 'heroine' therefore emerges as a deeply malevolent being. Again, the text is quite explicit about both the processes that have led to this, and about the significance of her reaction. 'Every day her self-esteem was insulted . . . and – poor girl! – every day annoyance, malice, envy, vengefulness little by little ruined her heart' (223). But it is not simply out of a desire to hurt those who have thwarted or slighted her. Rather,

Mimi is seeking to achieve a meaning for her life: 'Mimi saw that, if not by marriage, then by other means it was necessary to support herself in society, to give herself some kind of significance, to occupy some kind of space' (ibid.). And she acquires real power by these means, the power derived from being the 'soul of society', the leader of the 'female guardians of morality', primarily, as we have seen, by spreading lies and gossip about other women.

Not surprisingly, other women (apart from her fellow 'guardians') fear and avoid her, and this leads on to what I think is one of the central questions for an understanding of the politics of the text, namely, what attitude is the reader encouraged to adopt to a woman like Princess Mimi? Certainly, within the text the verdict is clear. Quite apart from the reactions of other women (including her own sister), the two unnamed men who discourse on sophisticated, 'abstract' topics find her loathesome. 'Oh, this woman produced horror in me' (239), one remarks, seeing her as a worthy heir of the 'fires of the inquisition' (ibid.). The reaction of the narrator is rather more ambivalent or, perhaps more accurately, duplicitous. Frequently, as already noted, he invites us not to blame her, but to pity her, exclaiming 'poor girl'. 'And do not blame her for this, but blame, deplore, curse the perverted morals of our society' (229) – this is a fairly typical narratorial apostrophe. At the same time, however, her portrait can be read as a quasi-Gogolian treatment, full of fear and loathing, of the female usurpation of power. Instances of this are the privileged male voice cited above ('horror', 'inquisition'); the logic of the plot, whereby Mimi's machinations lead to two deaths, or the grotesque account given of her toilet which, it seems to me, is intended to provoke disgust in the reader:

> how she suffered, corseting in her broad waist, – how she whitened her rough hands which had turned blue from the effort, . . . how she attached for the night – horror! – raw cutlets to her crimson cheeks! how she pulled out superfluous hairs from her brows, coloured the grey ones, and so on . (228)

The duplicity of the narrator is further corroborated by scenes which are the exact opposite of this one, that is where he invites the reader to gaze lovingly upon displays of parts of the female anatomy. Although such instances of narrative voyeurism and fetishisation are, in fact, rare in *Princess Mimi* they do occur. We have already seen the reference to 'little feet' in the gynæceum. This motif recurs in the scene between Lidiya and Granitsky. Even though, as already noted, this is one of the few scenes of genuine, positive emotion in the story, the narrator cannot resist drawing our attention to this detail, twice in a few lines, in fact. Lidiya has forgotten to put on her boots (and shoes are featured prominently in the gynæceum) so Granitsky 'tried to warm her charming little feet with his breath' (252); and then, 'Gabriel kissed her cold little feet, fashioned, it seemed, out of white marble and pressed them to his hot cheeks' (ibid.).

More generally, the whole story can be read as a discourse on sexuality, gender, power and the way each of these is mediated in discourse. Like other writers of the period, Odoevsky would seem to regard gender difference as absolute and this is particularly apparent in his discussion of the opposing gender relationships with the word. Moreover, for all the apparent 'feminism' of certain aspects of the story, power in discourse is seen to reside with men. This is shown, I think, by the two key digressions, that is, the discussion between the two unnamed male characters, and the *Foreword*. In reverse, women like Mimi's mother, do not like abstractions, and *their* discourse is represented as a 'witch's brew', if I may so put it, of trivialities, gossip and lies. As Mimi's plot shows, to be feminine is to misuse the power of the word. At the same time, female sexuality, and its relationship to language, is a central preoccupation of the text, from the very outset. We see this both in the second epigraph ('Cæsar's Wife') as well as in the brief conversation between Mimi and Eliza which opens the story: 'Tell me, who were you dancing with just now?' As the plot reveals, Mimi's opening sally proves to be an extremely loaded and highly charged question. Women's sexuality then is immediately established as central, and a problem. 'What should (married) women do?' is the underlying question which organises much of what follows. And, given the centrality of marriage as a problem, it can be argued that women's sexuality *is* their gender. Pulling these two propositions together, we can proceed to say that *Princess Mimi* concerns itself with women's relationship with the phallus, or rather, given the discourse about discourse within the story, their relationship (or rather lack of one) to phallogocentrism.

In this sense, the displaced *Foreword* must be seen as central to our understanding of the story. The power of this section is anticipated, in fact, by the narrator's earlier comments on what Mimi lacks in failing to find a husband. As we have already seen: 'Respect passed from the husbands to the wives; through their husbands wives had *a voice and power'* (223 – my italics). And it continues: 'only Princess Mimi remained alone, without a voice, without support' (ibid.). The *Foreword* returns to these themes to develop them and give them full meaning. As he approaches this section the narrator addresses 'my dear sirs!'[38] (243): this, most literary section of the tale, initially at least, excludes women from the discourse. He then offers a lengthy, jocular disquisition on the state of Russian literature and, in particular, the use of the Russian language. (Here, too, Odoevsky echoes Pushkin, most specifically the latter's similar remarks in his introduction to Tatyana's Letter to Onegin.[39]) In the course of this, the narrator does also turn to address 'my dear ladies' (ibid.), imploring them to begin to speak Russian (rather than the fashionable French, the language of Tatyana's letter, of course), and threatening not to write any more if they do not.

Once more, I think, we have a rather mixed message. On one level the narrator, however jokingly, deplores the exclusion of women from language (and literature). On the other hand, however, given this situation (and given everything else the text teaches us about women's exclusion from the dominant discourse), the *very literariness* of the *Foreword* (*pace* the address to the 'ladies') perpetuates this marginalisation. Mimi and her mother would not read it, as it were. So, both on the level of plot and on the level of the text's discourse, women have no voice and, *therefore*, no reality. The story and its narrator seem to protest against this, but, whether deliberately or not, collude in precisely the situation they deplore. *Princess Mimi*, then, would seem to be the story of the eponymous heroine. In the final analysis, it never could be because, as the narrator points out, she has no voice, and he continues to deprive her of one. In terms of gender, *Princess Mimi* reveals that language is male and to be female is to be silent.

3. PRINCESS ZIZI

Many of the paradoxes of *Princess Mimi* are repeated in this otherwise rather different story. Again the title leads the reader to expect a 'heroine's text' and in many ways this story too, on one level, seeks to protest against the invidious social position of women. However, the protest is once more to an extent invalidated both by the implications of the plot and by the narrative attitudes to the female characters. In this later work, the androcentrism is manifested in rather different ways (voyeurism and misogynistic caricature), and, ultimately, it remains as masculinist as its predecessor. Accordingly, it seems appropriate to begin a consideration of *Princess Mimi* with a discussion of the male characters in the story.

3.1 Images of Men

As *dramatis personae* male characters (Gorodkov and Radetsky) play a far larger part than any male personage in *Princess Mimi*, so it is perhaps fitting that the story opens with two unnamed men sitting, drinking and telling a story. Immediately, moreover, masculine values are established: one has just come from an all-male preserve (the stock-exchange), and they soon launch into the kind of literary polemic that both *New Year* and *Princess Mimi* have established as exclusively masculine (even if now under threat from authoresses!). Equally, although much of the narrative will be told from the point of view of its heroine, and the initial sections are in fact based on her own word (her letters), it remains significant that the first, and organising, narrators are male (one of whom just happens to have Zizi's letters on him!).[40]

In terms of character, however, it should be noted at the outset that one of the principal male characters (Gorodkov) is an unrelieved, melodramatic villain, while the other (Radetsky) is a Romantic, Lenskyesque fool.[41] In this sense, at least, the male is *not* privileged. For some time we see Gorodkov exclusively through the eyes of the besotted, love-lorn Zizi, for whom he arrives in their emotional wilderness as a Prince Charming and manages to please all three women – Zizi herself, her sister Lidiya and their mother. Retrospectively, we see him as a particularly skilled seducer, able to appeal to the individual tastes of all three women (although, equally, this reflects the gullibility of the women). Later, Marya Ivanovna, the recipient of the letters and a figure of some importance in the plot is equally impressed: 'she realised that not every woman could be indifferent to him. He was a fine young man ... was of a happy, even joking disposition' (268): he treats his wife Lidiya and sister-in-law Zizi appropriately. As the story develops, different facets are added to his characterisation. He becomes a stern paterfamilias, loving order in all things, and soon sees off the interfering Radetsky. Yet he is to be unmasked as a swindler, scheming seducer and mercenary adventurer. His wife Lidiya eventually warns that 'he is terribly cunning and terribly evil' (291). In other ways he remains merely a plot functionary, the Lovelacean villain who tests and nearly conquers Zizi's virtue. In this light it is perhaps injudicious to go too far in assessing him as a serious treatment of masculinity. What can be said, however, is that the story offers a warning to impressionable young women about believing too implicitly what they have read about men. This Prince Charming turns out to be a real frog.[42] Radetsky is even more schematically drawn and even less of a realised character. In essence he seems to be yet another parody (following Vladimir Lenksy in *Onegin*) of the ultra-Romantic hero who, like the heroine, believes too literally the books he reads. He considers it his 'holy duty' (280) to rescue the ensnared Princess, but in the end contributes nothing to her deliverance.

Overall, given the quasi-feminist approach to Zizi herself, it is significant that the male characters, while more central to the plot than in *Princess Mimi*, ultimately are revealed as either evil or inadequate. One theme of Zizi's story is the ability of the heroine to free herself and it is therefore important that the male characters remain subordinate to her heroic struggle: one is overcome and the other rejected.

3.2 Plot

As I have already noted, although Zizi's story will provide the main plot-line (and much of it will be narrated by her, in the form of her letters to Marya Ivanovna), the narrative commences from a traditional androcentric perspective. The two unnamed interlocutors will play no real part in the story but they lend the whole story a masculinist orientation, which persistently intrudes (especially, as one would expect, in those sections not based on Zizi's letters). Also important in this introductory frame is the deliberate confusion of time-scale and of the fabula/syuzhet relationship. (As Cornwell puts it, 'the narrative structure is complicated and contrived.'[43]) This confusion will have a number of effects and purposes.

Zizi's story then is introduced by the two men: she is first encountered as spoken about, and, moreover, as a profound enigma.[44] The second narrator, who introduces the story proper, remarks that in conversation in Moscow, where he had returned after ten years travelling, he had heard many names mentioned: 'One of them, I don't know why, attracted my attention more . . . in this name there was something special, [but] I involuntarily moved my chair towards the circle when this name was pronounced' (260–1). Seven different opinions are expressed, and each goes to stress how unusual Zizi is: indeed 'strange' (262) is used four times about her, and perhaps strangest of all is the fact that she had refused her allotted role by never marrying. In an ironic reversal of poor Mimi's tragicomedy Zizi had had the opportunity. As the narrator's aunt observes: 'She is a great coquette – however, though, she had good offers and didn't marry anyone . . . In her there's a great deal that's strange' (262). The prologue sets this up, then, as the main riddle, and motivates the whole plot, which is to answer the question: who can this strange woman be, who *refused* to marry? In other words, the plot can be encapsulated as 'what *does* a woman want?'[45]

After this androcentric (in several senses) prologue, one might have expected a proto-Turgenevan reminiscence by a middle-aged man about how he had met but never married Zizi. It comes as something of a surprise (and innovation) to find that the first sections of the story proper are related by Zizi herself, in the form of letters to Marya Ivanovna. In the first of these, while somewhat contrivedly offering the reader information we can assume Marya Ivanovna might already have (but thereby providing the prologue to her own story), Zizi, in a Belkinesque touch, anticipates her own plot by revealing that amongst the other books she continues to steal from her deceased father's library is *Clarissa*. Interestingly, the fourth volume drops down the back of a dictionary. This playful literary device[46] entails Zizi in not knowing the end of her own story and so she *mis-reads* the script she is to follow.

Her situation introduces one of the classic *topoi* of early Russian realism (although it has ancient fairy-tale origins[47]). The three women (Zizi, her mother and sister Lidiya), although resident in Moscow, lead a static, cloistered existence, going nowhere and receiving no-one. That is, they are immobile characters, identified with the chronotopic space they inhabit, the 'desert'[48] as Zizi calls it. Into this space comes the 'mobile' false hero, the frog in Prince Charming's clothes, 'Mr Gorodkov' (264), a dangerous city-dweller as his name suggests. At the very outset of the plot, as the newly arrived stranger plays his allotted role (that of providing the complication), the fabula/syuzhet disjunction becomes important. That is, the narrator of the overall story (who has Zizi's letters) presumably knows the outcome, which he chooses not to reveal. Consequently, the readerly suspense (and, ultimately, titillation) is maintained, and, equally, for some considerable time we are obliged to take Mr Gorodkov at face value, on trust, just as Zizi does. (At the same time, therefore, the reader not only hears the story from Zizi's point of view but is also placed in the position of identifying with her.)

As Gorodkov's visits become more frequent, and his suit is addressed to Lidiya, another important plot motif is introduced in that the mother colludes both in her daughter's seduction,[49] and in the thwarting of Zizi's hopes, as she is kept a virtual prisoner by her mother so that Gorodkov can concentrate on Lidiya. Soon Zizi herself introduces yet another element to the plot, that of the love-lorn heroine who has fallen in love with the first man she meets. She begins and ends her fifth letter to Marya Ivanovna with the tragicomic plea that her correspondent pray for her, and at this point, Marya herself takes up the narrative, remarking that 'The letters of Princess Zinaida . . . occupied and frightened me' (267). But she does nothing, until very much later, to intervene. Like Nelly Dean in *Wuthering Heights*, she too inadvertently colludes in the tragic events that are about to unfold.

She does, however, take herself to Moscow where she discovers that Lidiya has married Gorodkov, and that the mother had died, although not before imploring Zizi to look after her childish sister. Even from beyond the grave, it could be said, the mother will collude in her daughter's near destruction. Marya has to return to Kazan, and this allows the correspondence to resume. Once more, about a year later, Marya Ivanovna inadvertently interferes in the plot. Her increasing awareness of Zizi's hopeless (and incestuous) love for Gorodkov prompts her to send Radetsky to Moscow, and this will precipitate the peripeteia in that it will be his attempts to win Zizi that prompt Gorodkov's full-scale assault on her virtue.

It is at this stage that another major contrivance is introduced in that Zizi's letters now break off, because Radetsky's letters to Marya become the basis for the narrative, to be replaced by the quasi-omniscient third-person narrator, the source of whose information is Marya, who in turn had heard the story from Zizi. This switch in point of view has a number of effects. Certainly the fact that we no longer hear Zizi's own words directly adds greatly to the suspense in that the reader is left to guess at what may be the motives of her increasingly erratic behaviour. At the same time, the loss of Zizi's voice increases the possibilities of the narrator and reader *watching* her. And this will be of vital importance in our understanding of the semiotics of seduction in *Princess Zizi*.

The mystification at this juncture is also increased by Radetsky entering fully into the part of *buffo*. Clearly *he* doesn't know what's going on, so nor do we. His first letter finds him thanking Marya for the introduction, as he has fallen in love with Zizi. Two new motifs are thereby introduced: two men pursue the virtuous heroine, and male rivalry. At first Zizi avoids him, then she agrees to marry him, as long as it is 'as soon as possible' (279), but then she rescinds her decision: she cannot marry him because she does not love him. For all his confusion, Radetsky is able to see enough to lay bare what has now become the central plot motif. In typically lurid terms he writes to Marya: 'If I myself cannot be happy, then this does not prevent me from sacrificing, if necessary, my life, in order to save a poor girl from the inexplicable, but real snares which surround her' (280). Radetsky too, it would seem, is familiar with the eighteenth century novel of seduction.

After one more (and final) letter from Zizi to Marya in which she still eulogises Gorodkov and rejects 'your Childe Harold manqué' (281), we finally come to the peripeteia, narrated in the third person. (A great contrivance this: no-one could possibly have known all our narrator claims to know.[50]) He introduces this climactic account as follows: 'Later on Marya Ivanovna found out everything that had happened in the intervals between these letters' (282). Despite this 'everything' there are still contrivances, deliberate omissions and clear retardation devices (such as the literary discussion between Radetsky and Gorodkov). The effect is to delay the climax (the seduction of Zizi) and, therefore, to increase the anticipatory expectation of it in the reader.

And when this climactic scene does arrive, in direct contrast to the silence surrounding the rape of Clarissa,[51] it is certainly dwelt upon. First the narrator goes into great detail about Zizi's room in which she sits alone, waiting (to which I will return), before the actual arrival of Gorodkov. The scene and the events are very clearly foregrounded: *this* is to be the moment we have all been waiting for and which will answer all the questions which have been hanging in the airs since the framing prologue. The scene between Gorodkov and Zizi is, by some margin, the most intense *dramatic* scene in the story, so that the seduction of the virtuous heroine becomes the highlight of the story. (This will be very important for our overall understanding of the work's sexual politics.)

Bathetically, Gorodkov's designs are interrupted by the crying of Zizi's niece, but he is not to be deterred and his visits to her sanctuary become more frequent. To escape from this impossible situation, we now learn, Zizi had agreed to marry Radetsky, but this only prompts renewed and more insistent demands from her brother-in-law. Zizi breaks off her extremely short-lived engagement, only to be rescued once more from a fate-worse-than-death by another familial intervention, in the guise of Lidiya's illness, precipitated by dancing while pregnant.

Once again the story contrivedly is broken off by a switch to Marya Ivanovna and now at long last, for the final quarter, the fabula and syuzhet come together. The truth is revealed: all along, Gorodkov had had no interest in Zizi as such, nor even in Lidiya. The 'stock-exchange' motif (first mentioned in line 2 on the first page) comes to the fore in that all Gorodkov's machinations had been directed to acquiring Lidiya's and then Zizi's shares of the estate. He is finally despatched by an equestrian accident before Zizi, who is now devoting herself to her niece (Lidiya having died from her dancing lesson), resists yet another predatory male – the narrator himself who, it transpires, is only eighteen. The enigma of Princess Zizi is then finally clarified and she has shown herself to be not only a virtuous, but also a triumphant heroine. (Much of the latter part of the narrative is, in fact, taken up with her bitter legal battles against Gorodkov.) Whether, however, we can agree that she is a 'positive heroine' who achieves a *'podvig'*,[52] is a matter of some debate as a consideration of her and the other female characters will now reveal.

3.3 Images of Women

As in *Princess Mimi*, the title and epigraph immediately set up a number of tensions that will not be fully resolved. *Princess Zizi* once more suggests familiarity and intimacy, while promising that the heroine will be the subject rather than the object of the narrative. (In fact, she will be both.) The epigraph ('The Words of a Woman') also promise much: 'Sometimes in the domestic sphere there is need of more heroism than in the most glittering career of life. The domestic sphere is the field of honour and sacred feats for women' (258). Women and their world are thus immediately placed at the very centre of attention and their valorisation can be expected. At the same time, however, we should note the repeated emphasis on 'the domestic sphere': a hint, perhaps, of the Ruskinian 'equal but separate' spheres? Indeed, narrative ambivalence, if not duplicity, towards women will again be the key-note.

We see this, in fact, in a consideration of all the female characters in the story other than Zizi herself. If she is a 'positive heroine', then, like Turgenev's Elena[53] she will be entirely alone in her travails and quest. As we have already seen, Marya Ivanovna, although Zizi's confidante, fails to intervene to rescue her and is generally unreliable. From the outset she is thus characterised. The companion of the main narrator's aunt, she is discussed as 'a great chatter-box . . . and a passionate amateur of novels' (262).[54] This fallibility, and especially her love of a good story, are to prove nearly fatal for our heroine. Zizi's mother, as we have also seen, is even more directly implicated in her daughters' downfall, encouraging the attentions of Gorodkov toward Lidiya, while thwarting Zizi's hopes. Even after her death, her extraction of Zizi's promise to care for Lidiya ties Zizi to her potential seducer. In terms of her character, the mother is equally unmaternal.[55] Even though it is Zizi's account (in her first letter) which conveys this information, she is immediately presented in a typical misogynist sketch of the unattractive older woman: 'mummy is constantly ailing, constantly bored, dissatisfied with everything' (263). Zizi is so oppressed by her mother's irritating character that she even repeats her complaints later in the same letter: 'Whatever we say, she gets angry, ceaselessly complains about the weather, and her health, and other people' (ibid.).

We should also note in passing that Zizi is hardly filial in her sketch of her mother. Equally she shows no sign of sisterly feeling in her portrayal of Lidiya. Moreover, Lidiya is presented by all the different narrators in more or less exactly the same terms, that is, as a gross, misogynistic caricature of a feckless, irresponsible and thoroughly worthless individual. The sisters, as is so often the case in the literature of the period,[56] are presented as utterly contrastive types. We see this once more from the very outset: Gorodkov brings Zizi books, but for Lidiya embroidery patterns. We must assume that the calculating Gorodkov decides on Lidiya specifically because she is the more amenable. Once their engagement is announced, Zizi is vicious in her character assassination of her sister:

> And what has he found in her? She goes on as if nothing's happened! Can she make him happy? She's as cold as ice; for her to get married is like drinking a glass of water; she sleeps as much as before, embroiders just as much, eats just as much. (267)

Even allowing for Zizi's jealousy and envy these can hardly be read as the words of a 'positive heroine'. Her first letter after Lidiya's marriage takes up the same themes. *She* has to do everything because of the complete inability of Lidiya to do anything: 'She sleeps half the day and goes round the shops the other half; even there I have to keep her in check because, like a child, she's ready to buy everything she sees' (269). And she behaves even worse in society: 'sometimes, forgetting herself, she'll laugh fully-throatedly so that everyone looks round at her; especially at the theatre I have to keep pulling her by the sleeve so that she won't say anything indecorous' (271). Worse still in her complete neglect of her child, even though little Pasha is frequently ill. . . .

Lest this be seen merely as the jealous ravings of a woman scorned, it should be reiterated that later narrators completely endorse Zizi's view of her sister. Radetsky, for example, is glad of a chance to talk alone to Zizi because he could get no sense out of Lidiya: 'either she was silent, because she could not understand our conversation, or laughed out loud for no reason, or skipped away' (274). And the final narrator takes up the portrait, finally summarising Lidiya as a 'greatgranddaughter of Eve' (282), which, given the dynamics of her character, means we must dismiss her as unreliable – but also dangerous.

I have spent some time considering the portrayal of Lidiya because this certainly sheds light on the overall politics of the work. Even if we do eventually see Zizi as a positive heroine, then the excessive denigration of Lidiya undercuts any overall positive evaluation of the story from a feminist perspective. But what is the point of all this? Lidiya's main function is to provide contrastive illumination for her much more sensitive sister; at the same time her incredible stupidity and general worthlessness partially excuse Zizi's illicit love for her brother-in-law. In reverse, however, Lidiya's irresponsibility, taken together with the collusion of Marya Ivanovna and the mother, reveals how very alone Zizi is, without a shred of support from any other woman. In this last regard, Odoevsky's story is entirely consistent with the masculinist tradition.

Turning to Zizi, it is important to remind ourselves of the first impression we receive of her: she is a 'strange' being, whose riddle the plot will attempt to fathom. Later in the story this enigma is, in fact, deepened by her increasingly bizarre behaviour and sudden switches of mood, especially around her on/off marriage to Radetsky. He, in fact, encapsulates well the absurdity of her behaviour. He writes in some exasperation to Marya Ivanovna: 'The feelings of Princess Zinaida are impenetrable for me' (273). Her situation is even more incomprehensible: 'in the house she plays the role of some kind of governess or even housekeeper; – she is a woman of great intelligence, with erudition, with a passionate imagination! ... I don't understand' (273–4). And nor, for many pages, does the reader. Certainly, the contrivance of the *fabula/syuzhet* disjunction enhances the suspense of the story but it has this effect as well: Zizi is represented as being almost completely arbitrary in her behaviour, although in the end, at least, her story will be told. Nevertheless, for some considerable time she is created as a woman of mystery and this traditional image of the enigmatic, arbitrary woman persists in the reader's (as well as Radetsky's) imagination.

When we first encounter Zizi in the story proper she is located in the fixed space of the emotional 'desert' inhabited by the three friendless women. Immediately, however, an innovatory note is struck. The first narrator is handed Zizi's first epistle and remarks: 'Glancing at it I saw with surprise that it was written reasonably correctly in Russian, – and this alone, especially at that time, was very remarkable' (262). Implicitly, though fairly obviously, Odoevsky harks back both to his own *Princess Mimi* and beyond that to Pushkin's introduction to Tatyana's letter. Zizi is thus instantly valorised by the very simple fact of being able to write fairly accurately in her own language. More seriously, she and Marya Ivanovna thereby enter the phallogocentric world by appropriating the hitherto almost exclusively masculine symbolic code. At the same time, however, she is entering very dangerous literary territory. She and Marya construct between them an epistolary novel, thereby entering the eighteenth century world of *Liaisons Dangereuses* and, of course, *Clarissa*, which will prove to be the metatext for *Princess Zizi*.

Indeed, again echoing Tatyana, Zizi is now defined by her reading. This identification is also to have ambivalent resonances. Zizi introduces this motif by remarking: 'as before I continue to steal books from Father's library: this is my one joy' (263).[57] This is despite her mother's prohibition. Moreover, they are all 'masculine books' (ibid.). The engendered (and Œdipal) nexus could hardly be made more explicit by a post-Freudian writer. That is, Zizi is an undutiful daughter who appropriates, quite literally, the Word-of-the-Father,[58] and thereby compounds her breach of the ancient (and Biblical) taboo initiated by her 'stealing' of the Father's word (her writing in Russian). She then moves on to itemise her reading matter, including, as we know, a partial version of *Clarissa*. Although she shares this interest in eighteenth century fiction with Tatyana, she has gone beyond her and characterises herself as a thoroughly modern young woman by her professed liking for Zhukovsky and Pushkin (including, one assumes, *Evgeny Onegin*). Yet Zizi also displays anxiety about her 'erudition', afraid lest Gorodkov consider her a 'bluestocking'. (265). That is, Zizi is first characterised as progressive, indeed positive, but, understandably, is not fully comfortable in this role.

If Zizi has read *Onegin* she would be aware of the epigraph to the chapter which includes Tatyana's letter (Chapter 3): 'Elle était fille, elle était amoureuse.' For all her initial appropriation of the masculine code, once her plot is under way (the intrusion of Gorodkov), Zizi shows herself to be entirely compliant to life as 'fille' and *therefore* 'amoureuse': that is, she at once 'consents to femininity', and follows in Tatyana's footsteps by falling in love with the first man she meets. From now on, until her sudden (and miraculous) transformation towards the end, Zizi will cease not only to be a positive heroine, but even anything remotely resembling a 'character'. Rather, like many heroines of the period she will be an imbricated collage of almost all known stereotypes of the literary female.

Once in love, Zizi enters fully into the stereotype. She pours her heart out to Marya Ivanovna: 'I would comfort him every minute of my life, I would tend to his needs the live-long day, I would amuse him when he was bored, I would cherish him like a child . . .' (267). Up to a point, this dream is, in fact, fulfilled. Because of Lidiya's fecklessness, Zizi is the true mistress of the house, and everything she does, she does for HIM. Her only desire is to be his, later declaring that she will never marry, because she could never love another. Yet again, she echoes Tatyana's words, in her letter to Onegin, 'No, to no-one else in the world/Would I give my heart!', when she writes to Marya to explain her behaviour towards Radetsky: 'My fate is decided: I will never belong to anyone else' (281). Her devotion to Gorodkov reveals Zizi to be almost as stupid as her vilified sister. Indeed, what are we to make of her as a 'positive heroine', given that she falls in love with the first man to cross her path, that she continues to be besotted even after he has become her brother-in-law, (and that he is a villain and seducer)? Only when his malfeasance is revealed does she come to her senses! Indeed, even when something is clearly amiss and Radetsky tries to warn her, she asks Marya how dare he 'blacken a hero of virtue', an 'angel of goodness, selflessness?' (281).

To this traditional stereotype of gullibility, the story adds that of female self-sacrifice. Here too, Zizi enters the role whole-heartedly, heroically fulfilling her mother's death-bed wishes to care for Lidiya despite all the suffering this causes her. As Marya observes: 'she was calm: she understood the enormity of her sacrifice' (268). Closely related to this stereotype is that of the suffering victim, and Zizi appropriates this role almost as soon as she has met Gorodkov: she concludes her third letter to Marya with the plea: 'Do write to your poor prisoner' (266). Once the engagement is announced she enters completely the part of the abandoned heroine: 'Everything is over for me! My world is the grave, my hope – death' (267). A year later she writes once more to her confidante: 'What can I tell you about myself? the fever has passed; I don't spend nights on end in tears, but I can admit to you that there is often such a weight in my heart that it's impossible to describe' (269). Later she is to castigate Marya for reproaching her, Marya who knows 'all the agonies of my heart' (281). This intense emotionalism, yet another traditional icon of femininity, is carried over into the way she describes her bodily expression of feeling, and how others depict her. That is, she conforms to the *mechanistic iconography* of Russian neo-Sentimentalism. This motif is also heard almost from the very beginning. She tells Marya how she has fallen in love and waits the arrival of Gorodkov. Once she hears him coming 'the blood goes cold in my veins, my heart beats, I tremble all over, I'm all on fire, it goes dark before my eyes, my head goes round – I have no more strength' (266). This is all rather silly, but it is important that we note that Zizi writes this *of herself*. That is, it is an example not only of textual voyeurism, but also of ventriloquism, in that Zizi describes herself as being looked at.

The incidence of iconographic mechanism intensifies as the story develops, and as Zizi passes through the various cases of the dysphoric heroine's declension. Her spiritual agonies increase as she, Lidiya, Gorodkov and the child all live together and Zizi is forced into such close proximity to the man she desires but cannot have. Again she describes her own emotions as expressed through physical display, in highly Gothick language. She hears the baby's cry:

> What happened to me at the moment – I haven't got the strength to tell; it was – both inexpressible grief and inexpressible joy, both hell and heaven; I both cried and laughed, I prayed and cursed; I felt a quiver in every nerve, a ringing in my ears, my breath was taken away.... (270)

All these signs are part of the standard iconography of the period, and this is the point. Zizi is thus rendered a trembling, suffering victim, but also, *this is how she sees herself*. That is, like Tatyana before her, and others in the same period, she lives 'by the book', 'imagining herself a heroine'.[59]

However, this is not only a matter of self-definition, because Radetsky and the later narrator will depict her in very similar terms. Thus, when the former begins to make his feelings known to Zizi, he remarks in his letter to Marya: 'My words clearly made an impression on the Princess: she was in turmoil – now turning red, now going pale; her breast was heaving' (275). Later he finds her in that classic chronotope of Gothick neo-Sentimentalism, in church at prayer: 'she was praying fervently and weeping bitterly' (278). As she emerges from the service he is able to read all the tell-tale signs of this victim-heroine: 'her eyes were red, her cheeks sunken, her face bore the stamp of cruel inner suffering' (ibid.).

The problems with the portrait we are offered of Princess Zizi become increasingly apparent as we analyse it. Like so many female figures of the period she bears no resemblance to a literary *character*: rather, she is a *composite* of a bewildering profusion of contrasting and irreconcilable stereotypes,[60] a kind of blank screen onto which the masculine imagination may project more or less anything. To the motifs of 'blue-stocking', provincial Romantic, gullible fool, self-sacrificing, vulnerable victim, others may now be added. For example, Zizi both construes herself and is presented by the final narrator as a deeply maternal figure (one of the most marked contrasts with both her own mother and her sister Lidiya, another unmaternal mother). At times she clearly thinks she is Pasha's real mother or, at least, behaves more like it than Lidiya. She writes to Marya: 'Often I would wish to stay at home with *my* Pashenka' (271). Earlier she had gone even further in confessing these guilty desires: 'sometimes in my forgetfulness I think that on me has been laid the calling of mother, that I can say to him: "*our* child"' (270 – her italics). Certainly it *is* Zizi who plays the role of mother, dandling Pasha on her knees while Lidiya tries on a dress 'for the tenth time' (271). Once more, it should be noted, this is not only Zizi's self-definition: later Radetsky will also remark on Lidiya's neglect, while her sister cares for Pasha during one of her many illnesses.

Closely related to the maternal imagery in Zizi's representation is her identification with the sacred and the pure: that is, she is virgin *as well as* mother. From a relatively early stage she had sought consolation and refuge in religion and this motif is to grow in intensity. As she describes to Marya her growing suffering (just after the birth of Pasha has, as it were, confirmed the fact that Gorodkov *has* married Lidiya and not her), she writes 'my only consolation is prayer' (269). Later in the same letter, as she confesses her guilty desires, she remarks that when the clock chimes for bed, and Gorodkov remains alone with Lidiya, of course, 'I with constricted heart wander to my lonely cell and throw myself onto my cold bed' (ibid.). She takes this idea one logical stage further as the climax to the story approaches. Writing to explain to Marya the reasons for her strange behaviour towards Radetsky, she declares that she could never belong to any but Gorodkov. Once Lidiya and her children no longer need her 'the nunnery will hide the unfortunate one' (281).

The religious motif, I assume, is designed to strengthen the image of Zizi as a 'positive heroine'. At the same time, however, it has darker, somewhat Sadeian resonances, in that it will add a frisson of sacrilege to the seduction scene.[61] Moreover, it is somewhat at odds with other aspects of Zizi's 'character', most notably those elements clustered round her sexuality. As we have already seen, one motif in the delineation of Zizi is that of the 'suffering heroine'. There would also seem to be a marked streak of enjoyment of this suffering, in other words, of masochism. Once more her letter to Marya after the birth of Pasha is critical. Immediately after her evocation of her 'cell', she proceeds: 'But away with these thoughts, I will not rail against Providence: it has created me for agonising, daily, slow suffering; but it has also given me a consolation' (269). Indeed, she makes much of her suffering. She continues her letter: 'I look on myself as a victim, brought for his happiness, a pure, selfless victim – and this thought elevates my soul' (269–70). But again this should not be assigned merely to her writing herself as Clarissa. Radetsky once more corroborates the impression. As Zizi emerges tear-stained and red-eyed from her fervent prayer her suffering is both noted and appreciated: 'She had never before appeared so splendid to me' (278). And beyond him, perhaps, lurk the 'dear sirs' to whom *Princess Mimi* was addressed, who will also find the suffering of the pure victim 'splendid'!

Another Gothick element in Zizi's story, and perhaps the most obvious one, is the frisson provided by her strong and clearly incestuous feelings for her brother-in-law, Mr Gorodkov. We return once more to the 'cell' letter where Zizi enunciates her guilty desires: 'Lidiya dozes ... and then it seems to me that I am the real mistress in the house, that I am – I'm afraid to utter it – his wife' (269). Later in the same letter she returns to this theme and her guilty panic is indicative of the depth of her feeling (but also of the arousal both within her – and, perhaps, the 'dear sirs'):

> Oh, then my heart pounds, the blood rises to my head, and strange things pass through my thoughts, such thoughts that I am afraid of myself, I jump up and throw myself on my knees in front of the icon. (270)

Eventually she swoons away and when she revives all her desire, and guilt have passed. . . .

The portrait of Princess Zizi is, then, highly complex, but this suggests not psychological profundity but rather the familiar process of imbrication. This process is seen at its most striking in the remarkable scene of Gorodkov's virtual seduction of the heroine and, even more so, in the two pages of introduction to this scene by the narrator. To mark the onset of the peripeteia there is a perceptible increase in the semioticisation of the text. We are told that Gorodkov, having left Lidiya at the ball, enters Zizi's room. However, it is some time before we actually learn what happens after his entrance, as the narrator stops the narrative to describe the scene the seducer will see, offering it to the delectation of his listener:

> Zinaida . . . remained alone with Pashenka in her arms . . . Just imagine a little room, with dark-blue wall-paper, rugs; in the corner is a small Turkish divan . . . In the room it is dark; the dull light of the lamp illuminates only the divan, on which sits a fine girl in a white blouse . . . a darkish ribbon circles her slender waist; her black wavy hair falls over her shoulders in small curls; on her graceful little foot are velvet slippers. (284)

This is to be the scene of seduction, but first Zizi is seduced, gazed upon, by the narrator and his readers. We note the imbrication of images: first she is a mother; the chiaroscuro lighting (as well as the present historic) heightens the intimacy, romance and danger. The 'turkish divan' suggests the harem, while the white blouse is emblematic of virginity. Finally we note the exquisite detail of her fetishised body, culminating in the obligatory reference to her small feet.

Zizi waits, therefore, like a Madonna with child, waiting to be taken. And so it goes on. That this is to be the climactic moment is underscored by the fact that Zizi's whole life passes before her. She recalls the stolen poetry, how she had cried over the fate of the heroine of the first novel that had come her way. She is tormented once more at the agonies she has experienced. This is conveyed in a deeply Sadeian image: 'And so her whole life will flow away, an incomplete, false life, like the life of a brilliant insect, nailed to a piece of wood by a cold observer' (285). The text piles on the agony: 'There is no end to the sufferings of the poor girl' (ibid.).

Presumably we are to think that Gorodkov is this 'cold observer', but, equally, the reader is implicated in this position as we read and watch (and enjoy?) her suffering. The narrator wonders whether she will have the strength 'to survive this uninterrupted suffering' (ibid.). The narrative gradually builds to a crescendo of intensity: will she succumb to the temptation (of incest), or will she (switching to other motifs) fly to a nunnery, or, again, will she stay to observe her sacred promise to her mother, by being a mother herself to Lidiya's child?

Finally, we return to Gorodkov entering the room and he is immediately identified with the stance of the preceding pages: 'he was struck by the splendid picture before his eyes' (286). (Splendid for whom?). Gorodkov begins his seduction, only to be interrupted first by the cries of Pasha, and then the return of the singing and dancing Lidiya. But Zizi's sufferings are not yet over as Gorodkov resumes his assaults and she enters into new motifs of the vulnerable heroine: she cannot sleep, she can no longer pray in her own room. The virgin's inner sanctuary has been defiled and she begs 'Vladimir! in the name of God, leave me!' (289).

But she is saved from her illicit desires and the traditional fate-worse-than-death, first by Lidiya's miscarriage and then by the dramatic news of Gorodkov's swindling which comes from Kazan. It is at this stage, and really only at this stage, that Zizi becomes a 'positive heroine', immediately dashing off to seek help, and then engaging in lengthy legal processes to defeat Gorodkov. Yet it must be said that this miraculous transformation owes rather more to the fairy-tale than to realism: it is largely unprepared for in the previous narrative, except perhaps by her early appropriation of the masculine code in her writing and reading. Interestingly, indeed, her behaviour and demeanour are now characterised *as* masculine. Thus, on the very day she receives the letter she goes out to an important official to seek his assistance. On arriving at his house, she 'with unfeminine boldness, went straight into his study' (292). The official reacts in kind, 'struck by such an unusual scene' (293), as she comes straight to the point. Zizi herself is aware that her decisive, clear-minded behaviour is a kind of narrative cross-dressing, asking him to 'Forget that I am a girl' (ibid.).

Finally, after many trials and tribulations Princess Zizi is vindicated, showing 'heroism' on the 'field of honour and sacred feats'. She has become a 'new woman', overnight. But her trials are not completely over. Towards the very end of the story the final narrator meets her at a masked ball and he cannot resist describing her in the same voyeuristic terms as he had used in her room. 'In my whole life I had never seen such a slender waist, such marvellous little feet, which are, you know, almost everything for me in a woman' (301). As we already know, she refuses his proposal and so even at the end resists the traditional feminine role of marriage, prepared to accept being thought 'strange'. In the end, then, Princess Zinaida has become a 'positive heroine' but it should be remembered that she has absolutely no support from other women, that for most of the story she is a composite portrait of irreconcilable, traditional stereotypes and that the fairy-tale transformation is hardly convincing. In this sense, then, *Princess Zizi* certainly reveals the same masculine ambivalence to female power as Odoevsky's earlier *Princess Mimi*.

4
Elena Gan and *A Futile Gift*

> The Ideal *is unusual in its depiction of the oppressive atmosphere and stultifying routine of life in a provincial garrison town from which its heroine seeks to escape, but otherwise the story is improbable and the style sententious.*[1]

This recent dismissive comment from John Mersereau is, in fact, one of very few remarks of any kind passed on the work of Elena Gan in Western criticism. (Mirsky accords her ten, not very gracious lines.[2]) This ignorance of Gan's work, which is only now being redressed, is particularly to be regretted, given that, as Richard Stites has observed, she was 'one of a number, larger than is commonly held, of cultivated women . . . who passed the ordinary limits of women's consciousness of their age to look at the larger world around them', and thereby anticipated the 'woman question' by twenty years.[3] In her short life (she died in 1842 at the age of 28), Gan did, indeed, like many writers of *svetskiye povesti* (society tales),[4] place women at the centre of her work. What is striking about her *œuvre*, however, is not merely the questions she asked about women's roles, but also the challenging way she dealt with these problems. In the four works considered here (*The Ideal*, (1837) *The Locket*, (1839) *Society's Judgement*,[5] (1840) and *A Futile Gift*, (1842)), Gan's project was to subvert the literary imaging of women, as well as to offer new responses to the questions she was helping to formulate.

1. THE IDEAL[6]

1.1 Images of Women

In this, her first published work[7], Gan established what was to be one of her central motifs (and one that was deeply autobiographical), namely, the bitter fate of the exceptional woman, especially in provincial society.[8] Whereas her depiction of the central character,

Olga, will be almost entirely positive, the view presented of the mass of women is utterly negative, at times surpassing even the most misogynistic of male writers. Indeed, we first encounter women in Gan's work precisely in terms of a 'mass', an undifferentiated collectivity. The very first few lines of Gan's that we have set the approach that was to persist throughout all her work. *The Ideal* opens with a glittering ball: outside the assembly rooms 'carriages, landaus, traps, sleighs were bringing whole loads of grandmothers, mothers, daughters, grand-daughters' (435). At each social gathering that punctuates the narrative (both in the initial setting of the provincial town, and later in St Petersburg) women are introduced as these 'loads'. The opening scene-setting, however, also becomes more explicit (indeed, sententious, to use Mersereau's word). Olga enters the ball-room and the (female) narrator immediately draws out the invidious position in which this talented young women finds herself: 'it was sad to see this bright poetic *soul*[9] surrounded by a *poisonous swarm of wasps*, who found their pleasure in stinging her from all sides' (438 – my italics). The perhaps trite insect image makes the point: the 'society' whose 'judgement' will condemn Olga as viciously as it will later destroy Zenaida (*Society's Judgement*) is comprised almost entirely of women (very little mention is made of men in these settings) and their main aim is to exercise power and social control over the deviant (because talented) heroine. (And, as already noted, this applies just as much to 'sophisticated' Petersburg as to the 'benighted' provinces.) This policing (on behalf of patriarchy[10]) operates on the basis of envy and malice and by means of gossip: Olga Goltsberg is castigated because she reads books (and is even thought to be writing one!), and her every move is watched by this social hydra. Although the reader is made aware from the outset of her 'light poetic soul', *liaisons dangereuses* are invented for her. In the end, the point which is pretty clear from the first few pages is hammered home with deep (autobiographical) rancour and pathos: the mass of women is the worst enemy for the talented outsider. At the second provincial ball Olga hears more, completely unsubstantiated slander and attempts to slough off the mud clinging to her. The narrator, however, seems to lose patience and intervenes directly and heavily:

> And when one meets with women like these – thank God, these meetings are fairly rare,[11] – the question involuntarily is born in the mind, out of what special material are they created? Are they

demons' brood or nature's mockery of humanity, the wrath of God, sent down to earth together with famine and plague? (450)

This really breaches all narrative decorum,[12] of course, but this is precisely the point: so deep is the author's/narrator's feeling that she must speak out. Moreover, as we shall see, the biblical lexis is not mere rhetoric, but should be read literally: in this anathematising of the demon women we are close to the work of Gogol. We should also note the foregrounding of this narratorial vituperation in the work's rhetoric. Irony, dismissal, sarcasm are insufficient: the demons must be castigated and cast out. Moreover, no real attempt is made to explain the wasps' malice. Vera, friend and confidante (more the latter than the former[13]) attempts to explain their behaviour as an extrapolation of how they would behave themselves, but this is really rather a feeble attempt at narrative objectivity. Certainly, there is a marked contrast with Chernyshevsky's later redemptive strategy in *What Is To Be Done?*, in his 'Eulogy of Maria Alexeevna',[14] the heroine's 'wicked' mother. The present petty demons seem beyond redemption.

One woman, however, stands apart (other than Vera and Olga) and in this instance, too, Gan establishes what is to be a vital, recurrent point of reference. In all these four works, the Mother, or a surrogate (good) mother is deeply valorised. When Olga and Vera meet after six years apart, the narrator offers a brief glimpse of their shared childhood. They had been brought up together by Olga's mother, 'an intelligent, almost learned woman . . . something of a free-thinker'. She herself had read all the French thinkers (presumably of the Enlightenment) and had not only encouraged the two girls to read as widely as possible, but had also inculcated in them a sense of 'nobility' and 'self-sacrifice'. Moreover, she 'considered the immutable conditions of the everyday life of women as inventions, *suitable only for the crowd*' (442 – my italics).[15]

A number of issues arise here. The two girls have grown up in an exclusively feminine world, close to the mother: men have played little, if any part in their background. The maternal presence, in loose terms at least, certainly a pre-Oedipal point of reference, remains a lasting symbol of peace, purity and refuge from the 'demonic' world of society women and false heroes (Anatoly). The mother-daughter relationship emerges in Gan's work as the *most* valorised and is rarely challenged. Yet, these reverentially encoded, poetically recalled havens are in the past, a kind of lost Edenic world which has engendered feminine purity, but has not provided lasting protection against the world. The maternal is certainly not repressed, nor denigrated here, as in much of male-authored literature,[16] but it is rarely, in the end, sufficient to protect the daughters once they are forced to encounter the world of the Law. Indeed, even in this brief early remembrance of lost time, the emphasis is firstly on the fact that it was far away and long ago. Secondly, as the italicised words above indicate, the 'free-thinking' of the mother specifically *does not* prepare for living amongst the 'crowd' of 'demons' and 'wasps'.[17]

1.2 The Heroine

'Her sweet, silent, but passionate, heroines are pathetically naive and helpless, and invariably fall victims to the envy and slander of provincial gossip'.[18]

As we have already seen, the latter part of Mirsky's assertion is largely applicable to *The Ideal*. Olga, however, is passionate, but certainly not silent. (Indeed, mutism is very much not a defining aspect of Gan's heroines: on the contrary, one of the central aspects of her project was to find and give her principal women a voice). Olga Goltsberg enters the story as she enters the ball-room, already marked out as the object of narrative interest: who is this strange, socially-deviant 'blue-stocking'? Immediately, the narrator (not yet identified as female) offers a physical sketch of the 22-year-old woman: the emphasis is on how she differs from social expectations:

> [she was] not a beauty, not graceful; pleasant, dressed extremely simply: not a single flower, not a single bronze ornament. At first glance one could say about her – she's not bad looking – but the second glance gave birth to the wish to look more closely into her features.   (438)

Her dress, then is semiotically defined by its simplicity and lack of affectation. She is *physically* described here (and in the ensuing lines), but there is a marked lack of sexualisation of her features, still less the fetishisation so prevalent elsewhere in the period.[19] The chief impression is the valorisation of her *inner* life, instead of a concentration on her external attributes.

At the same time, there are stray traces of sentimentalist iconography:

Her *dark* eyes looked *fearfully* from under her *long black* eye-lashes;
... a shadow of *sadness* often flickered on this face.

(ibid. – my italics)

All of these features – the fear, the hidden sadness, the long, dark lashes – are the sign of the Sentimentalist[20] heroine and these signs are recurrent in this story, as in most of Gan's fiction. Yet if Olga is initially encoded as vulnerable, these features also denote her as a woman apart. The iconography intensifies as the story progresses. Soon she meets her old friend Vera and the depths of her emotion(alism), connoting her fragility are *physically* displayed: 'tears all but *spurted out* from under her lashes, and a bright *flush* lit up her *pale* cheeks' (439 – my italics). Overwritten[21] as this florid description now seems, each detail enhances her status as the essentially feminine (and, therefore, vulnerable) heroine.

But one of the features that differentiates Gan (and Zhukova) from most male writers of the period, is the attention paid to the inner life of the heroine. This is already hinted at in her introduction (her reading, writing, simplicity of dress, the hidden sadness). These are developed in the encounter the day after the first ball between Olga and Vera, where we learn of their childhood and their ensuing (largely negative) experiences of the world. Despite these experiences, Olga has retained her innocent idealism. The narrator even begs the reader's condescension on this point: 'Having reviewed her position, you will forgive her excessive *dreaminess*' (444 – my italics). The conflict between 'dreams' (*mechty*) and 'reality' was a central one in Russian Romanticism[22] and dreams were encoded both negatively and positively, as a flight from reality, or as a legitimate immersion in a higher, more ideal world. This ambivalence permeates *The Ideal*: like her lofty education, Olga's dreams set her apart from society and leave her ill-prepared to deal with its 'judgements'. At the same time, her dreams will lead her, not back to the maternal, perhaps, but to the revivifying power of the (Transcendental) Father.

One of the central negative moments here recapitulated is Olga's loveless marriage to the insensitive Lieutenant Goltsberg. Unlike her contrastive friend, this forced immersion in military life (another autobiographical instance) has not led to 'cold and sharp judgements' (443), but rather to a shrinking back into her inner, spiritual world and, indeed, to an increase in her potentially dangerous Idealism: 'And this discord [with her husband], this solitude of the *soul* reinforced within her the tendency to isolation and *dreaminess'* (447 – my italics). In Olga's case, a room of her own has to reside within her own body. But, as for Pushkin's Aleko, Olga's passions (her dreams) cannot be repressed forever and the potential catastrophe that awaits the return of the repressed is signalled when Olga first hears mention of the new *poema* by her Ideal, the false-hero, Anatoly the poet. As usual the repressed identity explodes in physical display:[23] 'And Olga with a flaming face, her hands tightly clenched, directed beseeching gazes' (448).

Much of the work's very extended prologue reiterates these motifs – her isolation, or rather alienation from the world, her spiritual sustenance in dreams and poetry, her repeated physical displays of repressed desire. When she moves to St. Petersburg with the stodgy Lieutenant her dreams and desires combine to provide a quasi-ecstatic response to her first sight of Anatoly, at the critical chronotope of the theatre (to which we will return shortly). His play is being performed and when the author is called for, Olga is likened to a Delphic priestess, 'awaiting the appearance of the spirit with rapture and longing' (457). Her clearly erotic ecstasy reaches a crescendo when he does appear. As the narrator had earlier, Olga breaches all decorum:

> Olga, not remembering the decencies, not noticing the looks which her exclamation brought upon her, clutched the back of the seat so as not to fall, and two enormous tears rolled from her eyes which were directed with an ineffable feeling at the poet, at her *ideal*.
> (458 – Gan's italics)

(Again, the narrator then intervenes to ask for condescension on the part of the reader.) The emphasis on liquefaction, on near hysteria cannot be avoided and the (excessive) iconographic representation of the heroine so apparent here and at every moment of intense emotion(alism) raises certain problems. Is this eroticisation, hysteresisation of the female body markedly different from the fetishisation already alluded to? Does the imaging implicate the reader in a titillated gaze? On the whole, I think not, in light of the overall project of Gan's approach to her heroines, however vulnerable she may make them. The stress here is not so much on the 'willing virgin's' surrender to the male (phallic) gaze, but on her idealisation of art, and, therefore, of the spiritual world more generally, or to use Gan's key lexical referent for feminine virtue and purity, the *soul*. Indeed, on the next page the narrator intervenes once more to emphasise that Olga's motives and behaviour are untainted. She [the narrator] admits that 'it is difficult to explain' (459) what has ensued, but that 'Her *spiritual* love for the poet had acquired more substance' (ibid. – my italics). And this is perhaps the main, radical point. The heroine is encoded in Sentimentalist, eroticised clichés, but this encoding does *not* lead to her becoming a seduced victim of the Rake (false hero), nor of the reader's gaze, but is part of her long, difficult and painful struggle to the spirit and the soul. The soul will become the true feminine heroine's space.

As the story progresses, increasing emphasis is placed on Olga's religious essence: this becomes the signified of the iconographic signifier. Anatoly, having taken full notice of Olga's emotionalism, soon begins his task of seduction and Olga through a combination of naive purity and idealism allows herself to be seduced emotionally, although never physically. At every stage of his encroachment, her spirituality is stressed, as if (and probably literally so) a guardian angel hovers to protect her. Thus, as she falls in love, the narrator exclaims: 'Yes! Olga already loved him with all the power of her fiery *soul*' (465 – my italics). Anatoly, well versed, it seems, in the 'tender science' sees clearly that 'Olga was giving herself to this love with utter faith in the sanctity of her feeling' (ibid.). As the actual seduction scene arrives we learn that 'her feelings spoke powerfully to Anatoly's advantage; they belonged to him indivisibly, but conscience, but religion battled with her love' (468). To the end, this conflict rages in Olga's soul and, equally, her emotions are always intense and are accorded full iconographic display, as when she finds Anatoly's revelatory venal letter, and as she returns to life after all her suffering, in the chapel scene which concludes the plot. In the end, we cannot consider Olga to be a fully realised character, but the repetitious emphasis on her sanctity and on her intense emotionalism serve the same purpose. Her sanctity saves her from the traditional fate of the vulnerable (virgin) heroine and, thereby, the iconography which clings to her takes on a new meaning. It denotes strength and ultimate victory rather than the sexual catastrophe which usually attaches to such iconography.

1.3 Images of Men

In *The Ideal*, sexual difference is more or less absolute. (Whether this apparent clarity about identity reflects certainly, or anxiety, is unclear, although the former is more likely). The depiction of Olga leaves her, in the end, as largely a stereotype (although I believe the stereotype is recast, renewed) and both the two principal males, Goltsberg and Anatoly, are certainly stereotypical, the one of the gross, insensitive husband, the other the Rake.[24] Within these limitations there are interesting notes, however, and both men are used to highlight[25] Olga's loftiness and sanctity. Goltsberg is thinly sketched and we know little of him beyond his eating habits. Married to a virtual stranger, Olga does her best to establish some kind of companionate marriage, but he is insensitive to her aspiration: 'but he would laugh, yawn, interrupt her ecstatic dreaming by a request that she order a little more ham for tomorrow's dinner' (447). The contrast between the spiritual world and the quotidian concerns of the 'ball-shaped' (458) lieutenant is nicely drawn. His insensitivity is doubly culpable. Not only does he thwart Olga's dreams, but his greater concern for his 'pie and porter' than with 'saving his beloved wife' (as Anatoly observes, 468) is directly instrumental in placing her at risk.

Anatoly features rather more prominently: indeed, as seen earlier, he may be the title character (although there are several possible interpretations in the end for the title). Much of his identity fits exactly the stereotype of the Rake. There is no ambiguity in his characterisation, and as is her wont the narrator intervenes to point up what is already obvious. Even before he has met Olga, he stands 'leaning against the wall and with a smile, in which flashed the shadow of *perfidy*, when Olga shuddered' (461 – my italics). This (devilish) cunning, as we shall see, will also take its part in the sacred/demonic lexicon which saturates the text. Lest the naive reader should miss this hint, two pages later the narrator spells out exactly what Anatoly is about:

> Anatoly's character was in complete disharmony with the feelings which he expressed in his works: fiery and elevated in verse, in essence he was a most ordinary man, greedy for all pleasures . . . and a Lovelace towards women. (463)

(There are several such direct narratorial interventions, and, indeed, Anatoly confirms the narrator's prejudice himself in the venal letter that Olga finds in his study (474).)

The critical point here is the contrast drawn above. That Anatoly is a self-proclaimed Rake is important to the sexual dialectics of the work. Even more central is the fact that he is construed by Olga as her *ideal*, the poet who speaks to her soul, and he betrays this sacred calling. As Belinsky put it at precisely this period, 'The poet, as the organ of the general and the universal, as the direct manifestation of the spirit, cannot be mistaken and talk falsehood'.[26] Olga (and probably Gan) would agree furiously with Belinsky and certainly Olga takes Anatoly (from his works) to be such an 'organ'. His greatest crime, then, is not so much to act out his gender stereotype as a heartless seducer (a role he relishes, but fails in), but rather to betray his (literally) sacred calling.

1.4 Setting

In this, her first work, Elena Gan, as we have already seen, established many of her own literary trademarks. In a sense, these could be summed up, to use the Formalist phrase, as 'revitalising the cliché' (stereotype), often with interesting implications for sexual identity (especially in her subsequent works). This approach largely holds for her use of setting, which is mainly comprised of a series of already well established chronotopes. As Bakhtin put it: [in the chronotope] 'Time here thickens; condenses, becomes visible in art; space is intensified and drawn into the moment of time, plot and history'.[27] As he suggests, the chronotope provides a kind of snapshot, a set-piece or tableau in which the actions of individuals engage with the wider currents of society, and history itself. In using this device as one of her main structuring principles, Gan is able to freeze the action for dialogue and character development, as well as to comment on the social factors (including gender identity) which underpin the given chronotope. Simultaneously, she locates her work quite specifically in certain generic developments, as Lermontov was also doing.[28]

As we have already seen, *The Ideal* opens with the central chronotope of the *svetskaya povest*, the society ball.[29] This chronotope, in fact, combines two which Bakhtin identified in French literature (of much the same period), the drawing-room,[30] and the small provincial town. As he says of the latter: 'There are no events here, only "recurring occurrences". Time is deprived of its progressive historical passage and moves in narrow circles . . . In this time people eat, drink, sleep, have wives and mistresses (without romance), make petty intrigue'.[31] This encapsulates very well the stultifying world in which Olga strives for the Ideal, and the opening ball scene lays down many critical clues as to the story's development. The ball (like the drawing-room or salon) is a place for meetings, intrigues: a place where women (with or without bronze ornaments, though usually with) will parade to be gazed upon. There is an emphasis here on the (relatively at least) glittering social scene – chandeliers, a thirteen-piece orchestra: every detail immediately alerts us to the fact that we will enter the world of the *svet*, with all the connotations this has at this period in generic literary development. All is typical, a 'recurring occurrence' – the flirting, the gossip and arrangement according to caste. It is a world where social and gender roles are seemingly *immutable* (whatever Olga's mother may think), where behaviour is ritualised and customs are repeated. In other terms, the power of the sociolect is absolute. All this leads to an emphasis on the narrowness of this (woman's) world, where everything is, moreover, mundane, trivial and banal. The specific gender and plot implications are further underscored by Olga's later avoidance of such occasions as the power of gossip intensifies around her. Her husband remarks that 'women love balls and finery' (448) and Olga deviates in this key semiotic determinant, as in many others.

When the plot proper finally gets under way the moment is signalled by the move to the 'Northern Babylon', St Petersburg.[32] By 1837, of course St Petersburg itself had become a chronotope in its own right in Russian literature (and thought)[33] – the symbol of Europe in Russia, of alienation, madness and despair and, above all, of artificiality. In this last sense, it was the intensification of all the values of the *svet* which Olga is a part but from which she is also an outcast. Immediately, the Goltsbergs are at the theatre, and the resonance of this situation is highlighted by a quotation (incorrect) from *Evgeny Onegin*. It is here that Olga displays her repressed passion for her ideal, but it is also a quintessentially *masculine* topos. Women may appear there, to be gazed upon with phallic lorgnettes[34] but it is part of the public domain in which, the story as a whole makes clear, they are excluded from playing a part in any meaningful sense. Because of the power of the resonance of this setting (and even before Olga's display), the rest of the plot is fatally coded in terms of her vulnerability and exposure to the rapacious male gaze.

Interspersed among these major, determining chronotopes are a number of other less developed, less powerful instances. Thus, there is the (again autobiographical) 'life of a military lady' with its Novikovian[35] details of provincial squalor and grimness, in which the emphasis is on constant change, but perpetual sameness, and which further reinforces the restricted nature of Olga's life; the scene where Olga and Vera stroll in pastoral, vernal quiet to have their sentimental conversation; the visit to the *dacha*, half nature, half urban where the seduction is pursued by means of another sentimental conversation, this time between Olga and Anatoly; and finally, Olga's fateful visit to Anatoly's study, the mirror of his soul, a fact Tatyana had already discovered concerning Onegin.

Two further scenes, however, deserve more detailed consideration, both standing as positive contrasts to the society world. Olga's childhood, we have seen, stands as a cherished memory of the maternal. The setting is deliberately not merely pre-Oedipal but almost pre-lapsarian in its Edenic tones:

> In a happy, southern land, on the southern shore of the Crimea, they lived not counting the days. The sun would awaken them for their lessons, for walks, for inexhaustible talks. (442)

The childhood scene is deliberately mythologised – the south (like Gogol's *Mirgorod*), the warmth, the carefree freedom where women walk untrammelled by men or the crowd (of women). Time stands still in this h(e)aven. It is indeed significant that, at her nadir of deception, when Olga finds Anatoly's letter, she recalls specifically this scene, just as she and Vera had earlier harked back to it. At this moment she returns to her childhood state: 'The suffering of the poor woman flowed out in bitter sobs. Olga sobbed like a child, as she had once sobbed in that distant region' (474).

A similar moment, in which several chronotopic motifs are intertwined, concludes the action of the plot. As Olga struggles to overcome her grief and desolation at Anatoly's perfidy and betrayal (of his sacred calling), she finds herself one *spring evening*, outside the city amongst the splendours of God's world. An invalid invites her to visit a wayside chapel. Inside she experiences a truly epiphanic moment as her life passes before her (another reference to her Eden) and she is plunged in despair. But, the, unseen (celestial?) instruments begin the evening prayer and the last rays of the sun burst out from behind the clouds and illuminate the Saviour. Each of these details is a cliché of Sentimentalism, but their combination has a powerful effect as Olga is reborn, and thereby, subverts the dysphoric declension she had almost completely played out. Gan's use of pastoral, then, again shows her ability to revitalise the cliché. Evening in a wayside chapel brings life, not the more usual final lachrymose moments of the fated victim.

1.5 Plot

The writer's creative use of cliché is also well illustrated in her handling of plot, in the sense that Gan takes an already well established plot motif (the Rake's seduction of the willing virgin[36] – and Olga certainly is this in an emotional/spiritual sense), leads us through almost all the stages of the paradigm, only to subvert the expected conclusion (illness and/or death) by the positive upswing with which the story concludes. In providing this unexpected ending, Gan illustrates the ability of the woman to overcome even the most dysphoric of circumstances and plots, even if the solution to her drama is, in one sense, an escape from the material world. In this way, Gan once more sets out one of her central creative projects and like *The Tales of Belkin*, she weaves 'new patterns on an old canvas [&] parodies the old literary stereotypes'.[37] In the instance of Gan, this project always has gender implications in that she allows her heroines, so often the victims of the plot, to find some kind of positive plot resolution.

One striking instance in *The Ideal* is the very prolonged prologue (with an interpolated pre-prologue). Both these sections, outlining Olga's present unhappy situation and the idyllic, but lost past, ensure that the readers' expectations are overdetermined to anticipate an 'unhappy ending'. Because the prologue is so prolonged, moreover (20 out of 45 pages) it is foregrounded. This has two effects. In retrospect, this seems the most important section (and therefore the narrative is more about the *context* of a contemporary woman than about her actual story); secondly, when the plot proper does commence, with the theatre scene, the action is much more dramatic, indeed, volcanic, after the largely static scene-setting which had preceded it. Yet another effect of the extended prologue is to off-set the interpolated pre-prologue. Because we know that this paradise *is* lost, the dislocation of the chronological order emphasises the seeming hopelessness of the diegetic present.

In the prologue, then, the reader learns of the power of 'society's judgement', Olga's 'deviancy', and of the factors which had brought about her gloomy present life. After the paradisaic childhood, the death of Olga's mother had left her dowerless, and had consequently propelled her, ill-prepared for the harshness of life, into a love-less marriage. Only days after the actual wedding (445), she is immersed in the coarse, unideal military environment. In much the same way that Tolstoy was to do in *Anna Karenina*, Olga is placed in an almost impossible situation. She is passionate, idealistic, yearning for love and her husband and his environment are the very antithesis of all she craves. Yet this too has a (proto-feminist) polemical point: Olga does not commit suicide, nor even die. In other words, Gan suggests, a woman can overcome even seemingly impossible odds.

One driving plot motif has already been identified, that of woman as enigma. The purpose of the pre-prologue and prologue is to explain where Olga has come from and the very telling of her story and its explanatory power (as well as seeing it from her point of view) has a further polemical function. Whereas most male-authored texts have the very purpose of showing that woman *is* enigma, *The Ideal*'s first 20 pages defuse this riddle.[38]

Towards the end of the prologue another critical motif is identified, and one that deliberately invokes the fairy-tale. As Olga attempts to explain to Vera the sources of her adoration of her ideal (Anatoly the poet), the more cynical and wordly-wise confidante shrugs and says with a smile 'Just wait, you'll wake up' (451). Indeed, Olga will be awoken from her dream, but the kiss will not be from the Prince, leading to a romantic happy ending. She will be awoken by the false hero, but, again, she will survive this potentially fatal encounter.

Finally, the plot does begin to emerge as we are told: 'And Olga is once more *thrown* into a new world' (455 – my italics). This is another telling detail. Although the plot eventually reveals Olga's true awakening, until the last few pages her desire plays no part in the activation of the narrative: at almost every stage, from the death of her mother until the chapel scene, she is acted upon, a passive and accidental recipient of men's desires. But, yet again, this traditional pattern will be broken in the end.

This 'new world' eventually leads to St Petersburg and to the theatre. The change in the story's direction is marked not only by the scene-shifting, but also by a sharp alteration in narrative rhythm. After the largely static, recurrent time of the prologue the remainder of the story, the complication, perpeteia(s) and dénouement unfold very rapidly, almost breathlessly at times. This breathlessness is precisely the point as it exactly enacts, speaks for Olga's condition. After the slow, unchanging empty years, her emotional/sexual life explodes and, at times, she herself is literally breathless. This general pattern is at its most intense in the theatre scene: the ecstatic moment of encounter with the ideal is conveyed in a rushing out of action (of emotion) after pages/years of refrigeration. And now that the action has commenced there are very few dislocations or digressions.

The principal plot motif now crystallises as the classic eighteenth-century paradigm of the Rake's seduction of the virgin. For most of this action, the story follows the paradigm almost exactly (except for the ending). Yet the *treatment* of the paradigm differs markedly from the most male-authored versions. Because of the point-of-view (the potential victim's, not the Rake's) and because of the narratorial interventions ('Anatoly is Lovelace') there is no false arousal of the reader. We are told exactly what is going on, although the euphoric rather than dysphoric conclusion still comes as a surprise. In other words (and this applies to several of Gan's works), we read the plot of *Princess Mary* as part of 'Mary's Journal', as it were. And the effect is certainly very different.

While Gan anticipates Lermontov's plot (although they both, of course, go back to a common origin), she also borrows that of *Evgeny Onegin* in a number of details, most obviously in the study (soul) scene.[39] This scene is significant in several ways. Olga is (mis)informed (at a ball) that Anatoly is 'dying for love', and so rushes to his flat: this is almost the only moment when *her* desire pushes the plot. Her need to know, to solve the enigma makes her momentarily, morphologically male.[40] Furthermore, it is here that, like Tatyana before her, Olga awakes, in her discovery that the hero is in fact, the false hero.[41] This moment is marked as the critical perpeteia/epiphany by the switch to the historic present, the extreme iconography attaching to Olga and the flash-back to her Edenic childhood. *She* discovers the truth and is thereby, again, rendered morphologically the hero.

That this has been the critical moment in her life is again marked by the narrator. On the next page (475), she declares: 'This is how the romance/novel[42] finished', and immediately she reverts to the generalised time adopted in the prologue. 'So months went by'. For a while, Olga behaves as the reader would expect the seduced and abandoned 'virgin' to behave. She enters the next stages of the declension, emotional disarray and actual physical illness, accompanied by a longing for death. But, as we know, there will be no suicide here. There is a kind of spiritual death, to be sure, but merely so that she may be reborn. (In this rebirth, Olga once more becomes the hero.[43]) This return to life shows yet again Gan's tendency to mark the switches in her stories from one section to another. After the generalised narrative ('months passed'), 'On one of the fine spring days' (spring), Olga finds herself outside the chapel. That her entry into God's house (and kingdom) will be significant is emphasised by another switch to the historic present: 'Olga enters the chapel' (477). Time sharpens yet further: 'enormous tears flow down her pale cheeks: *at this moment*' (ibid. – my italics), the celestial music commences. As she stares at the sacred images, a miracle occurs:

> With warm faith she prays, pouring out her soul before him; tears of repentance wash the marble, and a heavy feeling slipped from her burdened breast. She breathes easily, with childish joy she looks at the sacred face: she has found the aim of her life, – has found a friend, joy, comfort! From this minute her existence is complete. (478)

This resurrection completes the plot: like the mythical hero, this heroine dies, enters the grave, to emerge reborn. The Rake's plot ends with the victim's spiritual victory. Olga's letter to Vera now concludes the story and the fact that the heroine's own word provides a recapitulation symbolises Gan's new treatment of old material. The Sphinx speaks and tells her own story, the oppressed woman overcomes her circumstances and the plot expectations are subverted. In her letter, moreover, Olga not only reviews her life and makes sense of it, but is able to look forward to the rest of her life with calm, even joyous resignation. Her life now has meaning.

Before concluding my discussion of *The Ideal* by a review of the main thematic ideas, I would like to return for a moment to certain aspects of the plot, as they bear upon male/female relations which will again establish certain motifs and patterns recurrent in Gan's fiction. These considerations will also help to more exactly locate Gan's work in the generic and thematic development of this literary period (late Romanticism/early Realism).

Although the love plot (often, as here, in the form of pursuit and seduction) is to be central to nearly all Gan's work (with the notable exception of the unfinished *A Futile Gift*), it is, in a sense, decentred in *The Ideal*, primarily because of the considerable delay (the prologues) in introducing it. Consequently, the emphasis on Olga's inner world (the *soul*) is enhanced.

In another sense, however, the two motifs (seduction and Olga's soul) are directly interlocked and the concentration on the latter in the prologues leads directly to the former. On two occasions in these introductory sections the talk turns to Anatoly and his poetry and at both times Olga reveals the dangerous side of her passionate idealism, in that she shows herself to be *already ready* to be seduced. In other words, what we might call her 'Tatyanaism', her belief in the reality of fiction, predisposes her to the 'tender science' of the experienced Rake. Thus, when she receives a packet, containing Anatoly's verse, Olga exclaims 'He! He! Again I will hear his sounds, I will read his celestial feelings!' (451). The *on* of the Russian echoes exactly Tatyana's words (3:VIII) – '*éto on!* (it is he!)'.[44] And like Tatyana, Olga – indeed, her spiritual sister[45] – swoons with love on seeing her ideal.

At this encounter, another critical motif is immediately introduced. In her discussion of French and English texts from the eighteenth century (precisely the sort of books Tatyana had read, and, we might suspect, Olga had too[46]), Nancy K. Miller observes:

> The dialogue of meaningful looks is a necessary preliminary to the verbal exchange. In accordance with the canons of masculine and feminine behaviour (which presuppose naïveté on the part of the woman and experience on the part of the man), the man's gaze is a declaration, a communication that disconcerts; the woman's timorous . . . but compelled.[47]

This is precisely the situation here. After the commotion created by her 'hysterical' display, Olga becomes the centre of attention. 'She noticed . . . the deep, searching gaze of Anatoly' (458–9). This deeply phallic look is soon repeated and, if anything, intensified, with predetermined effects. As she and her husband attempt to get through the throng, 'At that minute Olga felt on her face the same searching gaze: it *penetrated* into her *soul*, and brought her to confusion and trembling' (459 – my italics). And Olga plays her part in this paradigm to perfection: 'Olga does not look back, does not dare to look up'. And then, 'She dared raise her eyes and they met the fiery, black eyes, which were looking at Olga with a caress, almost with love' (ibid.). Because both play their roles in this overdetermined plot motif, the dénouement is, seemingly, already prepared (except that, as we have seen, it is not: Olga's soul may be *penetrated*, but the breach will be healed).

There motifs are repeated as the seduction/pursuit plot unfolds in a series of eroticised encounters. Olga and Anatoly encounter each other at the dacha. Olga turns to be introduced to another guest, 'but further away by an open window, he stood . . . he!' (461). His 'sometimes sad, sometimes fiery glances' (ibid.) fall upon her. They talk of love, and Anatoly speaks in terms that exactly prefigure Pechorin's speech to Princess May, of avoiding love, to avoid the pain (463). Later, everywhere she goes in St Petersburg, Olga seems to see his eyes following her and when the actual (attempted) seduction scene arrives (467–9), Anatoly plays all the established cards of the seducer. He has absented himself for a while, he switches to the intimate *ty* form, declares his love for '*my*[48] Olga' (467 – my italics), he then turns cold, threatens to leave her and so on. The seduction scene is interesting in several respects. In terms of plot development, it is foregrounded by its very length (three pages) and its intensity, being comprised largely of (melo)dramatic dialogue. Potentially, for a woman writer, it is a tricky area, full of the risk of prurience or titillation of the (male) readers' gaze. Yet, by avoiding the sensualisation of the female body in this scene, Gan is able to present this *as* a climatic scene without falling into this trap. Furthermore, there is once again an implicit polemic in the actions of the two characters. Anatoly's game is so obvious and clichéd, he is deprived not only of originality, but also of the glamour that attached to his prototype, Lovelace, and that was soon to attach to Pechorin. Olga's reaction, in reverse, is valorised in that, despite the fierce struggle in her soul, she is neither seduced (like Bela and Mary) nor raped, like Clarissa. Her reactions may be full of the somewhat mechanistic iconography of the story, and of the period more generally (for example, 'she began to tremble in all her limbs' (469)), but her weakness under the assault, in the long run, denotes her strength. That is, despite her inner turmoil, despite her 'feminine' 'weakness', she does not surrender her citadel.[49]

1.6 Theme

As should be clear by now, many of the motifs and textual strategies of *The Ideal* indicate a central and explicit concern with gender issues, if not identities. Setting plot, characterisation, and now theme, are all organised, to a greater or lesser extent, around the principle of male/female. Certain themes make this organising principle even more obvious. For example, a recurrent problem in this work and throughout Gan's *oeuvre* (up to and including *A Futile Gift*) is that of female education. From the very first pages, as we have seen, Olga is marked out as deviant because of her education. Certainly, her upbringing *is* valorised, but the Ideal tuition from the mother also brings the problem of inappropriateness. Indeed, the narrator suggests as much: 'with her education, with her type of thinking and life up to the age of fifteen, how could she accept her lot, as thousands of women would have?' (444). A subset of the education discussion is that of reading. Developing Tatyana's situation, Gan echoes Pushkin by suggesting that over-identification with the world of heroes and heroines can be disastrous':[50] indeed, her 'love' for Anatoly is predicated on (his) fiction to a greater extent even than Tatyana's love for Onegin. This motif is once more crystallised by our ever-helpful (if 'sententious') narrator: Olga 'gave herself over to her books, her poetry and *fantasies*' (447 – my italics). The narrator takes this point up again later on. While commenting on the true (earthly) nature of Anatoly's interest in the (spiritual) Olga, she remarks that any hint at the earthly on his part 'will lead her out of her delusion and will show her things in their real aspect' (467). It is a central part of Olga's continuing ordeal that it is only when she reads Anatoly's letter (his real, rather than false word) that she finally emerges from her fantasy/delusion (again matching exactly Tatyana's path). (The theme of *mechty/mechtatel'nost* is very close to the *books/fantasies* motif.)

Implicit in all the above discussion is the lot of women in a restricted society.[51] As usual, the narrator leaves little to the reader's imagination and there are several very explicit *cris de coeur* on the subject of the oppression of women. In the opening pages she remarks upon how difficult life is for the exceptional man, 'but the position of a woman, which nature[52] has placed above the crowd, is truly awful' (438). The most direct exposition of this theme, however, comes from Olga herself in the course of a lengthy discussion with Vera. *No* woman's lot, they agree, can be happy, to which Olga adds with passion:

> But what evil genius has so distorted the destiny of women? Now she is born for the sole purpose of pleasing, flattering, entertaining men's leisure . . . Truly, it sometimes seems that God's world has been created for men alone; the universe is open to them, with all its mysteries, for them there are words, the arts and knowledge; for them there is freedom and all the joys of life. From the cradle a woman is fettered by the chains of decency. (454–5)

If Olga's words would seem to be a proto-feminist call for emancipation, then the overall logic of *The Ideal* suggests that no emancipation is, in the present circumstances, possible in the *temporal world*. For 'freedom and all the joys of life' a woman must look elsewhere. This leads us on, in fact, to the essentially religious themes of the story, which are, in the end (literally) more significant than the temporal aspects. The very title of the story leads in this direction. There are several contenders for the title. One might argue that the lost maternal represents an ideal state, while Olga herself, of course, believes that Anatoly (the poet) represents this quality. We know all along that he is a false-hero, and therefore an illusion, not an ideal, and Olga is eventually led to the same conclusion. More generally, she discovers, as Vera had already warned her, that to believe in an ideal in this world is a mere *mechta*.[53] As already indicated, another key word for understanding Olga's essence (and Gan does deal in essences) is *dusha* (the soul).[54] The importance of this word can be seen, for example, at the nadir of her fortunes. When she reads Anatoly's letter 'she stood for a second time over the grave and buried in it her soul' (474); and then, some time afterwards, 'everything around her was empty; just as it was empty in her soul' (476).

More generally, the story can also be read as an interplay between the sacred and the profane, largely on gender lines, Olga being the 'spiritual' feminine and Anatoly the blasphemer of her purity. (For example, 'indeed, in this look there was something authentically hellish' (470)). Consequently, the chapel scene and Olga's ensuing, concluding letter do provide the story with a fitting ending. She sums this up with the very last words of the story. After reviewing her life and finding resignation she instructs Vera:

> Nothing will fill up the emptiness of her [woman's] being, and she will exhaust herself in fruitless endeavours to attach herself to anything in the world. Unearthly attachments may satisfy her thirst. Her love should be the Saviour, her goal – the heavens!
> (480)

Olga thus finds her Ideal. The story therefore ends on a highly positive note and many traditional clichés have been reworked. A resolution to the story's many dilemmas and anxieties is found, although some may feel that this resolution is unsatisfactory. Be that as it may, it is one which accords with the dynamics of Olga's character and with the gender implications of the story as a whole, according to which the heroine is utterly feminine, and the essence of femininity is the soul, in the full Christian sense of the word.

2. THE LOCKET[55]

This story, also a *svetskaya povest*, repeats many of the political and parodic elements of *The Ideal*; indeed, the use of parody (especially of the Superfluous Man) and generic play ('Sternianism') are even more marked, and handled in a rather more sophisticated, subtle way.

2.1 Setting

While *The Ideal* declares its intentions by opening with the classic society tale chronotope of the ball, the present work does much the same by introducing us to the high society world, inhabited by Prince Yurevich and Baroness Sophia Engelsberg, of the spa town Pyatigorsk. Immediately, the contemporary reader would anticipate amorous intrigues, rivalry and deception, and is not disappointed, although the resolution of these motifs is very different from that offered by *Princess Mary*, for example.[56] As in this other, slightly later work, the Pyatigorsk setting excites other reader expectations: a kind of frontier town it stood on the boundary between 'civilisation' and 'the wilderness', promising the exotic, passion and danger.

In reality, by way of contrast with her more openly parodic *Memories of Zheleznovodsk*, Gan deliberately leaves these expectations hanging. Although a tragic drama unfolds in the tale-within-the tale, the first part of *The Locket* deliberately accentuates the venal superficiality of the high society world we have entered. The men here are Grushnitskys, not Pechorins. That we have entered such a world is succinctly made clear by a succession of well-chosen, evocative details – 'the foppish carriage' (210), the French phrases, the valet, the hunting dog and so on. It is a world of fashionable, idle young men at their leisure, into which a 'strange' woman has come, to wreak vengeance rather than to be destroyed.

As is her general tendency, Gan marks the stages of her narrative by a series of such evocative chronotopes – such as the promenade in the countryside, involving a Watteau-esque fête, and concluding in an alfresco ball. Later, and indoors, we visit a society evening, with singing and intimate conversations *à deux*, although in this last detail the (false) hero fails to achieve his goal.

In the first part of the narrative, in Pyatigorsk, the set-pieces act more as *tableaux vivants* and no particular point is made in the slightly mechanical use of the chronotope. In the second half (Baroness Engelberg's account of the events which had preceded the Pyatigorsk story), however, the use of chronotope is rather more effective and resonant. This story (the childhood of Sophia (the Baroness) and her sister, Olympia, and the fateful events that followed) begins with a deliberate and powerful recreation of the eighteenth century pastoral, in which the gender implications are developed. The first lines of Sophia's narrative set the scene of her childhood home: 'In one of our most picturesque regions there is a little corner, unnoticed by anyone and forgotten from time immemorial by historians and romantics' (259). Sophia has already apologised to her listeners that she is no writer, but Gan plays on this traditional modesty/anxiety[57] of the female author by having her heroine begin in this deliberately self-conscious way: the prologue, as it were, 'announces itself' as a literary cliché. As was also the case in *The Ideal* we enter an all-female h(e)aven of remote, simple peace and tranquillity, where the two contrastive sisters are brought up by their grandmother. All the details echo the Sentimentalist tradition, which is valorised rather than mocked.[58] We hear of the 'old woman'[59] and that 'the serious and slightly sad expression of her face would take on a shade of inexpressible tenderness; in her eyes, dimmed by time and tears, shone a reverential love' (260). It is a place where the absence of men is specifically commented upon and whose eighteenth century qualities are marked, even by the calling name of their estate, *Otradnoye* (Joy). As elsewhere in Gan's work the all-female community and the nurturing maternal presence suggest the ideal social organisation, one that is indeed heavenly perfection: 'At that time their dwelling represented the image of earthly paradise' (263). But the same problems as before arise when Eden must be abandoned, first by Sophia's journey abroad and then by Olympia's departure to the wicked world (Moscow) where her tragedy will begin. The feminine enclave and the maternal must some day be forsaken, but when they are, the loss is always immense. Nevertheless, it is significant that the final scenes of this, second narrative mark a return home. This return both underscores the cataclysmic changes that have occurred in the women's lives (by reminding them and us how much has been lost), but also acts as the locus for a partial recovery and reconciliation on the part of the tragic heroine and victim, Olympia.

Sophia further defines herself as a kind of female Belkin in her later handling of setting. Olympia's fall into the snares of the world, and into the Rake/victim paradigm is signalled by the move to the big city. As in *The Ideal* her (willing) seduction begins at the theatre and then is completed at the spa town of Lipetsk. Although less exotic than Pyatigorsk, this provincial watering-place excites the same reader expectation of amorous intrigue, which on this occasion are not disappointed. On the eve of her departure from Moscow to Lipetsk another chronotope is brilliantly developed, namely, a version of the 'ocular rape' scene, which occurs in a church, arousing marked undercurrents of Sadeian sacrilege. (I will return to this scene in more detail.)

2.2 Images of Men

Gan may rightly be considered one of the first Russian writers to place women (and gender issues) at the very centre of her work, but in this story she shows her ability to create an androcentric world. Although her aim in depicting the male characters of *The Locket* is primarily parodic and satirical, she does a successful job in establishing the world of all-male camaraderie and the ambience of the Superfluous Man. Here the 'Romantic Hero' is not merely uncrowned, but decapitated and in several ways, emasculated or, more accurately, *feminised*.

As the story opens in Pyatigorsk, the high society scene is swiftly sketched in. Initially, this is a world comprised of men, young men at their leisure, drinking champagne, gambling and discussing the local beauties. The central male character, Prince Yurevich is clearly marked as within the Onegin/Chatsky lineage, with several details deliberately lifted from the earlier works. The Prince has been abroad, having returned six months earlier, and since then he has been living on the estate of his invalid uncle, primarily because of the debts he has accrued. The Prince and his military comrades are quickly characterised as vain, worthless, puffed-up socialites. They discuss the news of the Prince's impending marriage (for entirely mercenary reasons), Baroness Engelsberg and other past and future (they think) conquests in a spirit of cynicism and boredom. Various ways of seducing women are suggested, with Prince Yurevich clearly at pains to establish himself as the cock of the walk.[60] He does this by displaying his gross misogyny: 'Women, my dear, belong in terms of their character, to the feline species; they scratch a child who approaches them fearfully, but submit before the stern gaze of a man' (213). His virility, however, is immediately deflated when it is revealed how dependent he is on his invalid uncle and, indeed, one of the central purposes of the story is for one of the cats to scratch his eyes out, metaphorically speaking.

Prince Yurevich's arrival in Pyatigorsk is soon noised abroad because of his fame 'for successes in society' (214), that is, of course, his many conquests. But having established his reputation, the narrator now interrupts the narrative to offer a brief biography, which stands as an exposé of the Superfluous Man/Romantic Hero, stripping him entirely of his glamour. He remains essentially a spoiled child: 'Spoiled in his youth, even when grown to be a man, he retained the self-assurance, persistence and all the caprices of a mother's[61] little boy' (214). The narrator then proceeds to give a kind of proto-psychoanalytic dissection of this man/child, which becomes, therefore, an account of the Pechorin-type without the self-justification:

> the world seemed to him a cradle, purposely created to cherish and lull his excellency; women seemed to be flowers,[62] with which he played, comforted himself, plucking them according to his caprice and weaving them into an endless garland of his conquests, while he regarded men as lads who were called together sometimes to play with the master's little son. (214)

This may be unsubtle, lacking in irony, but it is also a highly effective strategy.

The rest of the story follows this project. At every step of his attempted conquest of Sophia, Yurevich is thwarted and mocked by her superior wiles. Even when he retreats sulkily back to the all-male world of gambling, he loses heavily and is verbally thrashed by his (invalid!) uncle. Even in Part Two[63] where he *does* succeed in conquering the more naive and passionate sister, Olympia, his standing as a Romantic Hero is undercut, as, for example, when he rides majestically (he thinks) into Lipetsk on a 'black steed' (275).

Yet the treatment of men in *The Locket* is not altogether as black as Yurevich's horse. There are even signs that even he is not beyond redemption. Interestingly, these flickers of hope are depicted precisely in terms of his feminisation, reflecting Gan's developing concern to question gender identity, rather than merely construct her discourse in terms of immutable gender difference. At the end of Sophia's narrative (which also concludes the initial story) Yurevich is deeply affected and his reactions are encoded in terms of traditional *feminine* iconography: 'His face was *paler* than a midnight apparition, his eyes wandered with the strange expression of the absence of any thought, his lips were compressed with a *quivering* motion, drops of sweat had appeared on his brow' (297 – my italics). However, his loss of control is relatively brief and Sophia, at least, is convinced that in a few days he will have returned to his usual male rut/identity.

Elsewhere, however, there are other signs that the possibility exists of change in men, precisely in the direction of feminisation, and *therefore*, amelioration. Part Two, at times at least, adopts a less dualistic view. Sophia's husband, for example, admittedly a very shadowy figure, signals this possibility. When he proposes, Sophia is delighted, but cannot possibly accept because it would mean leaving her beloved sister. Colonel Engelsberg 'decided to offer his ambition to her as a sacrifice' (261). That this involves his leaving the all-male world of the army, and joining the previously all-female enclave is a detail of considerable significance in Gan's world (and one which, no doubt, represents great wish-fulfilment). Olympia's fiancé, Aleksin, also represents the good (feminine) man. As he begins to enter this world he behaves in a most virginal way: 'He was very young and extremely shy, spoke *quietly, blushed*, especially when talking to the ladies'[64] (264 – my italics). His 'mutism' and physical display are important details. But these glimpses are but details. In this work, for the most part, Gan again deals in more or less absolute gender categories, although, as we shall see, her heroine is capable of very forceful, 'male' action.

2.3 The Heroine

The Locket is, in its way, a kind of detective story: what is in the eponymous ornament (whose is it?), and will we be allowed to see inside, and with what effect? Analogously, the principal heroine, Baroness Sophia Engelsberg, for most of the story, and certainly for all of the first half, is presented to the reader as a riddle. However, as elsewhere in Gan's work, this has the very opposite purpose and result of suggesting that woman *is* a riddle. Rather, the polemical project of concealing her identity and the causation of her puzzling behaviour is to show that this particular woman has a secret role to play (on behalf of her sister) and a hidden strength. That is, her behaviour may be a mystery to the men of Yurevich's gang who see women as a lower species, but their misperception is a mark of their blindness to the truth about women.

Even before she appears, Sophia has been forged into this dominant image. She has been in Pyatigorsk for a month, but has hardly been seen. Then, very soon after Yurevich's arrival, she does emerge and everyone (including the reader) wonders whether her appearance is connected with his coming to town. The first sight of her is a telling icon: 'The Amazon sat calmly on her steed, although the stubborn Karabakhetz foamed and snorted under her, as if ashamed to obey the hand of a woman' (216). Not only is her (mythological) strength and serenity shown: her control of the (male) horse adumbrates in a few words the entire movement of the plot. This narratorial glimpse of her as(tr)ide, our initial impressions of Sophia are deliberately mediated through male perceptions and gazes. The point is again polemical: the masculine perspective is established, only to be subverted.

Now she begins to make herself the belle of all the balls and, a relatively rarity in Gan, we are given a fairly full *physical* description of a woman. She 'was wearing a light white dress, with one of those figures which ancient sculptors only gave to nymphs . . . her eyes [were] full of burning fire, covered with a mist of sadness' (220). The emphasis is on poeticisation of the woman (rather than sexualisation) as well as more mysterious hints ('sadness'). This mysteriousness is soon made more explicit. The Prince accosts her, and she responds to his overtures, but not, we are told, 'from coquetry', but from 'the action of a *secret*, deep feeling' . . . 'in her . . . each word seemed an echo of her *soul*' (222 – my italics). As soon as we see this last word, we know that she is the heroine, and that the victory will be hers. Very shortly, indeed, the narrator (who announces herself as *female*) decides to explain this mystery to her male readers, who may not wish 'to wander down the labyrinth of guesses' (223), and proceeds to tell us Sophia's history (deliberately, however, concealing a great deal). 'Her story is very brief' (ibid.), she begins, and then adopts a considered narrative strategy of rendering Sophia rather ordinary, or rather typical. This has the purpose not merely of deflating (male) reader expectations of a dramatic secret, but of suggesting that precisely because she is so ordinary any woman could do what Sophia is about to.[65] In terms of our overall understanding of gender issues in Gan's work, perhaps the most significant detail of her biography is the fact that she has come to this place of erotic intrigue partly for the sake of her ill son. This valorisation of motherhood becomes more obvious as we return to the diegetic present to apprehend Sophia in a deeply iconographic pose: 'Who would recognise the charming, brilliant Baroness in this sad woman, who with her arms crossed on her chest, with her head thrown back, white and pale, like mountain snow in the moonlight, more resembled a marble carving, than an animated being?' (224). Firstly, we should note the (later revealed) purpose of this iconography: that is, even a woman who is so deeply troubled *can* rise to great deeds. Secondly, her troubled reverie is broken by the disconnected words of her sleeping son: her maternal feelings bring her back to the world when all had seemed sunk in despair and immobility. Returned to life by care for her son, she soon declares: 'I will triumph! He will be at my feet!' (225). This vignette encapsulates Gan's conception of the good woman, which has moved on from her ideas in *The Ideal*. Her heroine now is deeply feminine, prone to despair and hopelessness (which will be displayed bodily); but she can act on behalf of others (her sister and her son), and defeat an experienced Rake (with 'many successes') – as well as writing a well-crafted tale. This second narrative has as its subject the contrastive type, Olympia, and her admonitory tale of Tatyanaism, to which we will return.

In conclusion to this section, however, there is another point that merits our attention. One of the most persistent features of male-authored Russian literature (and not only Russian), both before and after Gan's work, is the refusal even to consider the possibility of mutually supportive relationships between women. Zarema kills Mariya, Tatyana and Olga are complete opposites and strangers to each other, Elena stands alone on the eve of female emancipation and so on. (Chernyshevsky was to be a notable exception.) While Gan betrays great hostility to the 'crowd' of women (*The Ideal* and, especially, *Society's Judgement*), recurrent motifs are the power of the maternal (admittedly, usually paradise lost), and, especially in the present work, the joy, indeed passion, of sisterly love. This is the subject of the prologue to Part Two and, ultimately, the very *raison d'être* of the whole story.

Just as their estate and early life deliberately recall the eighteenth century tradition (the calling-name, the use of pastoral), so do their own 'calling-names', Sophia and Olympia. Like Tatyana and Olga, this pair of sisters are contrastive types, but their essences are complementary rather than antagonistic. Indeed, as already noted, so devoted to each other as they, that Sophia originally declines Englesberg's proposal. In turn, Olympia is reluctant at first to accept Aleksin's offer for the same reasons, avowing to Sophia that 'I feel even more strongly, that I cannot be happy anywhere without you; my only love has been and will be you' (265). Not long afterwards the two sisters do have to part, when Engelsberg's ill health requires that he and Sophia travel abroad. It is precisely during her prolonged absence that Olympia meets Yurevich and tragedy befalls her. The implication is that, bereft of her sister's love, or at least protection, Olympia is fatefully weakened. Olympia seems to sense this. As they are about to part she comments 'I'm afraid, sad, as if, with your departure, all *heavenly* powers must leave me. Who will be my *guardian*-genius? . . . Listen, I don't know what threatens me in the future, only I can't think of it without trembling' (267 – my italics).

Eventually, Sophia is able to return to her sister (after the death of her husband) and the three women are reunited. It is too late to rescue Olympia, the damage has been done. But to a certain extent Olympia recovers, at least in a spiritual sense, revealing an 'angelic meekness' (296) in the face of her broken heart (and blindness). Certainly, the logic of the plot is that the sisters would have been much better off if no men had ever entered their enclave. It should also be noted that Sophia does not display the same weakness: the humiliation of Prince Yurevich is her revenge, in the name of sisterly love.

2.4 Plot

As already indicated, from the title of the story onwards, *The Locket* can be read as a detective story (the reader as detective). The central plot typology, then, is that of the riddle, or rather riddles, as it soon becomes apparent (from the narrator's teasing clues – and red herrings) that a double plot is in operation. That is, Prince Yurevich thinks he is manipulating the solving of the riddle, and the capture of the prize, whereas, all along, Baroness Sophia is pulling at his strings. The motivation of the second riddle plot is, therefore, her secret, and the reader's desire to uncover it.

The prologue to the first part deliberately creates an androcentric world of male camaraderie, which we have already looked at. In this world women are objects, either for mercenary marriage, or for pursuit and conquest. One particular woman stands out for the latter sub-plot. It is typical of Gan's whole project as a writer that she erects the traditional masculine plots (solving the riddle of a woman/pursuit of a woman/trophy) only to subvert them by re-directing the desire that motivates this and other stories to the woman.[66] Yet another sub-plot typology is also touched upon in this prologue, namely, male rivalry, to become *primus Rake inter pares* and thereby to gain the prize. As Yurevich himself boasts: 'I don't like easy conquests' (213). That is, Sophia is particularly to be sought because of the difficulty her aloof behaviour has created.

The end of the prologue is marked by the unexpected appearance of Sophia. In terms of the riddle plot, as we know, the reader wonders if this entry is connected with Yurevich. It also suggests that it is she who will initiate the main thrust of the action: she enters the enclosed space, and, indeed, it will be she who proves to be morphologically the hero and the mobile rather than static character.[67]

A further variant on the basic plot typology occurs at the start of the exposition (at a ball). Yurevich notices the elegant stranger and asks his friend Mstislavov 'who is that lady in the white dress, with lilac in her hat?' (221). Thus, already, the classic paradigm is set in place: 1. The woman is an enigma. 2. How can I get to know her? 3. Pursuit planned. 4. Seduction/conquest envisaged. This would then be followed by the further 'cases of the declension', namely, abandoning the victim, her illness and/or death.[68] The desires of the hero and any expectant reader will suffer a painful *interruptus* during the course of the fourth stage.

As yet, the narrator deliberately teases the reader (mirroring Sophia's manipulation of Yurevich). She claims (223) that she will remove the enigma centring on the Baroness, but the brief biography here offered remains studiedly silent on the most important fact, namely, why *really* she is in Pyatigorsk and what is her previous connection with the Prince, and, therefore, what is the plot in which she is engaged. The narrator does, however, inform us that Sophia is acting 'against her own interest for the achievement of a noble goal' (ibid.). The battle is thus joined: as is typical for Gan's work, the issues at stake are essentially *moral* ('noble'). In terms of her plot, another factor is also important in this nocturnal visit by the narrator and reader to her home. As we saw earlier, she is initially in this scene deeply (iconographically) sorrowing. The polemic here is once more to subvert the masculinist paradigm. Even a woman who is plunged into grief can be transfigured, can arise 'from the grave'[69] and this will have critical implications for Olympia's plot.

In joining battle with Yurevich ('I will triumph! He will be at my feet! (225)), Sophia initiates another common plot typology of the period – that of the duel.[70] Once more Gan offers a nice 'feminist' twist to the tale. Not only is the metaphorical duel not between two men, but also the woman will score an easy victory.

The exposition then proceeds for twenty odd pages, consisting of a series of verbal thrusts and parries as Sophia gradually causes Yurevich to fall in love with her and abandon his engagement. He becomes more or less completely subject to her, following her to Kislovodsk (she is the mobile character), risking his uncle's wrath at the broken engagement and resolving to change his old wicked ways (with apparent sincerity). Finally, the Prince (and the reader) approach what they think will be the peripeteia. (The impending turning point is again *marked*, by the approach of Autumn, the end of the social season and the departure of most of the Summer visitors.) If we believe Yurevich's change of heart – and as we have seen from the last pages Sophia does not – then we would share his expectations for the perpeteia and dénouement, namely, marriage and some kind of ensuing resolution, happy or otherwise. Once again Yurevich has not realised in which plot he is a player, because this, of course, is not the perpeteia. Instead, all of Part Two can be seen as the turning point, with a very brief dénouement (Yurevich aghast), and equally brief epilogue (Sophia's words on his probable rapid recovery). This (at least partially) 'unexpected resolution' is significant in another way, and one which was typical for Gan. As she had already done in *The Ideal* and as she was to do a year later in *Society's Judgement*, literally the last word is given to the heroine. We are, therefore, not left wondering what became of the heroine (as in *Princess Mary* or *Asya*), but rather the woman is empowered to tell her own (and her sister's) story.

In terms of its basic plot typology, Part Two is a mirror image of Part One, reduced to its essentials of pursuit – seduction – abandonment – illness, with this time the last two 'cases' being acted out. It is, I think, quite deliberately a classic typology, both as a warning against 'Tatyanaism', but also to illuminate retrospectively the way Gan (and Sophia) have manipulated and thwarted this typology in Part One. The pace of the second story is also rather different, with fewer digressions and with the structuration more clearly exposed. The tone (apart from the florid iconography attached to Olympia) is rather bare, matter-of-fact, and to the point. (This also illustrates lack of artifice of Sophia as narrator.)

The prologue deals with the early, idyllic life of women alone in Nature. The ending of this stage is signalled in several ways. Sophia reaches the age of sixteen and must therefore leave the maternal presence and enter the symbolic order/the world of men. The dangers inherent in this are underscored by the arrival of the hussars who are billeted nearby. However, as we already know, this turns out to be a false danger, as Colonel Engelsberg leaves the military world rather than imposing it on the women. (A contrast both with Olga in *The Ideal* and Gan's own life.) But danger has been intimated and this is repeated when Olympia, in her turn, reaches 15 (although she looks older). As it turns out, this 'transition from a *childish age* to the *world*' (272 – my italics) only comes about rather later, but the anxiety is noted. This anxious note is touched on once again when Olympia accedes to Aleksin's proposal: Sophia's concern is whether the mild ('feminine') Aleksin will satisfy her sister's passionate nature (266).

The complication, then, begins not with Sophia's marriage, nor even when Olympia becomes engaged. This stage of the plot arrives and leads to tragic consequences when the three women leave their haven for the 'world' and, even more critically, when the two sisters are, for the first time, separated (with great trepidation on Olympia's part as we saw earlier). Sophia once more reveals her craft as a storyteller by locating the real commencement of the complication at the classic chronotope of the theatre, where Olympia becomes the latest innocent heroine to be espied by a phallic lorgnette, and the latest to display her emotions bodily: 'I[71] shuddered and threw myself back' (270). Given all the ominous notes already sounded this encounter overdetermines the eventual outcome.

Immediately the stranger with the lorgnette (who turns out to be Prince Yurevich, of course) has seen the reaction his gazing has produced, *he* initiates the rest of the action. He pursues Olympia to a church, and repeats his 'ocular rape'. Her willing submission to his attentions, her fall from grace are marked by the narrator: '*for the first time in her life* she lied [to her grandmother] in attributing her pensiveness and pallor to ill health' (271 – my italics). Olympia is indeed now lost as his relentless pursuit and seduction strategies are deployed. He follows them to Lipetsk, and soon inveigles himself into the grandmother's confidence. The paradigm unfolds inexorably, through the first time they are alone together, Olympia's breaking-off of her engagement and his immediate cooling off. Olympia does indeed decline into illness, especially after she reads in the newspaper of his departure for Paris with an actress. So great is her distress that she loses her sight.

In Part Two, then, Gan has quite consciously mapped out and developed a classic plot typology. This strategy has several points. It is a warning to young women like Olympia. As the story within the story it acts as a reproach and punishment for Prince Yurevich. Yet we should also note that the paradigm is not quite completed. Olympia does not die and, at least spiritually, she recovers. Implicitly, Gan suggests, even the most classic typological case can be thwarted in the end, even the most injured of innocent heroines can arise from her suffering. Moreover, the very act of the telling of her plot by her sister (and by herself, for that matter, as Olympia's letters to Sophia play an important part) validates Olympia's experience and acts as the peripeteia and dénouement to the plot the (false-) hero thought he was conducting, and by which he is punished.

In terms of character types (and stereotypes) as well as gender interaction, the narrative dynamics of *The Locket* should also be seen as essentially polemical. Taking the chronologically earlier plot (Part Two), Gan offers, in large measure, a re-run of *The Ideal*. The experienced rake (referred to variously as Lovelace (233) and Childe Harold (247)) encounters an innocent young woman at the theatre. She, in turn, echoes Olga (and before her Tatyana) by her over-identification with the 'fantasies' of literature (in this case Ophelia). He then proceeds to seduce her 'expertly' (although, again as in *The Ideal*, there is no actual physical seduction). The narrator (Sophia) persistently draws attention to the fact that this is all a game for him. At the very outset she remarks that Olympia did not suspect 'that it is possible to run after a pretty girl for several days from idleness and without any aim at all' (272). She thereby strips him of all glamour and exposes his worthlessness (as the first narrator has already done). Gan's intention would seem again to be deeply moral, Sophia referring to him as 'the tempter' (280) and noting that Olympia 'drank in the poison' (276). Returning to Part One, the Rake is further reduced in stature, both by the narrator's analysis of his childishness, and by Sophia's expert manipulation of the plot. At every stage she out-manoeuvres him and frequently mocks him. He is reduced to impotence. In reverse, the principal heroine, Sophia Engelsberg grows in stature as the two stories progress. In this way she and her sister should again be seen as contrastive types. Olympia is the traditional Sentimental heroine, all but destroyed and, like Olga in *The Ideal* only finding relief in quietistic resignation. Sophia enters the male world and the male plot and emerges triumphant.

2.5 Theme

As in *The Ideal*, gender identity runs as a kind of fault-line through *The Locket*, from the opening all-male scene, through the all-female enclave which acts as a mirror-image at the start of Part Two, and also in the conflicting stereotypes. As we have seen, this story does suggest some possibility of movement across gender lines (Yurevich's temporary 'feminisation', Engelsberg's leaving the army, Aleksin's shyness or, more significantly, Sophia's adoption of the morphologically male role of hero). The theme of love is also largely constructed on either side of this divide, although other aspects of this central theme for Gan also merit attention. Love has the power to redeem ('I am reborn' (252) the Prince claims); love must also be based on equality of feeling, as Olympia and Aleksin discover to their cost. It is significant that here, as elsewhere in Gan's work, the story does not end with a fulfilled love relationship.[72] Although we are meant to see the Engelsbergs as a successful union their story is very much peripheral to the work as a whole. No, it is the case here, as usual for this writer, that a tragic view of love is taken.

These two themes, gender and love, are intertwined in another of Gan's central motifs, the sacred. During one of their lengthy discussions about love the Prince, (mis)appropriating the feminine sacred lexis asserts that for him love is 'a moment of celestial bliss' (231) to which Sophia retorts 'Love is not a moment, but an eternity of bliss . . . But for this, love must be legitimised and sacred'[73] (ibid.). The sacred theme is to be more fully explored, however, in Olympia's story. From her very first sighting of her seducer, in tune with her fantasies, she identifies him with a painting of Orpheus at the *gates of hell*, seeing him as a 'fallen spirit' (273). This theme immediately receives a bravura variation in the church scene, where Olympia is completely seduced by his insistent gaze: 'His eloquent gaze beseeched forgiveness, demanded compassion and all presence of the girl's spirit disappeared . . . in a quiet, but extraordinarily expressive voice he tossed into the soul of the confused girl the words: "will you forgive me, angel of meekness?"' (271). We already know, of course, what his intentions are, so his misappropriation of the sacred lexis and the holy ground on which the seduction takes place lend the scene the resonance of quite literal sacrilege. As in *The Ideal* the satanism of the seducer is, for Gan, not merely modish Gothick, but is in deadly earnest. Sacred lexis occurs frequently as Olympia's fall ensues, and it is sufficient to save her from the ultimate calamity. As Yurevich attempts to mock everything she holds dear 'a good angel preserved her innocence' (287), and her 'angelic meekness' (296) saves her from despair. Indeed, in the end she echoes very closely Olga's words which conclude *The Ideal*: she cannot see the daylight but 'all the more clearly will seem to me the dawn of another, endless day . . .' (ibid.). Like Olga, Olympia finds her emancipation in the faithful hope for the other world.

She also recalls Olga in her over-investment in the world of literature: she plays Ophelia to Yurevich's Orpheus. As in *The Ideal* we are left in no doubt as to the dangers of such vicarious living. As she leaves Moscow the narrator comments on the 'chaos . . . the thousands of fantasies' (272) that fill her head. Later, as she awaits her seducer's arrival she flies off 'into the blossoming world of her fantasies' (286). Yet there, too, this story marks a progression. While Olympia allows herself to be manipulated and deceived by literature, her altogether more wordly (and, therefore, masculine) sister appropriates literature for her own purposes. In this sense as well, therefore, Sophia's telling of Part Two marks a victory. By speaking of another's tragedy she not only punishes the Prince, but also shows the ability of women to govern their own destinies by seizing the initiative, by speaking their own word.

3. SOCIETY'S JUDGEMENT[74]

This story also replays certain of the central themes of *The Ideal*, especially the dysphoric fate of the gifted woman and the malice of society, or rather, the viciousness of other women against her. As in nearly all of Gan's work the central plot motif and theme is romantic love (yet again with tragic implications for the heroine). This work, like both those already considered, culminates with the woman's word (Zenaida's letter) which vindicates the wrongs done to her and in which she finds peace, resolution and, here, forgiveness. But *Society's Judgement* is also markedly different from much of Gan's work in that most of the narrative is first person (as opposed to

Gan's preferred third-person more or less omniscient). Even more striking is the fact that the tale is narrated from the point of view of a man, the would-be hero Vlodinsky. Moreover, he differs profoundly from Anatoly and Prince Yurevich, although, in the end he is the prime cause of the heroine's tragedy. It is with a consideration of the typology of masculinity that the work offers that I will begin.

3.1 The Hero

Gan was clearly fond of the riddle plot: all four works considered here use this device as the initiatory plot mechanism. Here, after a general introduction to the awfulness of life in the provinces the female writer/narrator records how she had come to find Vlodinsky's notes (which are to form the main body of the tale) and gives an impression of him. (This prologue to the main story will be important for our understanding of his reaction to the events of the plot, sited as it is about twenty years after the main narrative.) He is introduced as a 'man of mystery'. Although only in his early forties he seems very much older, a burned-out case. He lives an almost eremitic existence. This is not, however, at all because of a misanthropic bitterness. On the contrary, he lives with a seventeen-year-old niece who is devoted to him and great emphasis is made on his philanthropy, although, equally, many details betoken his spiritual death. (For example, the narrator visits his study to find books scattered in disarray: reading, she surmises, acts as a narcotic for his pain.) On his actual death his notes are found and, in the spirit of *A Hero of Our Time*, she feels free to publish the account he has written of his life, as well as a copy of a letter which he has literally taken with him to the grave.

Vlodinsky's own preface enhances both the reader's sense of inquiring, as well as the notes of remorse already hinted at: he tells his niece, to whom the notes are addressed, what he had been unable to tell her orally 'the sad history of my errors, my sin' (158). There is much breast-beating, but little self-pity. So, then, we ask, what has produced this remorse and repentance: is the masculine life to be valorised in Gan's work?

What now follows is, I think, an attempt by Gan to create the typical masculine experience of the world, and the potentially ennobling (even *transfiguring*) effect that the love of a good woman can have. Significantly, perhaps, in terms of Gan's tendency to privilege the maternal, Vlodinsky had been orphaned at an early age and had, while still fairly young, joined the army during the Napoleonic Wars, in 1809. For the next six years he had lived to the full and unreservedly the life of a man, amongst other men in a world not only without women, but one which was both ignorant of and hostile to the feminine. It was a life 'full of alarms and debauchery, between yesterday's orgy in the tent and preparations for tomorrow's battle' (160). At the time, masculinity (in terms of stereotypical machismo) was deeply valorised by the young Vlodinsky: 'the preparedness to fight with a friend, even kill him because of a simple misunderstanding,[75] I took as proof of knightly bravery and nobility' (ibid.). He hardly knew women, considering man to be the crown of the entire visible chain of creation. Moreover, his juvenile view of women was explicitly based on ignorance and was deeply negative:

> Woman I considered a second-rate link [in the chain], a transition from man to dumb creatures: she seemed to me beautiful, but not deserving a great deal of attention, a flower which grew for the momentary diversion of man in his hours of leisure (160–1).

Quite explicitly and deliberately, therefore, Vlodinsky recreates the experience and views of the typical male of his time and class (albeit in rather general terms). What then follows is his transformation as a result of his separation from other men (he falls ill and is left by his regiment in Germany to recover). This transformation takes the specific form of his demasculinisation or feminisation. Initially this takes the form of traditional feminine iconography (extreme physical manifestation of emotion) being applied to him when he encounters the heroine, Zenaida. As he watches her from his bedroom window, and she approaches 'a feverish trembling ran through my body . . . my knees bent, more than once the light even became blurred in my eyes' (165). When they finally meet 'I could not recover from the confusion which had taken possession of me, I stumbled over my words, I was silent or answered inappropriately' (167). (Such are the first stages of this process of renewal/feminisation: I will return to the eventual outcome in my consideration of plot.)

3.2 Images of Women

Society's Judgement, in its contrast between the noble, gifted heroine and the 'crowd' of 'wasps', represents an intensification on Gan's first work, *The Ideal*. Here this theme both opens the story and is a chief ingredient in the causation of the tragedy. From the first pages the female writer (and frame narrator) introduces the viciousness of groups of women against other women as her initial central topic: 'The judges of the female sex regard their newly-arrived rivals with a not very benevolent eye' (150). It will be women who destroy other women; rivalry is the natural condition for women in society. The slightest deviation from the norm arouses the fury of these women and the worst thing of all is to be a woman of talent or, more specifically, a female writer.[76] Such a person enters provincial society as a kind of Elephant Man or Kaspar Hauser. She is regarded as 'a deformed whim of nature or, more accurately, a degenerate of the female sex' (152). She is invited to dinner as if a 'dancing monkey' (ibid.). All this is related in a tone of rather heavy-handed sarcasm (as in *The Ideal*, Gan's narrator, prompted by her own autobiographical fury, breaches decorum), but the point is made. As in the earlier story, moreover, no attempt is made to understand these women, still less to excuse or redeem them. Indeed, the narrator answers them in kind, returning their insults with rather cheap gibes, implicitly at least, *masculinising* them by endowing them with phallic lorgnettes,[77] and military metaphor: 'they armed themselves for a meeting with her with a hundred or more mental lorgnettes' (ibid.).

In terms of our understanding of Gan's view of the female writer, these pages stand as an important statement in their own right (and I will return to these points in my discussion of *A Futile Gift*). These remarks also, however, act as a fateful harbinger for the eventual destiny of Zenaida who in her own way is a kind of writer and, certainly, a 'deviant' woman.

When Vlodinsky returns home and is stationed in Lithuania he discovers that Zenaida is in the neighbourhood. At the mention of her name, 'society', that is, the 'crowd' of women (Vlodinsky's female cousins and his aunt) launch into a full-scale attack on and demolition of her character, all of which, we later learn, is based on no evidence whatsoever, but merely on petty, self-interested malice and envy. (Interestingly, one of the first charges laid at her door is that she likes to 'play the pedant, go on about Greek sages and metaphysics' (179).) Vlodinsky, of course, is aghast and uses language that is significant in terms of Gan's overall symbolic lexical system: 'I spent the whole night in cruel agitation, furious at the blackness of people, at the malice of my cousins, at the whole world,[78] which, unable to understand or value such an *angel*, hissed in the mud and poured *poison* over her name' (180 – my italics).

However, the tittering, innuendo and slander of Vlodinsky's cousins are as nothing compared to the astonishing diatribe which his aunt then pours forth before the shocked young man. (As a contrast to her usual treatment of the lost maternal, there is no valorisation of the older woman here.) All decency and proprieties are abandoned in this venomous attack which accuses Zenaida of almost every conceivable vice ever attributed to a woman: Zenaida, it is alleged, is a coquette, a woman of ambiguous behaviour, capricious, proud, self-willed, lacking in spiritual purity. Above all, she is condemned for daring to place herself above the crowd. She is, it is alleged, 'A woman, full of whims, ambitious, vain, a woman who wishes in every way possible to seem more excellent than her friends, even above her sex' (182). And so she goes on and on and on. Such calumny leaves us is in no doubt as to Gan's assessment of 'ordinary' women. But even this is not enough. Vlodinsky is battered into submission, admittedly also through his own weakness, and he comes to believe these lies, and the consequences of his belief in Zenaida's dubious character will be literally fatal. The title, therefore, has an ominous power. Society, that is women, passes its judgement and this verdict leads to death, and to the destruction of a pure woman.

3.3 Setting

By comparison with *The Ideal* and, especially *The Locket*, this story is more concerned with the inner life of its characters, first Vlodinsky and then Zenaida. Consequently, setting, and the use of chronotope, is less obtrusive, less pregnant with significance. This said, Gan again displays a skilful mastery of the established chronotopes of the period and genre; in a sense, indeed, the mastery is more marked, precisely because the 'set-pieces' are less insistently placed before us. They do not call attention to themselves in quite the same way as before.

There is recurrent use of the military environment. The story opens with a brief account of the life of military wives, the tedium of their existence, the scene ever changing but ever the same, recalling the initial section of *The Ideal* (as well as Gan's life). This setting recurs, as we know, as part of Vlodinsky's youth where its negative gender connotations are more fully explored. Significantly, after he and Zenaida go their separate ways he returns to the army and, he notes, 'my life flowed in its usual way; manège, lessons, inspections, my comrades surrounded me, as before' (177). His (partial) re-militarisation, and, therefore, re-masculinisation are to prove significant. This vaguely premonitory note reverberates as the tragic events of Part Two[79] unfold, and as we enter a series of negatively encoded *svetskaya povest* chronotopes. He first hears Zenaida's name mentioned at a ball: in turn, we know that their second encounter (which in the end does not eventuate) will be negative because they are due to meet at another ball. That his re-masculinisation is now more or less complete is signalled by his entry into the gaming-room,[80] an all-male environment where men are prepared to 'fight ... even kill ... because of a simple misunderstanding' (160). And, of course, the metaphorical duel of gambling leads directly to the real duel, the classic topos of masculinity.[81]

All of these *topoi* and chronotopes, as I have already noted, are passed over fairly briefly, really just as signals. The most important, extensive and interesting use of setting comes in Part One, in Vlodinsky's 'incarceration' in a German castle. Given that this is where he will undergo his rebirth, it is of significance that the scene here deliberately recreates the world of the fairy-tale. The estate is situated 'in a ravine between the mountains, surrounded on all sides by forest and a dense park'. The wind howls at night and 'all was desolate and wild' (161). Stress is placed on the Gothick elements, with part of the house, dating from feudal times, in ruins: Vlodinsky even has a Gothic window in his medieval-style room. (All this may well be parodic.) Similar evocative use is made of the passage of time, with a welter of pathetic fallacies. As the visitations by the strange figure in the park happen (it turns out to be Zenaida), Spring is just beginning: she usually appears at twilight. Vlodinsky's fascination with the stranger begins to blossom and the weather improves. He feels gloomy, so it rains that day. As their love finally emerges, we read 'Spring burst forth in all its beauty' (168). Most of this has occurred as Vlodinsky is merely a spectator of her strollings. When they do finally meet the author seems to mock him by refusing to collude with his romanticism. Their encounter does not take place in a picturesque ruin, nor even a leafy arbour, but in a drawing-room, where she is prosaically talking with a doctor. This deliberate deflation of his expectations apart (which is itself significant), this general use of setting serves a specific purpose, primarily to emphasise the magical, almost mystical essence of the change that is about to occur.

3.4 Plot

Generically and narratologically *Society's Judgement* is I think Gan's most interesting and complex work, rivalling the exactly contemporary *A Hero of Our Time* in its multiplicity of points of view, temporal dislocation and fusion of genres. Generically the work mingles society tale, Bildungsroman, fairy-tale, confession, the discovered document, a letter (which itself is a complex mix of genres) and others. There are three narrators – the unnamed female writer and frame-narrator, Vlodinsky and, having the last word, Zenaida.

In a manner that is again close to that of Lermontov's novel, the reader is led through a series of false starts before we reach the heart of the plot. A relatively extended pre-prologue (the narrator's description of provincial society and the invidious fate of a 'dancing monkey') seems to confirm what the title already suggests, that this will be a typical *svetskaya povest* along the lines of *The Ideal*. We then switch, however, to the prologue and its account of how the frame-narrator came across Vlodinsky's notes and we now begin to think that the principal plot motif will be, as elsewhere in Gan, the reader as detective, solving the riddle of his existence: why is he a recluse (but a philanthropist); why is he prematurely aged? 'Passions or grief have aged him' (155) the narrator suggests and we want to know which. Thus, the *fabula/syuzhet* disjunction creates a nice air of mystery and, moreover retrospectively this section (like *Maksim Maksimych*) will provide the dénouement to the overall plot. We know, therefore, when we enter the main narrative (Vlodinsky's notes) that there can be no 'happy ever after' resolution to his relationship with Zenaida.

More details add to this sense of mystery: why has his beautiful young niece abandoned all worldly interests to care for him? Gan plays nicely with current literary clichés in all this – various rumours see him as a Silvio figure, the perpetrator of some horrible crime. Or perhaps he had fallen in love with a princess, or maybe even his sister. (The *Island of Bornholm* is invoked at this stage.) Childe Harold also gets a mention and this prologue increasingly takes on the same function as *Bela*, or, in another way, that of some of *The Tales of Belkin* and *The Queen of Spades*. A Romantic image is created which the later narrative will explain and defuse.

After Vlodinsky's death Gan lays before us yet another literary cliché, that of the discovered manuscripts and, true to the eighteenth-century tradition (which Lermontov was also invoking and parodying in the same year) great stress is placed on both the authenticity and veracity of the documents.[82] 'Here is a copy, copied by me word for word' (158). At this point, however, the author/narrator springs a major surprise. Having led us along the labyrinth leading, we thought, to a solution to the enigma of the Romantic stranger, the narrator announces that Vlodinsky's story will give

> a sketch of the double life of a woman, a picture of a light and pure soul, which shone triumphantly in its own inner world, and of its false reflection in the opinion of people, in that treacherous mirror, which, like the kiss of Judas, flattering us to our face, prepares persecution, shame and often even death behind the back. (158)

A number of issues arise. Who is this, as yet, completely unknown woman? The posing of this question also completely shifts the line of our narrative inquiry and creates an even deeper riddle. It's a very clever and successful trick, in fact. In turn, the pre-dooming of the plot is immeasurably increased. After the rhetorical flourishes of these lines and the tolling last words we can expect nothing but tragedy, the immolation of a pure woman ('*soul*') on the altar of society's judgement, which here stands condemned in the most anathematising words possible for the Christian writer that Gan most assuredly was. (The kiss of Judas.)

This expectation of dysphoria is cranked up a further notch by Vlodinsky's opening remarks which strike a literally funereal note: 'The time of our parting is coming. I feel, the blessed moment of my release from earthly bonds is close' (ibid.). (And his remarks on his 'sin' which soon follow take us even further down this road.)

So, as we finally enter the main expository section of Vlodinsky's confession a great deal of narrative excitement has been raised. After more generic play by Gan (Vlodinsky's early life as an *éducation sentimentale*/primitive *Bildungsroman*) she has him announce what will be the central plot typology, and one which yet again lures the reader on to find out more. He concludes the prologue to his own story thus: 'Such were my ideas and my character in the 22nd year of my life: thus I was found by my *rebirth*' (161 – my italics). This last word suggests exactly the plot typology which is indeed to ensue, and which has been uncovered by Yury Lotman at the heart, and as the origin of much myth and later reworking of it.[83] Lotman distils this type of narrative down to a number of formulae, such as 'entry into enclosed space – emergence from it' or 'death – sexual relations – re-birth'.[84] And, indeed, much of Vlodinsky's narrative follows this (mythic) typological paradigm more or less exactly. Vlodinsky has, of course, fallen ill and left behind his old life, entering the enclosed space of the (fairy-tale) castle or, metaphorically/typologically, the grave (his illness). His story, with the assistance of Zenaida will detail his resurrection from death. The motif of rebirth/resurrection is persistently returned to, and Vlodinsky seems to be aware himself that this is precisely what is happening: 'it seemed as if, in being reborn, I began my existence a second time from a childhood age; I was weak, capricous, like a baby' (ibid.).

At this point, the heroine (who is an amalgam of several Proppian character types, Donor as well as Princess), appears on the scene, and with her more plot motifs and typologies are imbricated onto the basic paradigm as identified by Lotman. Again, Vlodinsky himself states the plot motif. When he first sees her he follows her 'with concentrated attention, vainly attempting to *decipher the riddle* of her presence' (162 – my italics). (It will be a mark of Gan's approach to issues of gender in narrativity that the riddle of this particular Sphinx will be answered by *her own story*.[85]) Gradually, his strength returns, and a new motif is added: 'how can I get to know her'. As yet, *his* desire is the plot motivation, although again Gan will subvert the androcentric plot, in that Zenaida will direct the action once they do meet. Gradually new stages arrive, each one being carefully marked (the on-set of full Spring, the switch from nocturnal gazing by him to diurnal encounters). As usual, Gan shows skill in handling narrative tempo. After a very slow build-up to their first meeting, the pace quickens dramatically as their relationship flourishes ('A month flew by unnoticed' (168)). Equally, Vlodinsky keeps returning to the lexis of rebirth as if to emphasise self-consciousness of his own plot: 'I had completely recovered from my illness' (168); 'I loved for the first time . . . with all the strength of my renewed existence' (169); 'the second epoch of my love arrived, the epoch of my rebirth' (ibid.). Indeed, the hero is 'reborn' through the agency of 'sexual relations'.

To this mythic or fairy-tale plot, specifically Christian motifs are added, deepening yet further the theme of resurrection from the dead. 'At that time everything within me and around me was transformed' (170) and he describes his rebirth in imagery that is derived from New Testament parables and miracles:

> I came to see like one who was blind from birth . . . gradually a new world unfurled before me . . . a world of elegance, of poetry, of everything that ennobles the human soul . . . With what awe I penetrated into the mysteries of this world! With what pride I arose from the insignificance that had oppressed me and, at last, like one created anew, I looked at God's world! (169–70)

There then follows two pages of rhythmic prose detailing these miraculous changes, a kind of litany. Truly an epiphanic moment, this perpeteia in his plot and in his life, is foregrounded by its length and by the loftiness of its language. The implications of this plot thus become apparent. This rebirth is through the agency of a pure woman; his rebirth is not a mere plot typology but (almost literally) a resurrection, which in turn leads to a transfiguration. And, as we have already seen, this process is also his demasculinisation and his feminisation.

Before long, however, Vlodinsky and Zenaida must part as he is summoned back to the world and, move particularly, back to the quintessential world of men (his regiment). As they part, the fairy-tale world is once more invoked in that he receives two tests from the still mysterious Zenaida. One is a wish: 'you can be useful to humanity; do not leave inactive so many fine gifts from heaven' (177). In other terms, will his return to the masculine world result in the reversal of his rebirth/feminisation? The second is an interdiction: he must promise never to seek to meet her in Russia, nor even to mention her name. Vlodinsky immediately shows his fallibility (he will only agree not to seek her out) and, indeed, he will fail both these tests, and his second transformation into a false hero, which takes him into the masculine worlds of the gaming-room and the duel, will lead to catastrophe.

At first, however, Vlodinsky cannot accommodate himself to the world of men and he spends a miserable year depressed and self-pitying, with only religion saving him from suicide. In other words, his rebirth is only partial, his new (feminine) identity is very fragile, and as we have already seen, he falls easy prey to the slanderous judgement of society and the fall back to his original state is swift indeed. As before, Vlodinsky announces, as it were, he seems to 'lay bare', the plot motif. That is, his regression to his former state is both self-conscious and explicitly stated: 'I called up from my memory the long forgotten philosophy against women' (191). Equally explicitly, his regression is in the form of his complete re-adoption of his masculinist persona.

After he has enacted the full masculinist plot and has murdered Zenaida's brother 'because of a simple misunderstanding' (Vlodinsky thought that his opponent was, in fact, a rival for his 'love' of Zenaida), he is carried from the field more dead than alive: 'I lay unconscious' (196). There is a nice circularity here, in that he has returned to the typological condition in which Zenaida had first found him. Once more he has 'descended into the grave'. But if Zenaida can be seen as a kind of Christ figure,[86] raising Lazarus/Vlodinsky, there is to be no second coming. And, as we have already seen from the displaced dénouement, even twenty years later, Vlodinsky remained spiritually and emotionally dead. In terms of gender, the plot would ultimately seem to take a pessimistic view of male identity. Vlodinsky fails his fairy-tale tests and returns to masculinity. Even the love of such a spiritual being as Zenaida can only bring a temporary feminisation and, in the end, the pull of masculinity is too strong, and masculinity is seen to be lethal.

But this is not the end of the story, literally so. As she had done in *The Ideal* and *The Locket*, Gan chooses to end her story with the direct word of the heroine (Olga's letter to Vera, Sophia's telling of Olympia's tale). Here the device is particularly telling in that Zenaida who had appeared as (at least partially) only inscribed in Vlodinsky's tale, a marker on his passage to a new life[87] now has the change to tell her own story and she, thereby, becomes a 'dancing monkey'.[88] This concluding document, Zenaida's letter to Vlodinsky, which, remember, he had literally taken to the grave, serves several functions. It validates the role of woman as a writer, it answers the slander of society's judgement, it allows us to hear the woman's own story from her own account of it, from her own point of view. (And, in terms of the generic complexity of the work as a whole, it adds yet further to the text's density and polyphony.) I feel it is most appropriate, then, that I also conclude with Zenaida's story.

3.5 The Heroine's Text

It is one of Gan's achievements in this work that she creates really rather well the masculine world and the male point of view. Given the work's structure (the order of the documents) Zenaida is initially seen (and literally so) almost entirely as mediated through the consciousness of an unreconstructed 'man of society'. Gazing (with or without a lorgnette) on an unknown woman has already featured prominently in Gan's work (as well as elsewhere in the literature of the period): Anatoly/Olga in *The Ideal* and Yurevich/Olympia in *The Locket*. In both these instances the motif is, in one sense, undeveloped as we see the scopophilia through the perception of the victim, so that the aims, purposes of the gazer remain on the level merely of device, virtually a plot cliché. Here, because Vlodinsky is the narrator and holder of the point of view the reader enters into his scopophilia (effectively is implicated in it). Because this gazing then leads to a more direct mutuality, however, we are also enabled to follow this process of signification at work. That is, to begin with, the woman, Zenaida, is merely a male-imagined signifier.[89] The signified is not Zenaida herself but Vlodinsky's fantasy of her: gradually, however, the woman as signified emerges into a real presence. Equally to look at the same nexus from a different perspective, Zenaida is, as already noted, the enigma who will herself solve the puzzle of her identity.

Her identity is, indeed, a crucial factor in the dynamics of the story. We have already seen much of the causation of the duel – the viciousness of women, Vlodinsky's susceptibility to this, his breach of the interdiction, his remasculinisation. Another aspect is Zenaida's identity, or more properly, Vlodinsky's understanding of it. Implicated in this is yet another aspect of his masculinity, namely, his myth-making around Zenaida's identity. In this he follows Gogol's Piskaryov (and many others). For him she had been a Goddess; because he 'discovers' she is not, she must be the lowest form of woman:

> The woman for whom I created an altar in my soul was simply a cunning, perfidious coquette . . . [she was] a woman without conscience, without a heart, without a *soul*.   (190 – my italics)

Jacqueline Rose (in discussing *Hamlet*) catches exactly this process of the male mind:

> Located by Freud at the point where the woman is first seen to be different, this moment can then have its effects in that familiar mystification of femininity which makes of the woman something both perfect and dangerous or obscene (obscene if *not* perfect).[90]
>
> (Rose's italics)

Unlike Piskaryov, however, Vlodinsky does not slide into opium, insanity and suicide but burns with a 'thirst for vengeance' (190), for the 'treachery' that Zenaida has enacted.

What, then, is her identity? After her initial series of 'apparitions' and their mediation by Vlodinsky Zenaida soon slips into the ideal image of the pure femininity with which Gan endows all her heroines. Vlodinsky, in getting to know her claims that 'all the fantastic visions were completely blotted out from my memory: I recognised in her a woman with a light, most fine *soul*, with high intelligence . . . with a *pure* heart, *innocent*, sensitive' (168 – my italics). Her behaviour, conversations and her own 'confession' largely confirm this first substantial impression. Significantly, as elsewhere in Gan, the heroine is not merely spiritual ('the soul'), but *asexual* ('pure', 'innocent'). These notes are reiterated persistently in Vlodinsky's tale, but are then totally reversed by society's judgement. Consequently, yet again, an enigma is erected centring on a woman's sexuality and Zenaida's letter will pass the true judgement. (The narrator's words, introducing Vlodinsky's notes should be recalled ('a picture of a light and pure soul'): we have no grounds for not believing that Zenaida utters the truth.)

Her letter echoes Vlodinsky's notes in the sense that it too is a testament: she will be dead when he reads it. It is also a 'confession of the most intimate secrets of my soul' (199). Zenaida, already twice encoded as a woman of the soul (by the narrator and Vlodinsky) speaks of herself in exactly the same terms. She now proceeds to lay before Vlodinsky, in a spirit of forgiveness rather than reproach (198), her life, the typology of which follows almost exactly that of Olga (*The Ideal*) and, in part, Olympia (*The Locket*). (It is also in certain respects autobiographical.) Like her predecessors Zenaida had grown up secluded from the world (society), nurtured by the all powerful love of the mother, which is here utterly valorised:

> O! what love! . . . If I tell you that she was our nurse, nanny, instructor, our angel of blessing on earth, then even so I will not express that infinite, self-less, all-sacrificing attachment with which she made happy our childhood (198).

The maternal presence, the pre-sexual world is again recalled as a haven of paradise on earth. This time, however, it is not an all-female enclave: Zenaida has both a brother and father, the former of which is twice to play a tragic part in her life. Consequently, as elsewhere in Gan, the implication is that a community of women is the perfect social arrangement.

However, as always, this idyll is set in the past and has been lost. Zenaida was only thirteen when her mother died and this loss, coupled with her emotional abandonment by her father, who was crushed with grief, has the by now expected consequence. That is, once maternal succour is removed, the girl is catapulted, ill-prepared, into the world, where she will meet predatory males and vicious women.[91] Zenaida goes to live with her aunt, very much part of society and its judgement (and also the fairy-tale 'wicked step-mother'). Soon, within a year 'all my innocent beliefs, my feelings . . . were trampled' (201). Like Olga, Zenaida's Romantic dreams leave her ill-fitted for the world. She is married, to save her brother from disgrace, to a man who laughs at her ideals, and who then proceeds systematically to rape her innocence: 'every day he stole from me some sweet hope, an innocent feeling. Everything to which I had bowed down since my childhood was mocked by his cold reason' (204). She is deprived of everything she holds sacred, even the chance to 'walk through life with a proud brow and a *light soul* to the end of a useful existence' (206 – my italics).

In this emotional and spiritual desert she carries her mother's memory as an icon, hiding her suffering, and carrying her cross. Indeed, the Christian note saturates her life and her reconstruction of it: 'The Merciful One heard my prayer: my mother's spirit sheltered me, I found tranquillity in the quiet of solitude and joy in my own soul' (209).

Finally she comes to their time together in Germany and here too she emphasises the key leitmotifs of her identity – innocence, purity and the spiritual. ('I saw you with my spiritual eyes' (210); 'I loved you with all the power of my first maidenly love' (ibid.); 'Your pure timid love did not frighten' (ibid.); 'in your presence the sacred conceptions of my childhood were resurrected' (211)). Even if she had been free, she would have rejected any 'union' with him. The ideal love then is a *celestial* bond, becoming one soul rather than one flesh. In the same way, Zenaida is constructed (by the narrator, by Vlodinsky and now by herself) as pure spirit. I am sure that Gan wished her readers to see Zenaida (her pseudonym) as the ideal woman and she certainly does emerge from this 'confession' as a perfect icon of feminine spirituality. As in the similarly structured *The Ideal* the woman not only has the last word, but her word recuperates all her worldly suffering, as she anticipates *the* perfect union with Christ her Saviour. In this sense, the heroine's text represents her victory over false male imaging and over 'society's judgement', but it also involves the total repression of any hint of sexuality.

4. A FUTILE GIFT[92]

This last and unfinished work by Elena Gan is doubly tragic. The story of Anyuta the poet who dies at an early age, virtually unknown and unrecognised speaks for Gan's own premature death and her own often difficult life as a woman writer in the almost universally male literary world of Russia in the 1830s. I assume Gan must have known she was dying when she wrote it. It is, therefore, also her testament and represents an heroic statement. The work is also a valuable resource for us today because it is one of the first prose accounts in Russian (in fact I know of none earlier) of the pain, suffering and anxiety of a woman who becomes a writer.

A Futile Gift also represents a summation of Gan's work. From the very first pages she published in 1837 (*The Ideal*) she had placed the difficulties encountered by the outstanding woman at the very centre of her fiction and returns to this theme in all the works I have considered, as well as elsewhere. With increasing insistence she had defined this theme more narrowly as the problem of the creative woman. At the same time, she had valorised the woman as writer and each of the works I have discussed ends with a woman's story told by a woman – Olga's letter, Sophia's telling of her sister's tale, Zenaida's letter/confession. Gan had also tackled the nature of women's writing, seeing it as antithetical to the world of men's writing, in terms of the public versus the private, the outer world of action and adventure, versus the life of the emotions.[93] Gan had also shown herself to be highly self-conscious as a writer, engaging in the 'Sternianism'[94] so popular in the 1830s – temporal disjunction, variety of narrators, fusion of genres within a single work and so on. Her self-consciousness often takes on a polemical gender-oriented project in that she tends to use traditional masculinist plots (scopophilia; woman as enigma; pursuit – seduction – abandonment and so on) only to subvert them, to punish the rake and valorise the maternal. Indeed, more generally, although the image of women in her work is usually deeply traditional, her manipulation of plot is very often very radical, feminist in a sense. Many of these issues receive a more explicit and definitive form in *A Futile Gift*.

I will begin my consideration of these problems with a description of the epistemological parameters set by Gan around the question of woman as writer. The story opens with two women travelling by carriage through an exceedingly desolate landscape. One of them, the narrator, ponders on metaphysical questions, prompted by the tale she has already heard and the events she has witnessed (only later conveyed to the reader). Her general theme is the arbitrary inequality of the distribution of gifts and talents: 'Tell me, whence proceeds this inequality, this endless variety in the handing out of divine sparks which enliven man?' (710). More specifically she sees the inequality as underpinned by gender divisions:

> And how, moreover, are we to interpret the inappropriate location of souls in frames which are often incompatible with them? How to explain the manifestation of enterprising, firm, fearless characters in the weak bodies of women and the lack of character, the lack of passion which demeans humanity in the mighty hearts of men? (ibid.)

She cannot answer these questions properly, but muses 'Is this a mistake of nature, or the finger of a higher plan?' (ibid.)

It is important to note the terms of reference which this opening lucubration sets. Although specifically social, man-made conditions will impede Anyuta's development as a writer, the more general frame suggests that these chances and inequalities are either God-given or natural. In other words, if a gift *is* futile, then that's just the way things are. Here too, as we will see, while the end of Anyuta's story recuperates her tragedy by virtue of celestial reward, there is an underlying, profound pessimism about the very possibility of change in *this* world. Nature's Law or God's Plan pre-determines individual destinies.

If these opening metaphysical musings set a decidedly doom-laden frame for Anyuta's tragic story, this is immediately intensified by the setting which is now sketched in. As usual, Gan employs (a rather obvious) pathetic fallacy to set the scene: 'Around, everything was empty and wild: nowhere was there a dwelling place or a human voice . . . Around me the earth and sky gave no answer, my thought remained unanswered' (712). The two women ride through a natural desert, which echoes and anticipates the emotional desert in which the creative woman always finds herself in Gan's work. (As Anyuta's Lemm-ish mentor, Geilfreind will say 'a [talented] woman must freeze in a wilderness, in obscurity . . . simply because she is a woman' (752).) Not everything is wilderness, however. On the estate in which the action (such as it is) of the story takes place a library has survived the death of a previous landowner, and it is this library which both stands as a symbol of civilisation in the wilderness, and as a sign of the Father's word which Anyuta will attempt to enter and appropriate.

Gan's account of Anyuta's brief life encapsulates extremely well the anxieties and problematics of the woman as writer. Gilbert and Gubar call their account of this process in nineteenth century English literature, *The Madwoman in the Attic*. Anyuta first enters the story as the Madwoman in the Garden, an almost ghostly figure who wanders at night in the grounds of Countess Belskaya's estate, drawn and captivated by the music she hears there. Gan's basic plot mechanism (woman as riddle) is established. After a few such visitations, the narrator, Belskaya and their entourage begin to receive clues to enable them to decipher this enigma, culminating in an account of her life narrated by Belskaya's doctor. First the narrator encounters her in the garden, devouring a book by a French poet the narrator had dropped. Even by daylight Anyuta seems 'more a spectre than a person' (719), and she runs off when she hears the narrator approach.

Shortly afterwards Anyuta's mother approaches the household seeking assistance for her daughter who is not 'ill', she says, but 'deranged' (721). Her mother now offers a brief biography of her strange child, which reveals Anyuta as yet another daughter of Tatyana. As a child she had been different from the others, preferring solitude, but also highly intelligent, learning French and German very quickly, from the tutor Geilfreind, who had been hired for her brother.[95] The doctor investigates her case and diagnoses galloping consumption, but no clinical signs of madness. Her illness and general spiritual malaise were not caused by 'some unhappy love – the most ordinary of all the illnesses of the female heart' (725). At the commencement of Anyuta's story, then, Gan makes an important polemical point, against herself as well as against the masculinist tradition. This is her only important story where love is not at the very centre of the work: in this her testamental statement the underlying polemic is, to paraphrase Karamzin, that 'even women know how to be a Romantic poet' – and to suffer all the agonies of that privileged, yet alienated position.

The doctor now proceeds to relate the information he has gathered about the causation of Anyuta's malaise. Even as a child she had occupied that Romantic space, seeming like a foundling in her own family, not at home in this world. As well as being a narrative about the Romantic poet, the story is also a fairy-tale. Anyuta begins to come to life when her 'real father' Geilfreind arrives (and Countess Belskaya will prove to be her 'real mother'). He recognises her natural talent and encourages her: much use is made of the disused library which had belonged to Countess Belskaya's father: the girl-child is quite specifically, therefore, introduced to the Symbolic Order of the father's word, and as we shall see, this transition will be deeply problematical. Indeed, the problems begin when Anyuta reaches puberty (twelve), and wishes to enter the world of the symbolic, in which, in Lacanian terms she (the woman) has no place. As E. Ann Kaplan puts it:

> For Lacan, woman cannot enter the world of the symbolic, of language, because at the very moment of the acquisition of language, she learns that she lacks the phallus, the symbol that sets language going through a recognition of difference; her relation to language is a negative one, a lack. In patriarchal structures, thus, woman is located as other (enigma, mystery), and is thereby viewed as outside of (male) language.[96]

Although Anyuta is twelve years and not twelve months old, this seems to me to sum up exactly the problematics that Gan has identified in her story (and elsewhere, of course, enigma, mystery being the central metaphors for the appearance of the heroine in her plots). Geilfreind it is, in fact, who identifies the problems surrounding Anyuta's desired entry into the phallogocentric world. What fate awaits her, he ponders, either in remaining in her own world 'in the provincial depths, surrounded by simple people' or in the wider world which she would try to enter without status or patronage? (729–30). He recognises her 'gift' but fears (correctly so) that it will be 'futile' *in any circumstances*. As elsewhere in Gan's work (*The Ideal, The Locket*) the question is posed: is education for women actually counterproductive in that it prepares them for a world *they cannot enter?*

Nevertheless, Geilfreind presses on, inculcating in her an almost comically Lomonosovian delight in science and the natural world. But Anyuta wants more, her *'soul* thirsts for poetic impressions' (732 – my italics). At the age of fifteen she plunges into a somewhat clichéd Romantic *weltschmertz*, whereby all seems pointless and empty. Her position recalls that expressed in Lermontov's juvenilia (1828–32) – or the 'works' of Vladimir Lensky. However trivial and hackneyed her lamentations may be, the important point is that, most unusually, they are applied to a poor provincial *girl*. Her principal longing is for some kind of 'ideal world' (736). The thirst for the ideal has been the quest for all Gan's heroines from her very first story (*The Ideal*). Again a new twist is introduced in this valedictory work, in that the ideal is not sought in the perfect romantic union, but in art. (There will also be a reversion, however, to the answer Gan's fiction always gives her questing heroines: the only 'ideal world' any of them obtains is in the arms of their Saviour.)

Anyuta is saved from her present despair, ironically, by death. She and her mother become even poorer when her father (of whom we have heard almost nothing) dies, but the 'Sacred obligation of a daughter' (738) brings her out of her despair to care for her distraught mother. As yet, then, she remains a *dutiful daughter* both in this literal sense, but also in the psychoanalytic nexus, in that she accepts the limits (rational thought) placed on her learning by the 'good father', Geilfreind. The rest of the library, the locked away poetry (the soul, the ideal) remains for her *'forbidden fruit'* (738 – my italics). This phrase is, of course, a hackneyed poeticism, but I also feel that we are entitled, indeed *must* read it literally, given Gan's pervasive use of Biblical imagery, with its full original force. This reading adds further dimensions to the problematics of the process of the woman-becoming-writer. When Anyuta eats of the Tree of Knowledge (which she very soon does) must we read her as Eve and her reading which then becomes writing as a breach of a sacred prohibition, which in turn will lead to her fall?

The suggested motif of temptation leading to fall (or seduction) gradually becomes explicit, and it is specifically a temptation to break the prohibition of the father. Anyuta wonders what is in these other books: '"What is hidden in them?" the *tempting* thought whispered to her. With what ruin had Geilfreind threatened her, should she open even one book buried on these shelves?' (741 – my italics). Her thoughts wander on: 'But she is already sixteen; she is *not a child*' (ibid. – my italics). The whole episode carries not merely Biblical baggage, but, it seems to me, a clearly sexual frisson. Anyuta is faced with the choice: now she is (or desires to be) a woman she must go against the father, to appropriate his word, to be initiated into the phallologic world.

Finally, in a state of excitation ('her eyes were blurred, the letters were moving . . . ' (ibid.)) she snatches a book (of German poetry[97]) and reads it in an enraptured, ecstatic state. We then have two pages of virtual stream-of-(un)consciousness as she races through the 'divine poetry'. All this is taking place at night, to reinforce yet further the nexus of imagery of sexual initiation into rapture. Now she has found her 'ideal world': 'Oh, so this is it, this is the heaven of which, in anguish, her soul had dreamed' (744). Gan thus fuses the two dimensions – her own spiritual (Christian) theme of the feminine desire for the ideal, and the theme of the woman becoming a writer (with its concomitant initiation into the world of the phallus). Anyuta, in discovering her 'paradise . . . happiness on earth' (ibid.), achieves a genuine epiphany. And yet, the reader must pause. In achieving her desire the girl becomes a woman, but by breaking the father's prohibition. Will she be, in fact, like Eve before her, expelled from Eden? Moreover, we must always remember the potentially awful implications of the oxymoronic title. That is, she has discovered her 'gift': we have already been led to believe (the prologue) that it *must* remain 'futile'.

Once the dam has been breached Anyuta's ecstasy now floods out in her nocturnal devouring of poetry. Soon she begins writing herself. Interestingly, it is a kind of automatic writing (Romantic inspiration? writing the body?): 'At first she took up the pencil almost unbeknownst to herself: something pressed her inside, something asked for release from her heart to the wide outside: feelings agitated her breast' (748). Certainly, the language for Anyuta's writing seems to me to be saturated with (no longer) repressed sexuality. Equally, her writing is both valorised and is restorative in that she now rediscovers her joy in the world. At this stage, euphoria dominates. To become a (woman) writer is not merely a release, and a fulfilment in itself, but also leads to communion with the Ideal. In a sense, to be a (woman) writer *is* the Ideal.

But almost immediately more warning notes are sounded. Anyuta becomes even more alienated from reality than before, preferring to 'befriend the heroes and heroines of utopia' (749). As before in Gan's work the detachment from the real world in favour of the Ideal is a real pull, but one which is also fraught with real dangers. Another and more actual threat now emerges. Geilfreind discovers her work and her 'father' (as Anyuta now calls him (750)) declares 'it is good' and decides to attempt to publish it, in St Petersburg. This second temptation, this endeavour *in reality* to enter the phallogocentric world is to prove to be catastrophic. Her hopes are raised, only to be dashed, her living conditions worsen, she and her mother now being sunk in abject poverty, and all Anyuta's former despair and depression return. Even worse, she has to relinquish her writing as a condition of the offer of employment as a governess as neither her mother nor her employer considers such nocturnal emissions as suitable in a young woman. She reluctantly agrees to this condition, burns her work, and attempts once more to become a dutiful daughter. But the cost of this renewed repression soon become obvious and Anyuta displays clear symptoms of hysteria – deathly pallors, brilliant flushes, insomnia.

It is at this point that Anyuta became the Madwoman in the Garden, at least in the eyes of those who surround her, 'even her own mother' (773) as Anyuta reflects bitterly.[98] What is even worse, she wonders whether her gift had been a mere chimera: 'Her poetry, her heavenly gift – was it a lie, an illusion?' (773). Finally she enters the house of God to appeal for his succour, only to collapse with blood gushing from her throat.

This concludes the doctor's narrative and the finished section of *A Futile Gift* concludes with the attempts of Countess Belskaya and the others to restore Anyuta's spirits, if not her physical health which has been so undermined that Anyuta passes into the (only) real ideal world in scenes of high (but effective) Sentimentalism. A few days before her death they had managed to persuade Anyuta that she had never been mad and that her gift was a reality. This scene provides the resolution of the debate the story has offered around the issue of the woman writer. After some persuasion Anyuta recognises that 'all this was the action of inspiration and not of a disordered mind' (780–1). Her enthusiasm for writing returns and she exclaims: 'Yes, I have happiness, peace, fame, friends . . . and my poetry . . . my wonderful, celestial gift' (781). We are left with the opposition: the gift (of being a woman writer) is 'futile', or it is 'celestial'. In the end, perhaps, the conclusion Gan leads us to, is that it is both. Her reading and writing had given Anyuta not merely self-fulfilment but also a vision of earthly paradise, had led her to the Ideal. Yet it had also been a breach of the Father's Law, for which she seems to be punished by frustration and despair, because her talent was not recognised until a few days before her death. *A Futile Gift*, as we know, was to be Gan's last work (and she probably knew it would be). Its discussion of what it is to become a woman writer is deeply moving and full of insight, but it also seems to suggest that the price to be paid is excessively high and may, in the end – at this time, in this place – not be worth paying.

It would be silly to suggest that Elena Gan was a Lacanian *avant la lettre*. Certainly, her thrilling description of how Anyuta dares to eat from the Tree of knowledge, and the consequences of this, do fit a Lacanian view of the relationship (or non-relationship) of woman to language. *A Futile Gift* sees it in rather more materialist terms. Before Geilfreind makes the fateful decision of sending her work to St Petersburg, he too wonders whether her gift will be futile, because a woman cannot enter the world of language/literature in the *present* conditions. A man of talent, he cries, may achieve anything, all paths are open to him,

> whereas a woman, equal to a man in talent, and greatly surpassing him in her heart, must freeze in the wilderness, in obscurity, far from the world, from all the great models, from all resources for learning for which her soul thirsts, simply because she is a woman! . . . And futile is her gift. (752)

As we have already seen, this is a deliberate echo of the narrator's opening metaphysical ponderings (as well as of the title). So, are we to think that the futility of a woman's gift is decreed by Nature and/or God? Are the conditions which eventually lead to Anyuta's despair, and, in a sense, at least, her premature death (and Gan's) immutable? Geilfreind, the valorised Old Man/Father thinks not: 'But, in truth, after all, it is not nature which blocks for a woman the path preordained for her on high! People, laws, societies, conditions . . . the strongest have established their laws'[99] (753).

A Futile Gift, then, provides a compelling testament from the dying writer. Anyuta dies in 'the wilderness, in obscurity' and her gift has brought more agony than joy. In the end, however, her gift was not futile, and nor was that of Elena Gan in the sense that she had 'passed the ordinary limits of women's consciousness of [her] age' and had at least posed the problem. In the same year Lermontov commented on a different problem. 'Let it be enough that the disease is indicated but how to cure it – God alone knows!'[100] Using these last words rather more literally, the Christian Gan would probably have agreed with her more celebrated contemporary.

5
Mariya Zhukova and Patriarchal Power

In a sense even more fundamental than is the case for her younger contemporary, Elena Gan, Mariya Zhukova's life[1] and works have been 'hidden from history'. Where Mirsky makes a few rather condescending remarks about Gan, he is completely silent on the subject of her more prolific fellow writer. The situation is no better in the much more recent *Cambridge History of Russian Literature* of 1989 which also has not a single reference to Zhukova, although a number of minor male prosaicists of the period feature. (Richard Stites also fails to mention her.) Finally, however, this silence is ending. Zhukova's major works have recently been republished in Russia[2] (rather more extensively than those of Gan, in fact), while a lengthy section on Zhukova is to be included in Catriona Kelly's forthcoming *Russian Women's Writing 1830–1990: A History*.

Zhukova and Gan have much in common and certainly deserve at least equal attention. Both were highly acclaimed in their life-times (especially by Belinsky[3]); both contributed to a significant and original degree to the development of Russian prose in the 1830s and 1840s, in its move from 'small' to 'large' forms, and, most importantly, not least from my present perspective, 'they both set at the very heart of their creative efforts the depiction of contemporary Russian womanhood',[4] to an extent that surpasses by far any of their male contemporaries, Pushkin and Odoevsky included. It is impossible, therefore, to have a complete understanding of the paths of Russian fiction in this critical, formative period without including Zhukova and Gan in this appraisal. It is my intention, therefore, in this chapter (as it was in the previous one) to present an examination of certain major works by Zhukova and Gan which attempts to locate them in the development of Russian prose (including the question of generic experimentation[5]), while concentrating on their examination of the 'woman question' (and gender more generally) in its formative period.[6] Here I will discuss two of the tales which make up Part One of *Evenings at Karpovka*, namely, *Baron Reykhman* (1837) and *The Locket* (1837) as well as the later *The Dacha on the Peterhof Road*[7] (1845). Each of these works, roughly speaking, can be accommodated into one of the dominant genres of the 1830s, the 'society tale', practised by Pushkin, Lermontov and, as we have seen in Chapter 3, Odoevsky as well as many others. Both Zhukova and Gan used the society tale to explore the confining role allotted to women of the period. Whereas Gan was seeking to go beyond these roles (particularly in her increasing concentration on the struggles of the creative woman), Zhukova tended to adopt a rather more resignatory tone. In her work she may explore the pathos, even the tragedy of women trapped within a cage not of their own making, but in the end, the power of the sociolect, or as she calls it explicitly in another story from *Evenings (The Monk)* of 'patriarchal power', is inviolable.

1. BARON REYKHMAN

1.1 Setting

Because *Baron Reykhman* largely concerns itself with the inner life of its heroine and the price she has to pay for contravening the rules of society, there is little attention paid to the physical surroundings of the Reykhmans and their society. In much the same way as Gan was doing at exactly the same time, however, Zhukova (or rather the narrator of this story, Aleksandr Pronovsky) uses a series of set locales, or *chronotopes* to illuminate and condense in clear focus not only the story's social ambience, but also the themes of the work.

In this sense, the opening lines of *Baron Reykhman* are highly significant. Whereas Gan was adopting a slow narrative pace at the outset of her stories (especially in *Society's Judgement* and *A Futile Gift*), gradually leading the reader through a labyrinthine series of puzzles and false starts, we are here plunged straight, *in medias res*, into the heart of the story's world. The first few lines are, in fact, a conversation between a four-year-old boy, Koko and his mother, Natalya Vasilevna Reykhman. At once, anticipating as in other ways *Anna Karenina*,[8] we are in the very specifically familial and the tension between maternal duties and social glamour is immediately established in that, in a manner that is reminiscent of *Evgeny Onegin* we encounter a denizen of high society (Baroness Reykhman) preparing herself in front of her mirror. Her husband, the rather older Baron Reykhman is also present. This conflict, between the maternal and familial on the one hand, and the superficial attractions of appearances will be one of the *dominantas* of the text.

Soon the story switches from the private, domestic world of a woman's boudoir to the classic chronotope of the society tale, the ball. Indeed, the narrator even lays bare the fact that such a scene has become a cliché:

> No; I will not describe the ball! The glitter of lights, the glitter of diamonds, of outfits and beauty, the assembly place of passions, which stroll about in festive half-masks: to whom is all this unknown? (46)

Nonetheless, the narrator does then proceed to give a kind of sketch of the sensations produced by attendance at a ball, commenting that rarely does one leave a ball without 'emptiness in one's soul and a feeling of cheated expectation' (ibid.). This particular ball is later recalled through the eyes of Natalya Vasilevna (a scene to which I shall return), but for the moment, a number of points need to be noted. Just as a tension was established at the outset between the maternal and the social, this scene takes the latter value to emphasise the conflict once more between inner and outer. To all appearances, and this is precisely the word, this summarising moment (the ball) provides glamour and excitement. In reality (inside – the soul) it offers only emptiness and disillusion. In microcosm, we have encapsulated the story's plot.

The next day (and this is the title of the following chapter) a further semiotic dichotomy is established, between the social and the natural,[9] which Zhukova was to retain as a dominant theme in her work, especially in *The Locket, The Last Evening* and *Dacha*. Here it is dealt with only fleetingly, but motifs are again established which are important for our overall understanding of the work. For almost a full page the narrator outlines in rhapsodic vein the glorious winter scenery of the northern city: 'The sun luxuriously scattered diamonds and gold over the snowy shrouds in which nature wraps our northern region for six long months' (50). In a deliberate lexical echo ('diamonds') the natural scene is contrasted with the real (but false!) jewels of society. Whereas the scene outside her window is full of vivacious action 'This picture of *life* did not gladden Natalya Vasilevna' (ibid. – my italics). Nature can offer an antidote to the 'emptiness in one's soul', but Natalya is too enmeshed in the toils of society to relate to this.

Much of the rest of the story is based on this pattern of successive *tableaux* which highlight both the mores of society and the deepening drama of Natalya's search for happiness within or beyond it. After 'On the Next Day' there follows 'The Morning Visit', offering a further vignette of the empty amusements of high society (singing, the piano, gossip: this latter motif will be crucial in the story's plot dynamics and I shall return to it later). The scene now switches to another commonplace of the period, the dismal provincial town, to which Levin (Natalya's lover) has been posted. This section ('The Bracelet') not only provides the scene for the most dramatic plot development, but also once more allows for effective use of setting to develop the underlying themes. Given the motivation for the move to the provincial town (the redeployment of Levin's regiment) we enter a specifically masculine milieu, where we see the brave young officers drinking, gambling and, ultimately, preparing to fight to the death around the issue of a woman's (sexual) honour. Although Natalya's 'good name' will be of crucial importance in these scenes (and the 'good name' of her husband to an even greater extent), it is a milieu in which women themselves are, by definition, absent. Again the use of setting encapsulates theme: men dispose of women's reputations among themselves (on the gambling table, or by duelling – although this motif is, in the end, not actualised), but women are unable directly to contribute, in high society, to the resolution of their own destinies. The story's setting returns for its final resolution to 'Another Ball', offering an explicit echo and plot rhyme of the earlier scene, while the final lines of the tale see Natalya Vasilevna, lost in France, banished from the world in which her reputation has been lost.

1.2 Plot

This level of *Baron Reykhman* offers the same degree of manipulation of *topoi* of the period, presenting the classic 'society tale' story of amorous intrigue and infidelity as well as a certain ingredient of 'Sternian' narrative experimentation, involving, as we have already seen, *in medias res* opening, and consequently the use of flashback, as well as deliberate retardation devices and the laying bare of clichés.

The initial situation/exposition, coming before the prologue, delineates the social norm of the period, a marriage of convenience (although of benefit to both sides) which will be tested by the 'passions' whose 'assembly place' will be the balls, as well as the gaming-room. As in the setting, conflicts and tensions are immediately hinted at. Although Baron and Baroness Reykhman are satisfied with their arranged marriage, there are, equally, profound gaps. Quite apart from the considerable age difference, there is (again anticipating *Anna Karenina*) an emotional void at the heart of their relationship:

> The Baroness was dissatisfied with one thing: she found Serge too material, too attached to the prosaic side of life. He could not understand her heart. (42)

This motif of conflict between 'prose' and the 'heart' ('poetry') will prove the main engine of the plot: although the woman's 'heart' will be valorised, the 'prose' (of men) will prove triumphant. Indeed, this is anticipated by another implicit tension. The opening sections lead us into the world of Natalya Reykhman (to her 'heart'), but the title of the tale suggests that she will not be the dominant persona, and so it proves.

Soon, the complication emerges, by means of the flashback to the prologue provided by Natalya's reverie 'On the Next Day', in which we learn of her relatively long-standing liaison (of precisely what kind remains unclear) with Levin, a junior officer under the command of Reykhman (and this latter, official, relationship will be crucial). The *in medias res* opening thus serves to decentre the sexual plot, removing the potential readerly voyeurism of a seduction motif. Another kind of decentring now arises in that, although the first third of the story focuses on Natalya, once her plot situation and its etiology are established, she virtually disappears until the closing few pages. Indeed, as the title suggests, the text does not focus on her, but rather on how Baron Reykhman (and others) organise her destiny.

This decentring of Natalya occurs by a series of 'Sternian' switches, first to another society lady Lidiya Ezerskaya, who is also linked to Levin and who will, indeed, be engaged to him by the end of the story. This section then moves to the motif of 'society's judgement'. In the Ezersky household (during 'The Morning Visit') various éminences are gathered who set in motion the engine of rumour which will ultimately catalyse the Baron's wrath against his wife. Although not as fully developed as in Odoevsky's *Princess Mimi* or

Society's Judgement, the motif of rumour (and therefore the loss of the society woman's only real commodity, her 'good name'/sexual honour) has a critical plot function. The narrator sums up the effect of 'society's judgement' simply:

> And so, thanks to . . . Ezerskaya's annoyance with Levin because he had almost completely abandoned her house . . . rumours spread around the city, passed from mouth to mouth, grew, increased and fell like a dark cloud on the horizon of the baroness's life. (55–6)

In keeping with the 'prosaic' tone of the eponymous Baron which also characterises Pronovsky's narrative, the sense of futility over the destruction of a passionate woman is simply stated, without the emotional rhetoric that Gan's narratives would use.

We now move yet further away from the initial narrative focus (Natalya) as we follow Levin's regiment to the provinces, although her fate will underly all the masculine machinations which now ensue. The first of these is another classic *topos* from the period, the rivalry between two men (Levin and his fellow officer Gotovitsky) for a woman (Ezerskaya), which mirrors, on the one hand, the Baron–Levin–Natalya triangle, and on the other, the Ezerskaya–Natalya–Levin nexus. When Levin catches Gotovitsky not only losing heavily, but also cheating at the card table, an argument ensues, during which Natalya's bracelet (given originally to her by the baron, and then by her to Levin) is thrown on the table. Once again, a single detail of *Baron Reykhman* encapsulates the macrocosm. A woman's honour becomes the subject for public dispute, and is cavalierly tossed, as if a gambling chip. Men fight over her virtue, but their pride and passion preclude any real concern for her genuine interests. Indeed, the bracelet has a profound metonymic resonance: Natalya becomes the token of exchange and rivalry between the three men concerned.[10]

The fight between the two 'sons' does not go the usual course, however, as the 'Father' Reykhman intervenes to sort out their quarrel. By now the story's centre of gravity has completely shifted to the implications of the title as the 'prosaic', but imperious Baron now arranges the affairs not only of Gotovitsky and Levin, but also of his wife. Natalya in 'Another Ball' declares her willingness to anticipate Anna Karenina in this respect too, namely, to abandon not only unloved husband, but beloved son as well. But Levin refuses, declaring not only where his own interests are (with the Baron) but also what are the governing values of this society:

> Should I forget the magnanimous step of your husband ... Make *his name* a fable throughout the city and repay with black ingratitude the trust with which he released me? (71 – my italics)

In the end, it is his name, The Name of the Father, which is the central value of the story and the society it depicts and Levin will be willingly obedient to this name. So too, willingly or unwillingly, must Natalya and her banishment to France, while Baron Reykhman keeps the child, is only confirmation of the main plot motifs: 'patriarchal power' is threatened by a woman's 'heart' and 'passion', but will reassert itself and the woman who loses *her* name is cast beyond the pale.

The plot of *Baron Reykhman* offers, then, an admonitory lesson for women (however sympathetically their plight may be depicted) and this view is confirmed by a closer look at the emotional, sexual and social relations between men and women.

1.3   Male/Female Relations

Like nearly all the other stories in *Evenings at Karpovka*, *Baron Reykhman* places the relationships between men and women, as well as an examination of (seemingly immutable) gender differences at the very centre of its discourse. It is significant, therefore, that scenes between husband and wife both open and close the narrative. As we know, theirs is a marriage, if not of convenience in the strictest, negative sense, then of mutual advantage, which has received the blessing of Natalya's father. The Baron's glittering ancestry and army record had proved a fitting complement for her 2000 serfs. The opening scene (apart from swiftly and succinctly sketching in all this background) provides warning notes in plenty. Quite apart from his 'prosaic' attitude to the emotions, they spar, quite light-heartedly on the whole, around issues of jealousy, with particular reference to Levin. The Baron disdains to be jealous, arguing that this would 'restrict his wife's freedom' (44) which he has no wish to do, before, however, making his authority – and Law – quite clear: 'My business is to concern myself with the purity of *my name, and that is all*. No jealousy, no precautions will save a wife without good morals' (ibid. – my italics). First and last, it is his *own* honour that counts, and it is this concern which will shape the story rather than 'love', whether between them, or between Natalya and Levin. His wife is very unhappy about his rational approach: indeed, she wants his jealous love and cries despairingly: 'No, you men are terrible! You will never understand the heart of a woman' (45). And therein lies the problem. In this story, as elsewhere in Zhukova, men and women are implacably engendered, constructed almost as separate species. Men inhabit the world of 'prose' and rationalism, while women are drawn by 'poetry', the 'heart' and the 'passions'. And it will be significant that no Zhukova heroine in these stories will ever find happiness by following these 'feminine' attributes: only those who are able happily to accept marriage on society's (that is, men's) terms will find some kind of contentment.

Natalya Reykhman, however, makes the mistake of following her heart, of seeking passion with Levin. But he is to prove as 'male' as her husband. Although their liaison is of some standing he too fails to understand her, mentally exclaiming: 'Oh, women, women! What will one do here?' (48), anticipating, as other male characters in the period do, Freud's famous question. And, as we have already seen, he will sacrifice Natalya on the altar of her husband's good name. She, in fact, had not sought, at first at least, a great deal from her liaison: 'Was she really never to find happiness? Dreams, dreams! Were they really never to come true? Was she really never to hear "I love" from dear lips, never to know poetic love?' (51). She desired only to be 'loved, understood' (ibid.). Deliberately, it seems to me, Zhukova presents her heroine with a harsh choice. Her wants are modest, merely to be loved, but even so, if the woman seeks fulfilment even of this limited ambition outside the proper bounds, that is, if she does not submit to society's code, then she will be ruined. Later, before the dénouement makes the point clear, the narrator sums up her position: 'This is why a woman who loses the love of her husband, even if she does not love him herself, is the unhappiest creature in the world' (60). And this is precisely what Natalya Vasilevna Reykhman becomes by the end of the story.

1.4 Women and Society

Indeed, one of the paradoxes of Zhukova is that, although women's lives are at the every centre of her fiction, her resolution of their plots tends to be conservative, androcentric in some senses. If she seems to counsel her heroines to accept 'patriarchal power', then this is because she appears to have done so herself. The main female character in *Baron Reykhman*, is of course, Baroness Natalya Vasilevna, but before examining her portrait and role in the story, I will look briefly at the other women in the story.

One of the striking features of 'patriarchal' literature in this period in Russia, but equally elsewhere, is the approach to older (that is no longer sexually 'interesting') women. On the whole they are either ignored, and so marginalised, or the object of masculinist disgust. Both Zhukova (especially in *Dacha*) and Gan valorise the older woman (in Gan's case, quite specifically, the Mother). Here we have only a brief harbinger of this tendency, in the depiction of Lidiya Ezerskaya's mother, who is quite explicitly past her first flush of youth. But denigration is absent from this sketch: her advancing years (and lack – to male eyes – of physical attraction) is delicately touched upon: we are introduced to 'Ezerskaya, a fairly weighty lady . . . of those years when every morning carries off a new beauty and bestows in return new, alas! artificial roses' (53). Similarly, the mother-daughter relationship (to be *the* central reference point in Gan), which is absent or difficult in, say, Turgenev, is here shown to be amicable and mutually supportive.

Physical scrutiny of the nubile heroine is also a repetitious *topos* in Russian fiction in its formative years, frequently accompanied by a degree of fetishisation which borders on the pornographic.[11] This too is eschewed by Gan and Zhukova alike. Here, for example, we are shown Lidiya singing and playing and she is described physically, and as attractive, but, as in the case of her mother, her appearance is simply stated: 'a young pretty girl, rosy as a rose, and with two dimples on her plump little cheeks' (ibid.).

In turning to Natalya Vasilevna we need to recall her opening situation, which in a few lines establishes the duality of her position and sets in train the conflicting motifs, the tensions between which are eventually to destroy her. On the one hand (and firstly) she is a mother; on the other, she is a full participant in the ethos of high society. It is, indeed, of vital significance that the maternal is the first motif in the story, because this is her central attribute as a woman and her preparedness later to abandon *even* her young son is a sign of both her desperation and of the depths to which she has sunk. This is encapsulated both when we learn that Koko 'so as not to disturb them [Natalya and Levin] is locked in the nursery for days on end' (54) and in the conversation between the two lovers near the end. Natalya offers herself to Levin, who, quite apart from reminding her of her conjugal duties, twice asks 'But Koko?', to which she can only cry 'Oh, you are cruel, Aleksander!' (71). And, in the end, of course, her ultimate punishment is that she is deprived of this central, defining role, in that the Baron keeps the boy.

Although Natalya is initially defined as mother, more emphasis is actually placed on her whole-hearted enthusiasm for society life. First adumbrated in the opening lines (as she arranges her curls before her dressing-table mirror), this theme is developed in the first few pages. Unlike Gan's heroines (*The Ideal, Society's Judgement*, for example), Natalya is no unwilling martyr to society's rules. Instead, her vanity and shallow enjoyment of the flattering admiration she receives at the first ball are emphasised. Both in her marriage and in her everyday life, she is presented as a woman who is fully part of this world. Yet, as we know, neither role will be sufficient for her because Zhukova reveals within her (as she will in later stories) a deep tension which, ultimately, cannot be resolved. If her principal defining *role* is the maternal, then her (woman's) central attribute is 'the heart', her unfulfilled (and unfulfillable in society's terms) longing 'to be loved and to be understood'. (I shall return to Zhukova's master concepts for gender difference shortly.)

It seems to me that, by placing Natalya in an impossible situation, and by punishing her by the final textual exclusion, Zhukova displays a deep-seated ambivalence to her heroine: she is allowed deep feeling and real needs, but then shown that she must either suppress these or face terrible retribution (and it is terrible for all the relative lightness of narrative tone). This ambivalence is also shown very clearly in the handling of narrative and, especially, point of view. The opening pages would seem to suggest that Natalya will be our 'sentient centre': certainly, efforts are made, especially after the first ball scene, to enter into her inner life (51). But the fact that the point-of-view moves completely away from her is critical. Again there is an illuminating parallel with Gan. In *Society's Judgement*, for example, the heroine, Zenaida, is the object of an orchestrated campaign of malicious vilification, but the story ends with a lengthy memoir from her to justify and explain her completely innocent behaviour. The woman's word is, literally, final, and is valorised. Here, however, in Zhukova's as well as society's judgement, Natalya is in the wrong, and the deprivation of point of view, her narrative silencing at least implies that she has no defence. The silencing is only relative, however, in that, towards the end, the point of view does return to her and renewed attempts are made to understand (empathetically) her troubled situation. But the author's ambivalence, as well as her views of moral rectitude, permeate even the thoughts of her heroine: 'Who will assure him [her husband] that my love is pure, innocent? But is not this very love, is it not already a crime? How to bear his reproach, how to meet his gaze?' (68). A real effort seems to be made to understand the anguish of the 'guilty' wife (and mother) but 'guilty' remains the verdict.

These latter stages of the narrative also mark an intensification of the dysphoric iconography which is so characteristic of the depiction in this period of suffering heroines. Again there is a shift relative to the opening of the story. At the start (after the first ball) Natalya is unhappy about her relationships, and there are only glimpses of what is later to come: 'She looked *sadly* at the lively scene . . . [her annoyance] had given way to *quiet sadness* . . . but the sun was not rising for the *poor* Baroness' (50). All this italicised lexis is typical of the series of clichés usually attached to the suffering or rejected woman, but here a tone of mockery pervades the narrator's depiction of her rather childishly self-indulgent vanity. But this is to change.

At first we have a glimpse of her decline through the thoughts of Levin (and this may, therefore, only be a reflection of *his* view of her): 'What will become of her, this dear, light-hearted creature, flighty, but loving, weak, but devoted?' (60). As his lucubrations, and the story more generally, unfold, we too come to see her – or, at least, are encouraged to see her – as 'light-hearted', 'flighty', and 'weak'. Soon Levin again envisages her: 'he only saw the Baroness, timid, weak, powerless against the storm which threatened her' (61). When we do finally return to her the narrator presents her in very similar terms and as the 'storm' bursts, she enters into the iconography of the destroyed woman fully, whereby she betrays her 'timidity' and, especially, 'weakness' by tell-tale *physical* displays, which becomes *signs* of her collapse. She is handed the packet containing the emblematic bracelet and 'Her hand began to tremble' (67). A few days later we enter her study where 'Natalya Vasilevna sat, or almost lay. . . . Her thrown-back head, pale face, her lowered hands, the position of her whole body indicated complete moral destruction' (67–8). Indeed, (the last clause), the function of such iconography, the relationship between the signifier and signified is laid bare and, as so often, the woman becomes pure sign.

The last half-dozen pages concentrate on Natalya and on her mental and, physically expressed, agony as she wrestles with what is the essentially Classical dichotomy of duty and desire. She makes up her mind declaring 'You know, Alexander, that my whole life, all my being belongs to you' (70). Given the decorous value system underlying the story, and given that this declaration takes place at the quintessential locus of public display and erotic intrigue, the ball, Natalya reveals herself to be, indeed, a woman without shame. Her moments of immodest bravado over, she relapses into iconographic signs and again the connection between the signifier and signified is made manifest: 'With her soul torn to pieces the Baroness, pale as death, ran into her study' (71). Indeed, morally, socially – and narratively – she is dead.

Several forces and pressures contribute to her fall. Apart from her own fallibility, the central power impinging upon her is 'society's judgement', the sociolect which declares that a woman's honour, her good name and, *a fortiori*, that of her husband, are the only things that count. As we have already seen, this has a critical catalysing impact in terms of the plot, but it is also vital to our understanding of Zhukova's conception of women and their place in society. The significance of these opinions can be gauged firstly by the foregrounding of the section 'The Morning Visit' in the narrative flow. After the exposition and prologues the story is arrested so that this latter-day chorus can comment upon it.

The impulse to their deliberations is Natalya's increasingly deviant behaviour, deviant in the sense that she has absented herself from society, to devote herself to music, or rather to the performance of it *à deux* with Levin (the Baron having no liking for music, and Koko, as we know, locked in the nursery). The initial verdict is passed: 'she is too careless: she is doing unforgivable things. One feels sorry for her!' (54). In both Odoevsky's *Princess Mimi* and Gan's *Society's Judgement* the power of society is shown, but also it is attacked, in that the rumours surrounding the heroine in each case have no justification: here this is not the case. As Princess Ezerskaya sums it up, 'she is sacrificing her good name, the opinion of society' (55).

The central issue in *Baron Reykhman*, to which the story repeatedly returns, is precisely this: a woman's sexuality and how she handles it. If, as already noted, Zhukova is dualistic in her approach to her heroine, then this is because her very conception of gender is dichotomous. Men and women are different, have different needs, different roles and, therefore, totally different expectations. This is touched upon in the initial exchanges between Natalya and her husband, but is most fully explored in another foregrounded, plot-retarding section where Levin muses on Natalya's behaviour and her lot. (Although this section (pp. 60–1) begins as his thinking, there is considerable slippage in the point of view, so that the ideas are presented somewhat *ex cathedra* and, I think, reflect the narrator's and Zhukova's views rather than simply those of their utterer, Levin.)

These views are stated simply and very explicitly: 'The life of a man is two-fold: he is a family man and at the same time, the duties of a citizen fall to him. . . . Woman is created solely for the family; the area of activity beyond it is alien to her' (60). The phrasing is such that these lines read as a kind of immutable set of laws: indeed, this dichotomy seems to be fixed, permanent ('created'). The thinking continues to be as lapidary, as one statement follows another, and becomes quite explicit about the underlying causes of this dualism: 'The first foundation of her domestic happiness is the love of her husband; because, let us not deceive ourselves, power is situated in the hands of the man' (ibid.). There is no protest, implicit or otherwise, nor even any questioning of these assertions. Indeed, they are seen as having the status of Law: 'men have on their side rights which they have appropriated or which belong to them from time immemorial' (ibid.). These days men may not resort to the cruelties of the past (murder, imprisonment, banishment to nunneries[12]) but the hegemony of patriarchy is as potent for all that. If a woman does step beyond her allotted sphere then there awaits a 'Terrible thought! The long, tormenting trial of a life-time' (61). Long before the end of the narrative proper, Natalya's eventual fate is anticipated, as is the lesson to be drawn from it. Levin recapitulates this two-edged argument as he presents Natalya with his decision: 'There is the life of the heart, dear friend; but there is also the life of society' (71). The latter (the world and rights of men) take precedence over the former (love, the 'natural' sphere of women).

1.5 Images of Men

The thoughts of Levin (and behind him, the narrator and the author) make clear where power lies. This is also apparent from an analysis of the role men play in the story. In particular, Baron Reykhman is seen, from the very title onwards, to control everything that happens: he has all narrative power and his desire, the Law of the Father, governs.

Fittingly, then, although the first third of the story will concentrate on Natalya, we learn first about the Baron's history. He is rather older than his wife, according to the conventions of the day, although his precise age is not specified. Both in his background, and the later plot, emphasis is placed on military motifs: he is, indeed, a dashing veteran of the Napoleonic campaigns, and his Livonian ancestors had first come to Russia to serve 'The Giant' (42), that is, Peter the Great 'who was creating a new state' (ibid.). This link with the semi-mythic Father of modern Russia will have important resonances later. At first, after this brief biography, the Baron remains a somewhat shadowy figure, yet his presence is always felt. Natalya and Levin in their musical encounters usually had the Baron present: now, as the complication of the plot (their liaison dangereuse) develops the Baron leaves them alone. This is because he can afford to, given that, as we will see, his will is ubiquitous.

The Baron intervenes in the plot proper during the gambling party, where both his and Levin's close identification with the quintessentially masculinist military ethos emerge. For Levin this is in the diegetic present (his proposed, but aborted duel with Gotovitsky): for the Baron it is by way of memories of his 'youth with its storms, passions, losses' (57). Soon Reykhman's authority as the Father of the story comes into even clearer focus. As a crowd of hot-headed young officers cluster round the gaming table, on which Natalya's honour lies in the metonymic bracelet, the Baron steps forward to pick up this highly charged adornment, declaring 'Honni [sic] soit qui mal y pense' (59). He, then, is the ultimate guardian of his wife's honour and, while the young men are ready to fight to the death, he behaves with dignity and decorum, laying a friendly hand on Levin's shoulder and claiming that the bracelet is a gift from Levin's sister. His gesture towards his rival Levin is significant. As the dominant figure, he has no need to challenge Levin, but can patronise and disarm him. Another conclusion can also be drawn, which emphasises yet further the increasingly androcentric tendency of the story. All this fuss is really about nothing, and can be sorted out, in a rational way, man to man. Finally, we should note that the bracelet bears the Baron's coat-of-arms: his presence and authority are indeed ubiquitous.

Mariya Zhukova and Patriarchal Power   153

It is no accident, therefore, that the foregrounded digression on gender differences ('power is situated in the hands of the man') should come at precisely this point, thereby acting as a commentary on the scene that has preceded it. In the course of these meditations which are, of course, at least partially a reflection of Levin's thinking, he remembers that Reykhman is his commanding officer. Quite apart from the obviously Oedipal resonance that this nexus gives to the plot dynamics, this relationship between the two men is important in two other ways. Firstly, as the later development of the plot reveals all too clearly, his primary obligation will be to his superior officer/Father, rather than to the woman he claims to love. Secondly, 'the man' in whose hands power is situated in this story, is precisely the man to whom Levin (and the other young men) are subordinate – as, in no lesser measure, is the wife, Natalya.

It is from this point onwards that the narrative focus concentrates on the world and values of men, especially the Baron, at the expense of Natalya and the feminine values her story represents. He has learned about the duel, and prevents its occurrence, thereby drawing Levin even further into his debt, and his patronage (for which, as we have already seen, Levin will be a dutifully grateful son and will relinquish any claim to Natalya). The Baron is now presented as the true Father, in terms redolent of Old Testament Patriarchs. Levin himself offers this characterisation of the Baron: 'He is passionate, but kind; hot-tempered, but magnanimous' (64). The father will be angry with the squabbling sons, but will show condescension. He also shows ability to rise above such petty concerns as human passions. Weeks go by. Levin waits impatiently for some resolution, while, as we later learn, Natalya is in agony, but 'The general seemed to have forgotten completely about Levin ... all went on in its usual way' (ibid.). Levin is summoned before his commanding officer who, although betraying signs of suppressed emotion, returns to him his things (including the bracelet) and acts with dignified aloofness: 'I have no need to know anything, Mr Levin. Take this bracelet; I leave it to your heart to tell you what you must do' (65). And he leaves him without a further word.

Levin learns the lesson of true manhood from the Baron and this 'father-son' relationship becomes the dominant one. It is at this point that, after a considerable absence, Natalya now re-enters the story. She too regards Baron Reykhman as a kind of Old Testament Patriarch, but one whose stern judgement she awaits with dread and trepidation. 'How to bear his reproach, how to meet his gaze', she wonders and this emphasis on his seemingly all-seeing eye once more reflects the increasing all-pervasiveness of the Baron's power. Natalya cannot return this gaze: at the climactic second ball she cries to Alexander: 'I cannot see the Baron: the very thought of this meeting terrifies me' (70). He may be 'kind' and 'magnanimous' to his wayward 'sons', but he will be pitiless to his errant wife. What is even worse for Natalya, as the ensuing discussion with him reveals, is that the reformed (and forgiven) 'son' will collude with the omnipotent father to cast her adrift, literally in the 'name' of the Baron.

The epigraph for the final chapter is, fittingly from the Old Testament (the Psalms): 'O Dieu, aye pitié de moi selon ta miséricorde' (71). We can read this as voicing Natalya's position: certainly she will have no pity from Reykhman. Equally appropriate is the title of this concluding section, simply and starkly 'The Husband'. He is given final authority and has the last word as he announces to Natalya her wretched destiny. In keeping with the strict engendering of the story 'She stopped . . . as if turned to stone', while 'The Baron went up to her freely and with a completely unrestrained air' (72). His final words to her ring out with chilling authority: 'I leave to myself only the right to dispose of the destiny of my Konstantin and the certainty that he will remain the sole heir to my name. Good night, Baroness!' (ibid.).

By the end of the story, then, Baron Reykhman has, indeed, all the power, both social and narrative while Natalya is left with nothing. The moral implications of the story seem clear enough as, indeed, are the rigid gender differences established.

2. THE LOCKET

2.1 Setting

Like *Baron Reykhman*, this story largely concerns itself with the inner life, this time of its two contrastive heroines, Mariya and Sofiya, and, accordingly, little attention is paid to external features of the setting. Despite this, use is made of a number of chronotopes which are typical of the period.

Indeed, the opening of *The Locket* is significant in this respect. Echoing the nameless (female) compiler of *Evenings*, as well as the principal female character at whose house the 'evenings' occur,

Natalya Dmitrievna (who is also the narrator of the lead story, *The Monk*), the narrator of the present story (Gorsky) begins his narrative with a contrast between the unsalubrious climate of the northern capital and the joys of the Russian countryside. Pushkin opens Chapter Two of *Evgeny Onegin* (which introduces 'wild, sad, silent' (II:xxv) Tatyana to the reader) with the punning epigraph 'O rus! . . ./ O Rus'.' This homonymic identification of ancient ('Holy') Russia and all its traditional values with the countryside runs as a red thread through much of the thinking of the period (the Slavophiles, Gogol) as well as the literature of the entire century (Tolstoy, for example). Certainly, it is one of the master chronotopes of *Evenings at Karpovka*. Gorsky, then, opens the tale with an account of how he had been sent from St Petersburg to his aunt's estates in the Simbirsk province and remarks 'in my soul I blessed both the doctors and the fashion for emigration [from city to countryside]. In Russia too, in its broad valleys, there are villages which can be considered paradise' (76). He then goes on, in terms which anticipate the ambience of Turgenev's *Notes of a Hunter*, to recount the bucolic pleasures of strolling with his gun and his dog, book in hand, which leads on to a sketch of his favourite spot, which is also the preferred place of Mariya and Sofiya, the two heroines. This extended lyrical opening, then, not only establishes the values of *Rus'* as the dominant ones, but links the two young women ineluctably with these traditions and they thereby become implicitly daughters of Tatyana and all she represents. Indeed, as we shall see, Romantic adoration of nature is a key-note in the portrait of Mariya. In turn, we are to see her in a pastoral vignette, typical of the neo-Sentimentalism of the 1830s and 1840s, sitting under the willow that shades her mother's grave, discussing her hopeless love for the *raznochinets* doctor, Velsky. Nearby in the village church . . .

Equally significant in terms of the chronotopes of the period is the dramatic switch back to St Petersburg towards the end of the story. Given the *Onegin*-inspired opening, as well as the explicit denigration of St Petersburg, to say nothing of the overall resonance of this setting in the literature of the period (and later[13]), we know that the values that have permeated most of the story will be sacrificed in favour of the glamour, superficiality and falseness of the high society which dominates the capital. The potential for tragedy, or at least, disappointed hopes, is immediately intensified by the specific locale we enter, the most powerful (and negative) chronotope of the society tale, namely, the ball. Significantly, moreover, the moral (as well as sentient) centre of the tale, Mariya, is absent from the plot for the first time. And, true to expectations, Sofiya, not altogether unwillingly, blows her head before the exigencies of society's code (or 'patriarchal power') to marry a complete stranger, thereby arriving at the same terminus as her literary mother, Tatyana.

2.2 Plot

For two rather different reasons, the ostensible story-line of *The Locket* proves to be of little importance. On the one hand about half of the text is taken up with a recapitulation of the background, so that we have in essence two portraits (Sofiya and, especially, Mariya) rather than a developing narrative. When the story proper does get under way the main motif (will Mariya or Sofiya win Velsky?) is thwarted because the one he loves, Sofiya, is socially superior, and marries the man chosen by her parents, while Mariya, who truly loves him, is, in turn, married off to a relative of Sofiya's mother. Nevertheless, an examination of the plot, such as it is, sheds interesting light on the main issues at play.

The title is foregrounded in the opening situation. We encounter Sofiya, with Mariya at her feet, in the picturesque locale lyricised by Gorsky, playing with the eponymous adornment. This proves to be a locket which seems to be emblematic of both women: what will be their hidden secret? In the pages that follow we learn much about the heroines from which several determining points emerge. Their contrastive appearances (particularly that of the 'ugly' Mariya) are much dwelled upon, leading, in fact, to the conclusion that '(physical) appearance is (for a woman) destiny'. In turn, the flashback pre-prologue (their education) suggests that social origin is equally an insuperable conditioning factor. Indeed, as in *Baron Reykhman*, the laws and codes which surround women seem to be immutable.

This lengthy, recapitulating pre-prologue concentrates exclusively on the world of women. Certainly, they are established as, and remain, the primary narrative focus (indeed, male characters are largely peripheral to the *plot* of *The Locket* except at the end), and the expectations created are that a woman's desire (first Mariya's and then Sofiya's) will shape the story. The dénouement, however, thwarts these expectations and, thereby, female desire, for all the concentration on it for most of the work, is seen to count for little. Indeed, the conclusion that the plot leads to, is anticipated very much earlier.

After the near-drowning of Mariya (after a playful tussle between the two women over the locket), Sofiya's mother reads her a *poucheniye*, a religious word conveying both 'lesson' and 'sermon', warning her to forsake any interest in the 'lowly' doctor: 'you should not think about him; your father would never forgive you such an inclination: his prejudices are known to you' (83). As in *Baron Reykhman*, the Law of the Father will conquer all. Equally, this *poucheniye* (like the meditation on gender in the earlier tale) is foregrounded, both by its length, and its plot-retarding position, coming as it does immediately after the first dramatic incident.

For the next dozen or so pages, narrative attention and point of view switch almost completely to Mariya, and her inner life, her relationship with Sofiya, and her hopeless love for Velsky. This section like the rest of the plot teaches the heroine – and the expectant reader – a stern lesson. However valorised Mariya may be (morally and narratively) her desire in particular will be discounted.

After these lengthy prologues, we finally return to the diegetic present, about half way through. Mariya is in love with Velsky, while he keeps his distance from Sofiya, because he knows full well that the sociolect will never allow him to marry her. In any event, he is more intrigued, at least at first, by the more spiritual Mariya. Here another motif is introduced, to be thwarted, in that Velsky 'wished to solve her enigma' (94). The solving of the enigma of the mystery woman was to prove a popular and recurrent topos in nineteenth century Russian literature (in Lermontov and, especially, Turgenev, for example). But here the motif is deliberately stunted, aborted almost at its inception. That is, Velsky's desire *too* will be thwarted as the exigencies of 'patriarchal power', the 'prejudices' of the Father subvert *all* other plot expectations. Those of Sofiya are frustrated because she is a dutiful daughter (and more generally because she is a woman): those of Velsky because he is of the wrong social origins; while those of Mariya go nowhere because she is *both* female *and* socially inferior.

Once the main plot does finally come into proper focus we are presented with yet another motif which has, in fact, lain dormant from the very first, contrastive description of the two women, namely the rivalry between the two for the same man. Although Sofiya initially has no real interest in Velsky, her vanity is pricked by his clear preference for Mariya and she goes out of her way, successfully, to win his heart. Velsky succumbs to Sofiya's greater personal charms and, particularly after the dramatic climax of Velsky's near death by drowning, their mutuality seems assured. *Amor vincit omnia* the reader is led to believe for a few pages. But at this point the attentive reader of the whole cycle should remember Levin's *poucheniye* to Baroness Reykhman: 'Love is the happiness of life . . . But there is something higher than love – honour!' (71). And, even though Sofiya's father is almost completely absent from the diegesis, his 'honour' and 'prejudices' prove dominant. As Levin learns to be a dutiful son to his 'Father', so too Sofiya bows down before the same iron Law. As her mother says to her: 'So, Sofiya, God will reward you for your obedience; filial love never goes unrewarded' (106). Sofiya, in fact, is delighted by this arranged match, while Velsky and Mariya (who later dies at the age of 29) go their own, separate ways. Certainly, the plot of *The Locket* confirms the lessons to be drawn from *Baron Reykhman*: women may be the narrative centre of Zhukova's tales, but in these two, at least, their desire must be subjugated to the will of the father. Equally, the arranged marriage is valorised. As Sofiya's mother also remarks at her daughter's betrothal, harking back to the latter's brief flirtation with love for the unsuitable doctor: 'Dreams will remain dreams, my dear . . . love, wealth, the historic name of the Count will reward you for their loss' (ibid.). In this she echoes not only other plot situations in Zhukova, but also her own life which had been briefly delineated as part of our introduction to Sofiya. Like the Reykhmans she and her husband had married entirely for mutual benefit and many years later she clearly does not regret her choice. In Zhukova's world (and this is a very marked contrast to Gan) love matches come a very poor second to 'rationally' organised society arrangements.[14] In this sense, too, all the plot expectations around Mariya, Sofiya and Velsky were doomed even before they were aroused.

2.3 Relations between Women

In no text covered in my earlier work *Women in Russian Literature, 1780–1863*, before Chernyshevsky's revolutionary *What Is To Be Done?*, is there anything resembling a close, intimate relationship between two women. Even where a relationship of any kind exists it is usually presented as one of conflict or inadequacy. To take just two examples from works which more or less frame the period under study in the present work, *Evgeny Onegin* presents the two sisters Tatyana and Olga who had nothing in common beyond the same parents, while *On the Eve* has Elena and her companion Zoya who do not exchange a single word to each other in the course of the entire novel. In Gan's work, for the most part, close relationships between women (especially mothers and daughters) feature as a crucial ingredient of her contribution to Russian literature. Zhukova's position would seem to lie somewhere between these two poles. She displays here, in fact, the same ambivalence as she does to female desire more generally, which she presents sympathetically, even positively, only to severely curb it by the codes of society which, overall, she endorses.

The opening of the story sets this pattern. Like Pushkin's sisters, the two young women are more or less complete opposites, both physically and spiritually. Indeed, the narrator draws our attention to this polarity: 'It would have been difficult to find the slightest similarity between the two friends' (77). Nevertheless, they appear to be genuinely close, although it is not a relationship between equals. Later we learn that 'Sofiya became Mariya's idol' (87) as they grew to know each other, and it is surely significant that we first encounter them while Sofiya sits, looking at 'the girl, who was lying at her feet' (77). And, indeed, although Sofiya is chronologically the younger, Mariya is definitely cast in the role of junior partner, or *confidante*.

For all that, the bond between the two women is set before us as the introduction to the story and is, thereby, established as the *given* of the narrative; the initial situation and the lengthy scene as they sit in the lap of nature, coming immediately after the narrator's paean to *rus/Rus'*, certainly valorise them and their relationship. The trouble begins as Mariya's feelings for Velsky become clear and, in part, are reciprocated. Here Zhukova's position shifts more towards the 'androcentric' view found in almost all other works of the period, according to which no two women can ever remain friends for long, especially if an eligible man is around. Initially, Sofiya's interest in Velsky is based on wounded vanity, his apparent slighting of her out of preference for Mariya: 'He looks down on me from the heights of his Germanic erudition; for hours on end he talks to Mariya about Schiller, Goethe, Jean-Paul; not a single word to me! It's as if he thinks me incapable of understanding him' (83). Mariya, used to rejection and isolation, is, in turn thrown into agonies of jealousy when Velsky is enticed away by Sofiya's 'coquetry' (as her mother had earlier called it (83)), but once Sofiya's feelings seem to deepen and become real love for the noble, Lenskyan doctor, Mariya is prepared to embrace her rival, who is, for all that, still her friend, and implores Sofiya to make Velsky happy (102). Again, a harsh realism underpins Zhukova's world: women *can* be true friends to each other, provided the socially inferior (and 'ugly') partner is ready to submit to what Sofiya considers her natural entitlement (because of her birth and beauty).

A critical motif in Gan's writing is the paradisiacal girlhood of her heroine, who is nurtured by a perfect mother, who becomes and remains the emblem of all that is good and holy, although nearly always the mother has died before the story proper begins. This pattern is replicated here in the biographical background to Mariya's story. However, whereas the idealistic education of Gan's heroines at their mothers' knees usually leaves them ill-prepared for the harshness of 'patriarchal power', Mariya, 'from her childhood years' (86) had had inculcated into her a harsh lesson: 'My plain one, you are not pretty, my plain one; there is nothing for you to do in the world; you will be a nun' (ibid.). Given the realities of 'the world' from which Zhukova does not shrink, this is a sound lesson, and one that Mariya learns well. Indeed, the mother becomes everything to Mariya, the symbol of all that is finest: 'the heart of her mother replaced the universe for her; in it she lived like a queen . . . It [her mother's heart] surrounded her with an entire world of the magic of maternal love' (87). As in Gan, then, the mother/daughter relationship is presented, in this vignette, as the supreme, most nurturing bond. But, also as in Gan, the maternal is lost: Mariya's mother dies and 'she remained alone, and a desert surrounded her' (ibid.). Often in male writers it is the death of the father (the loss of patriarchal protection) which precipitates the plot, and leads to catastrophe (as, for example, in *Poor Liza* and *The Fountain of Bakhchisaray*[15]): here, it is the death of the mother. It is significant, therefore, that twice the grave of Mariya's mother becomes a refuge for the daughter – in the scene already described above, and, when, having implored Sofiya to make Velsky happy, Mariya 'went out to her mother's grave and there for a long, long time her tears dropped onto the cold marble' (102).

Sofiya's mother is still alive and plays an important part in this daughter's acclimatisation to the rules of society. We see them together in two critical scenes, that of the *poucheniye* and at Sofiya's betrothal. In each instance, Sofiya's mother, Princess Z. plays a dual role. Certainly, there is real intimacy and affection between the two women (such a rapport is a real rarity in the fiction of the period), yet the mother's essential role in the plot, on both occasions, is to impart the lessons of society, of patriarchy. (In this respect both mothers have the same function.) It is she, rather than Sofiya's father, who remains a very shadowy figure, who reads the 'lesson', while it is also Sofiya's mother who instructs her daughter as to the value (and rewards) of a match made according to mutual self-interest, as we have seen. Once more emphasis is placed on the real bond between mother and daughter (Velsky espies the Princess 'holding Sofiya in her arms' (106)) but, at the same time, the older woman is the one who perpetuates the conditions which restrain the natural inclinations of the woman's heart. The older woman is certainly important in Zhukova's work, as someone with real power and authority, but this authority is shown to be used in the interests of the 'prejudices' of the fathers.

2.4 Images of Women

Without doubt *The Locket* has as its primary focus the inner world of women, and this, in itself (sections of *Evgeny Onegin* apart) was fairly novel for Russian literature. As already noted, the narrative development as such plays only a small role. The two heroines are contrastive types and *The Locket* is also remarkable in that (again in some senses following Pushkin) it concentrates on the 'ugly' heroine, 'plain' Mariya. This concentration is, indeed, signalled even before the story begins, in the conversation between the frame characters, where the narrator announces that his story will concern 'the complaints and sufferings of a woman offended by nature' (74) – that is, lacking in beauty.

The first thing we learn of the heroines is, precisely, their physical appearance. Sofiya takes precedence (narratively as well as socially), even though the plot will ignore her for long periods. She is immediately announced as the pretty one, and to the narrator at this initial stage, *therefore* of more interest. The narrator emphasises her great beauty, as well as the mixture of sensations her appearance seems to arouse:

An artist, the spoiled child of Italy, without hesitation would take as a model the splendid forms of her body; her features were regular; her eyes, half-concealed by long lashes, which jealously hid a glittering moistness, which gave to the eyes an enchanting charm, already burned with the fire of developing passions, whereas the frank smile of childhood still at times appeared on her pink lips. (77)

Gorsky then goes on to detail further aspects of her appearance – 'fine skin', a 'tender blush' and so on. The emphasis throughout this long description is on the sensual and is quite in keeping, in fact, with the masculinist tradition of sexualisation (verging on the fetishisation) of the female form, even if these tendencies are slightly restrained. Nevertheless, it should be noted that readerly voyeurism is definitely encouraged: Zhukova successfully writing as a *male* narrator, perhaps?

Much emphasis is placed on this portrait because, as we shall see in more detail with regard to Mariya, one of the central motifs of the story is that (for women) 'appearance is destiny'. In Sofiya's case this motif is developed into that of 'coquetry': because she is physically striking (and knows it), she is 'so used to conquests and admirers' (83), as she herself says to her mother. Indeed, Zhukova does appear to follow the male tradition (running, say, from *Evgeny Onegin* right through to *Uncle Vanya* and beyond) according to which the beautiful woman will be vain and flirtatious, while the plain woman will develop compensatory spiritual beauty. Certainly, in this story, Sofiya does deserve the label 'coquette', in the sense that, as we have seen, she plays with Velsky's feelings, and with those of Mariya, for that matter. Indeed, Sofiya had already made this clear in the two women's discussion of love. She laughs at Mariya's Romantic notions: 'God knows what you see in love, whereas it is a highly amusing plaything, the doll of a seven-year-old child' (81). It should be noted that some efforts are made by the narrator/author to redeem Sofiya. Religious feeling will be a key motif in Mariya's portrait and Sofiya is not entirely lacking in this regard. After Mariya has nearly drowned Sofiya kneels to pray thankfully for her rescue.

This is a brief moment, however. Rather more important are Sofiya's obedience, in the first instance to the laws of physical appearance, and in the end, to the laws of society. One of the key-notes of her mother's *poucheniye*, as we have seen, is a keen sense of class proprieties and, although, we are led to believe, she does develop genuine feelings for Velsky, these are swiftly abandoned (as Olga swiftly abandons the memory of Lensky) once she is reminded of her role as a dutiful daughter. Sofiya herself had realised this in her discussion with her mother, clarifying the latter's euphemisms to put the following words into her mother's mouth: 'My daughter knows her duties too well to love a doctor'[16] (82–3). And so it proves.

Running through *The Locket* are a number of dichotomies and tensions, which display, I think, Zhukova's deeply ambiguous position as a woman writing about women. Sofiya in some ways triumphs, winning not only the love of Velsky, but also making a successful social match (with which she is delighted), while Mariya loses the man she loves, is married off, and dies young. Yet the feeling one persistently has is that Sofiya's role in the story is really only as a foil to the real interest, which is Mariya. I shall open my discussion of her by returning to the beginning, to start as the narrator does, with her physical appearance. In this she is presented as a stark contrast to Sofiya and for Mariya even more than for Sofiya, appearance is destiny.

In this initial characterisation, stress is placed not only on how different Mariya's appearance is, but also on how, in conventional terms, unprepossessing she is:

> a sickly pallor, permanently red eyelids which almost concealed the small grey eyes; unattractive features, although not without, incidentally, a certain pleasantness, and the thoughtful sad air formed a sharp contrast with the lively, playful, somewhat haughty physiognomy of the other. (77)

This opening account, as was the case with Sofiya, not only states the physical details, but also attempts to interpret them. Consequently, the reader is left with the impression of someone who is unattractive, because of inner problems. Indeed, we are soon told that Mariya even appears to be physically weak. As we soon learn, in her biographical background, Mariya's mother had inculcated into her the lesson that such a *durnushka* ('a plain woman') can have no life in the world, and should become a nun. This theme is treated with the utmost seriousness and with great persistence. Thus, we visit Mariya alone at night in her room. She is secretly excited and pleased because she has managed to keep her beloved Velsky's miniature in the tussle with Sofiya that had nearly ended in tragedy. But she looks in the mirror: 'In a single moment the expression of pleasure which enlivened her face disappeared' (85). Seeing her reflection, Mariya must abandon all hope (indeed, Dante's celebrated epigraph is later quoted):

> Poor girl! In this nocturnal dishevelment, with this animated look, in this picturesque position how splendid another would be! But she! – The mirror reminded her of her plainness: it was not for her to give herself up to the heart's rapture; the dreams of gullible youth were not for her! (ibid.)

Such a curse (her plainness) is a hell on earth. (Later on we are told that, as a child, Mariya had even taken to covering her face!) This scene is recapitulated almost word for word as Mariya again looks at her reflection. Recalling her mother's words 'she understood everything: she was plain, an orphan, poor!' A long discussion of this problem ensues, with the narrator finally apostrophising:

> The flattering sensations of self-love were not for her! She did not know the pleasure of admiring herself. Oh! Women will understand how much this means. (90)

There is no irony here, it seems to me. Nor, given the dynamics of the plot, should there be, as it is precisely Mariya's 'plainness' which causes her to lose Velsky and which constitutes, in part at least, her being. And, as with the general acceptance on the part of the author of the social dynamics which restrain women and their desire, the pathos of Mariya's situation is certainly emphasised, but no real alternative is proposed.

Equally, and although she will be proved spiritually superior in the long run, Mariya is also frequently and persistently characterised by the application to her of the mechanistic dysphoric iconography so common in the period. That is, she suffers much, and this emotional inner turmoil is displayed outwardly, as a *sign*. Thus, as she retires to her lonely room with Velsky's portrait 'her heart beats violently, a blush plays on her cheeks: something violently agitates the girl's breast' (85). The switch to the dramatic present, the repeated adverb merely emphasise the emotionalism, the physicality of the vulnerable heroine's response. More stereotypical language is soon used after she has looked at her own reflection: 'she *sadly bowed* her head, and her hand *involuntarily* fell to her lap' (ibid. – my italics). This iconographisation of the emotional woman is not, however, total and, indeed, this tendency in literature is laid bare by Mariya herself in that she will later resist such display. She tells Gutengertz, her German music teacher, of her great love and admiration for Velsky, but also of how she had responded to his work amongst the poor. Sofiya had wept watching him 'but I did not cry; I don't know how to cry: people only cry who have grown accustomed to giving their feelings free expression' (98).

Indeed, like Jane Eyre (and the two heroines have much in common), Mariya has learned the lesson that her mother had taught her, and has become spiritually independent. This has come not merely from what the mirror teaches her, but also from her social situation as a poor orphan, brought up, however kindly and charitably, by wealthy relatives. And, just as appearance is immutable so too, in Zhukova, is social standing: this plain orphan will not even be allowed to marry the humble *raznochinets*. However, Mariya does learn and develop. Although her orphanhood and consequent status as *vospitannitsa* (ward) mean that she is only allowed to share the benefits that Sofiya has of right, and although Mariya has grown used to a life of emotional solitude, she has not grown bitter. On the contrary, Zhukova's portrait has a sharp polemical, even if not subversive, edge. That is, Mariya 'the plain orphan' rises above her disadvantages, to show great self-sacrifice, spiritual feelings and the power of love.

Mariya's self-sacrifice, and self-effacement are particularly apparent in her love for Velsky. In the initial stages, merely to love him is sufficient for her ('I want nothing more. I only want to love him, to look at him' (86)). Later, as poor Mariya is deprived even of her spiritual conversations with him, as Velsky turns to the greater personal charms of Sofiya, this self-effacement gets much harder: her already bitter life becomes almost intolerable. Yet, here the narrator intervenes with one of his many *dicta* to counsel resignation, to suffer and be still, for this is a woman's lot. Velsky, who has been rescued from drowning by Mariya, mistakenly thanks Sofiya, 'My guardian angel' (101), for this service. Will Mariya intervene to stake her rightful claim? The narrator rejects such an eventuality:

> No; I know you. Timidity will never allow you to say that. To sacrifice everything for others, leaving nothing for yourself, is the lot of a fine soul in this world; to love with self-sacrifice is the lot of a woman. (101)

As in *Baron Reykhman*, the status quo is presented as a *given* (the twice repeated 'lot'). Mariya rises above Sofiya here as elsewhere because *she* is the 'fine soul'. And so, as we already know, once Velsky declares his love for Sofiya, Mariya embraces her and asks only that she make Velsky happy. The doctor recovers and his attachment to Sofiya survives his delirium. Once more Mariya nobly accepts the happiness of the pair and once more the narrator asserts that, in so doing, she is acting as a true woman: 'but Mariya's love was the true love of a woman, whose *essence* is self-sacrifice, life in another' (103 – my italics). Here too, the 'nature' of woman is immutable.

If Mariya, then, is given the moral high ground by her resignation and acceptance, her self-effacement, then this privileging of the essential feminine is seen in even clearer relief in her response to nature, religion, and spirituality more generally. As we saw earlier, *rus/Rus'*, the celebration of the traditions of Holy Russia and its natural 'paradise', is an important moment in the story's opening setting. Both Sofiya and Mariya are immediately identified with this chronotope[17] and the values it represents, but it is Mariya who proves to be the true *Rus-ist*. As we penetrate, in her biographical background, deeper into the heart and mind of this solitary creature, we learn of her profound need for consolation and love. Rejected by society, cast out because of her 'plainness', 'her heart, created for love, sought fellow feeling ... and her passion for landscape opened to her a rich source of comfort: nature!' (91). Thereby, she becomes identified with the narrator and his values, and beyond him the other privileged frame characters, including the cycle's compiler. Moreover, given the centrality of the Mother in this story, as elsewhere in the collection, a further thematic link is soon to be vital. Nature is not only her consolation, but 'Nature was becoming her *mother*' (ibid. – my italics), and through her discovery of it, her whole being is transformed: indeed, it is this that leads to her resignation and acceptance as 'She ceased to demand from them [people] sincere feeling or to expect anything solid' (92). Nature, *rus/Rus'* is her joy.

This spiritualisation of the landscape and, thereby, of Mariya, is taken one stage further, in that Mariya discovers not only the maternal in the fields, but, echoing the pastoral traditions of eighteenth century Sentimentalism, to which she (and Zhukova) is a true heir, Mariya experiences a specifically Deist epiphany:

> Her soul soared: something holy, great, which transcended everything earthly, illuminated her thoughts; she was carried up to the source of nature and the thought of the Omnipresent One took possession of her, the thought before which all earthly passions were stilled. (91)

Yet another value is imbricated onto the panoply of privileged indicators of Mariya's value, namely, love itself. Whereas, as we have seen, for Sofiya love is a 'plaything', for Mariya 'Love is the religion of the heart', and in her devoted, self-less, religious feelings for Velsky, Mariya rises above the worldly. Indeed, her feelings for the doctor are virtually a religious rather than an erotic passion. For her, he is almost a Christ: she rhapsodises his healing work to her confidant Gutengertz, wondering 'But will he not say to the sufferer: take up thy bed and walk!' (98).

As I have already noted, the portrayal of Mariya has an important polemical point. In her Zhukova has taken the 'ugly' heroine and not only made her the centre of the story (and it is largely her point of view we follow) but has also transfigured her by virtue of her identification with Nature (and, therefore, Russia), the maternal, the spiritual and the religious. This polemic, in tune with the neo-Sentimentalism of the story as a whole, seems to me to be a reworking of Karamzin's most famous line. *'I krest'yanki umeyut lyubit''* ('Even peasant women know how to love') becomes *'I durnushki umeyut lyubit''* ('Even plain women know how to love'). Although this conforms with the traditional line of 'spiritual beauty' to compensate for the supposed lack of physical charms, nevertheless Zhukova is here saying something important and new. That is, by taking the contrasting pair and highlighting, and privileging the 'plain' one, she is challenging the androcentric tendency according to which, generally speaking, only sexually interesting women are interesting narratively. Again, there is an important parallel with 'plain' Jane Eyre (who appeared ten years later, of course). Jane is such a revolutionary heroine precisely because of (amongst other things) her despised appearance. (Even Elizabeth Gaskell's working-class heroine Mary Barton is strikingly beautiful.) Yet, equally, we see once again Zhukova's ambivalence. Jane marries Rochester: the woman's desire, albeit after many tribulations, is fulfilled. Here Mariya's great worth counts as nothing. She is married off – and off-stage. Indeed, there is an even deeper conservatism underlying the contrastive heroines' stories, in that *neither* woman is allowed to follow 'the religion of the heart'. The laws of society demand that the desires of these women will count for little. Equally, all the high estimation of Mariya is futile – she follows the lot she would have had anyway and Zhukova seems to be able only to recognise women's worth and the sufferings they are caused by 'patriarchal power', rather than to suggest alternatives. Things are as they are.

3. THE DACHA ON THE PETERHOF ROAD

3.1 Setting

Although this story appeared eight years later than the first part of *Evenings* cycle, Zhukova makes much the same use of contrastive chronotopes, although she shows greater complexity than in either of the two stories discussed in her handling of setting, in that three main locales feature – the world of high society in St Petersburg, the suburban, eponymous dacha and the provincial town. Essentially, though, the same points are made as in the earlier works.

Dacha opens with an extended account of life in the northern capital and the marital plans of the poor-rich Evgeny and his female relations. Throughout emphasis is placed on the false, the trivial and, above all, the mercenary. The main motif here is how best to keep up appearances. (There is little description, however, of the physical setting of the city.)

We are then taken off to the dacha, where there is a long, picturesque setting of scene, to be introduced to another pair of contrastive heroines, Zoya and Mary. Significantly, given the thematics of the story, this is only *half* nature, a crossing-point between civilisation and the natural. Like Sofiya and Mariya, the two young women here are first apprehended 'in the lap of nature': indeed, we are introduced to them through the eyes of wandering shepherds (260). As elsewhere in the story (and as elsewhere in her *œuvre*) Zhukova nicely mediates literary expectations. By invoking explicitly the pastorale of eighteenth century Sentimentalism, she leads us to expect a grand-daughter of Poor Liza. And, indeed, one of the main arguments in this work will be the conflict between neo-Sentimentalism and the realism of the story's dominant genre, the society tale. Similarly, the actual dacha (Mary's house) hovers half-way between two literary worlds. It is a very substantial and well-appointed edifice, which also allows for 'raptures and feelings *à la Byron*' (264 – French/English in original). Once more a very neat use is made of this chronotope given that in the story's dénouement this house will be the scene, simultaneously,[18] of both the most banal of society, mercenary transactions (the arranged marriage of mutual self-interest) and of wild melodrama in the insanity of Zoya. (Once more we see a parallel with the almost exactly contemporary *Jane Eyre* in which Thornfield is the site of both social frivolity and a near marriage of mutual self-interest (Rochester and Blanche Ingram) as well as the original 'madwoman in the attic', Bertha Mason-Rochester.) Throughout these opening scenes in the countryside we see Mary and Zoya together more than once, and nearly always in scenes where Sentimentalist clichés are invoked. For example, they had first met when 'in the garden it was quiet; the trees dozed half-asleep, dressed in the light dusk of the northern, May night' (264). Later, at the end of the season we are given another picturesque tableau of the young women:

> One morning, a splendid summer morning at the end of August, the two girls sat in a small gallery, decked out with flowers. The sun's rays, penetrating the gallery through the thick branches of an old lime, played on the floor.

and so on (270). Again there is a tension between different expectations: Zoya believes in the picturesqueness of her setting, it is her natural ambience, while Mary will show herself to be a follower of Marie Antoinette and not Rousseau.

In turning to Zoya's original setting, the provincial town, Zhukova's narrator invokes other, more recent literary resonances, in that much of the scene (especially the climactic provincial ball at which Zoya willingly is seduced by Prince Evgeny) is conveyed in a style redolent of Pushkin's Belkin and the Gogol of *Dead Souls*. The introduction to the ball is a delicious pastiche of the latter:

> In the nobles' assembly a ball was being given, for the purpose of ... no doubt, for the most well-intentioned purpose ... The fruits, the sweets – my dear Lord! ... And the champagne! ... The results of the abundance in this regard I cannot even describe; I will only say that everyone was very satisfied and only on the second or even on the third day rumours went about, to the effect that the provisioners for the ball had stocked up for their own days of celebration. (289)

Shortly after this opening to the ball scene, Zoya will be lost forever. The point of this deliberate banalisation of the scene is, again, to mediate the story's polemic: the contrast between reality and the Romantic (or rather neo-Sentimentalist) heroine's perception of it. For the reader, the chronotope of the provincial ball, as mediated *à la* Gogol, has one value: for Zoya, the child of Rousseau, it has another altogether.

3.2 Plot

Dacha follows *The Locket* in its introduction to the main plot-line (in the present) followed by an extended flash-back to the biography of the neo-Sentimentalist heroine. Consequently, when we read the latter it is with the consciousness of this *fabula/syuzhet* disjunction. Similarly, although Zoya's story will increasingly become the narrative focus, we know even before it begins that her destiny will not follow the lines mapped out by her desire, but by the stricter exigencies of the real world.

Indeed, the opening of the story is very much set in a world in which all the values that Zoya comes to represent are conspicuously absent. The initial situation is that of Evgeny, a glittering young man of society who has to find a way out of his debt-ridden situation. Various options are suggested, culminating in the idea of an arranged marriage, and it is all presented in a deliberately mocking, ironic tone, involving much use of exclamation and question marks. The knowing, colluding narrative voice makes it clear that this – on the whole – will not be a tragic or Sentimental tale, and that a way out of Evgeny's troubles will be found soon enough. The plot motifs in this introductory, prologue section are 'the ways of the world' and mercenary self-interest: a locus where 'money is the prime mover of our age' (248). Given this dictum, the ensuing love plots are predetermined to a dysphoric conclusion.

Finally, after discounting all other possibilities, a suitable heiress is sought, and it is at this point that the narrative switches to Mary and Zoya at the dacha. Almost immediately it becomes apparent that the iconographically suffering and half-insane Zoya cannot possibly be the chosen one, but several enigmas are posed to become the engine of the rest of the story. Who is this strange creature; why is she reduced to this state; and why is the sensible Mary, who is clearly the chosen one, so friendly with her? These questions provide the raw material on which the plot development will be based. Here again *Dacha* replicates the architectonics of *The Locket* in that we first concentrate on the society woman (Mary), whose expected engagement is now on everyone's lips, only for the bulk of the narrative to focus on the pathetic tragedy of Zoya. Once more we follow in some detail the lineaments of the woman of feeling, only for female desire to be crushed by both the ineluctable power of society and, in this instance, by the effects of the narrative dislocation. That is, as we follow Zoya's early life (which occupies nearly half the story) we have already been told of its culmination. Given that we know how the romance of her youth will end, we can learn the lessons of her disappointment more easily, without any expectation of a 'happy ending'. Thereby, the reader can also see more clearly the dangers of the romantic illusions in which she indulges.

At first, Zoya's *éducation sentimentale* mirrors that of the (chronologically later) story of Mary in that a marriage is arranged for her with a local *sovetnik*. For all her romantic expectations, she is quite happy to go along with this arrangement, until the fateful and fatal irruption of the Romantic, in the shape of the Byronic rake, Prince Evgeny. Such is the power of her romantic beliefs that she falls almost without any real seduction on his part. For a while, the reader is even led to believe that Zoya and the Prince may find happiness – yet we must remember that we have already seen Zoya (and, indeed, the Prince) at a later stage. Insistently, that is, the polemical point is made: Romantic infatuation cannot lead to happiness, but only to disillusionment and even madness (for the woman).

On the advice of his aunt and others, Prince Evgeny sees the impossibility of such a *mésalliance* and leaves Zoya to her madness (in both the clinical and Romantic senses), and, finally, at this point we return to the diegetic present. As before, several questions hang in the air, all centring on the question of whose desire will push the narrative to its conclusion: will Evgeny revert to Zoya; will Mary (who comes to learn much of Zoya's story) nobly reject him out of sisterly solidarity; will Romance or 'money' win the day? Given the opening situation, and given Mary's equally hard-headed approach there can only be one resolution. Mary, like Sofiya before her, realises where her own self-interest lies, as does Evgeny after a rather feeble attempt to re-establish contact with the woman he had 'seduced' and abandoned, while Zoya, who earns the title of 'poor', retreats into madness and death. The values of society once again triumph and there can be no place for the extremes of feeling that Zoya represents.

3.3 Images of the Male

As in *The Locket*, male characters impinge very little on the development of the plot, although, as elsewhere in Zhukova's work, their values, their desire remain paramount. In Prince Evgeny, however, Zhukova has given an interesting reflection of the obverse of her ambivalence to the female. He is persistently mocked, yet, narratively at least, he is shown to have his desires pandered to from beginning to end. In Zhukova's fiction, it would seem, it's a man's world.

Certainly, the story begins androcentrically enough, with a concentration on him and his financial problems. By virtue of his name and his situation, Zhukova again is clearly seeking resonances with her literary 'fathers'. Indeed, two of the classic texts from the previous fifteen years, *Evgeny Onegin* and *A Hero of Our Time*, their types of hero and heroine and plot situations, are consistently modulated in Zhukova's work, although this process is perhaps most explicit in *Dacha* (by the end of which Evgeny marries a woman who thereby becomes Princess Mary).

The exposition of the story, then, concerns Prince Evgeny who is a deliberate amalgam of many details and plot references which had by now become clichés. He is a man from the highest society, but now regrettably in debt, a gentleman of leisure, a former army officer, living with his mother. Certain narrative expectations are immediately aroused: will he be a Rake of the old school; will he be a superfluous man, bored, spoiled and superficially Westernised? In his youth he had, indeed, lived the life of a 'rake' (246), gambling and enjoying all the other pleasures of life as a hussar. Quite specifically, the narrator is introducing the contemporary reader to a type that would be very familiar, indeed, a cliché. The tone adopted throughout these opening sections is deeply mocking, and, moreover, his circumstances mock him. He is not in charge of his affairs, either here or later. Instead, a series of women, his mother and, especially, his aunt Elena Pavlovna at the beginning and, at the end, Mary clearly organise his life for him. He thinks he is in control, but at every stage his proud position is subverted: *he* is the one who will be married off like a prize horse, to a rich heiress, so that the family debts may be paid. The polemical purpose of all this is to deflate completely the hero of the preceding literary period: the Romantic, Byronic hero will be the passive recipient of female desire, and, for the most part, his actions are dictated by *older* women.

Evgeny also features, of course, in an earlier incarnation, as the agent of Zoya's destruction in the flash-back to her youth. Here we see the darker side of the Rake in that he first decides to seduce her simply to win a bet (with his aunt). For a little while he actually persuades himself that he has fallen in love with Zoya but, again, he does the bidding of older women who persuade him of the inappropriateness of such a match. In the final sections of the tale Evgeny continues his worthless path. In the moral debates of the last few pages (in which Mary decides not to assist Zoya's attempts to reconnect with Evgeny) he is largely absent. Indeed, all in all, Prince Evgeny the noble scion and former rake plays little real part in the movement of the plot, or in its moral world. As in *The Locket*, men are presented as being largely peripheral to a world which is dominated by women, although it should be remembered that the same paradox applies to this latter work. In the diegesis, men feature very little. Zhukova presents an almost all-female world, yet these women always have to operate in situations which, in the final analysis, exist and are maintained for the benefit of men – however insignificant or worthless these beings may be. She may mock them or ignore them, but is not able to imagine a different way or a different world.

3.4 Male/Female Relations

In this area *Dacha* re-enacts the dualism found elsewhere in Zhukova's work, that between the arranged marriage which is of benefit to women as much as to men on the one hand, and, on the other, the social and marital catastrophe that awaits women (but not men) when the passions are unleashed in romantic love which in this story, in particular, is seen to be based on illusions and self-delusions on the part of the heroine.

With the exception of Zoya's brief entanglement with Evgeny (although the effects of these few days are with her to her premature and tragic death), the whole story is constructed around a series of arranged marriages both in the diegetic present and in the various past lives that are merely glimpsed. The main plot-line, with which the story opens, is, of course, organised by this motif: will Mary be a socially acceptable heiress who will be able to rescue the finances of Prince Evgeny and his family? Fittingly, in terms of the story's themes, these arrangements provide both the exposition, and the dénouement and epilogue to the events: the very last lines, indeed, give us a brief cameo of Prince Evgeny and Princess Mary engaged in the everyday trivialities of the social round. (Mary's background and genealogy are also plotted in precisely these terms.)

But it is not only the *svet* which organises its marital arrangements on such 'rational' principles. Before Zoya encounters Evgeny she had been about to enter an arranged match with Councillor Il'in. As she is a decently educated and promising young woman, while he is a widower with two daughters, it is seen by all concerned (including Zoya herself) as an eminently suitable and – again –

mutually beneficial arrangement. Even more telling is the fact that it had been arranged by Vera Yakovlevna and Avdotya Vasilevna, two of the valorised older women of the story.

So, then, Mary's family background, her betrothal and eventual marriage to Evgeny, Zoya's prospective match with Il'in – all of these are the norm across various social strata and one which the narrative and its author, seemingly, fully endorse. Consequently, Evgeny's callous seduction and, *a fortiori*, Zoya's reckless and naive infatuation are presented as gross solecisms, both socially and in terms of literary genres. As I shall argue more fully in my discussion of Zoya's portrayal, one of her many difficulties is that she acts according to the wrong script, as it were: that is, her behaviour is inappropriate *generically*.

Although their liaison is brief, the narrator goes to great pains to lay out its meaning and to demystify, in particular, Zoya's Romanticism. Certainly, Evgeny is reproached for his calculated callousness, but, just as the text is ultimately pitiless in its exclusion of Baroness Reykhman, so too here, Zoya seems more at fault. At the beginning of the ball (which, remember, has already been demystified by the Gogolian pastiche), Zoya is identified with the luxuriant foliage which decorates the hall. 'But here by one of the columns . . . is a little tree, as tall and graceful as Zoya herself. . . . The tree is strewn with [these] red flowers. And how pliant are its boughs, how light! If there were the slightest puff of breeze – they would begin to shake . . .' (290). That is, Zoya's heightened emotional state (based on her Romantic expectations/delusions, derived in turn from her reading) renders her ready to be plucked. And so it happens. Almost as soon as Prince Evgeny turns his penetrating gaze upon her, she is in love. 'She was so happy! Judge for yourself: a prince, – yes, the guards officer was a prince, – the prince was a musician himself and a passionate musician!' (291). After the ball Zoya returns home in raptures, remembering her ecstatic experiences (at the Gogolian provincial dance) and, especially, 'the pale face with its black moustaches and with the gaze . . . with the gaze, which promised the whole gamut of sounds, and all of them inspired, all full of feeling, like a Schubert motif. . . .' (293). The very next day she decides she can marry none other than this dashing guards officer (who, the reader knows, has now won his bet). And so, she rejects the worthy, if prosaic Councillor, the 'advantageous fiancé' (300) who had been found for her, and whom she had been perfectly happy to marry.

All this would be rather comical and silly if, again in line with the neo-Sentimentalism which permeates the tale, Zoya had not entered and completed the full paradigmatic declension of the dysphoric heroine: – seduction – abandonment – illness – madness – death. Zoya learns an even more painful and tragic lesson than Baroness Reykhman and the story, when stripped of its melodramatic coloration, offers a stark warning to Romantic young women as regards their emotional and sexual relations. Zoya re-enacts the plot of Lermontov's Princess Mary, while Zhukova's Princess Mary has learned many lessons from her literary elder sisters.

3.5 The World of Women

As already noted, one of the characteristic features of both *The Locket* and *Dacha* is the relative unimportance of male characters in the diegetic world. Whether in high-society St Petersburg or the provincial town in which Zoya is reared, nearly all the significant characters are female, and men are acted upon rather than acting. Evgeny is surrounded by his mother and aunts, especially Elena Pavlovna; Mary, an orphan, has almost only female associates, while Zoya is brought up by female relations as well. In terms of the plot dynamics (Mary's marriage to Evgeny), the action is always propelled by women, especially Elena Pavlovna. *Prima facie*, Zhukova presents a world that is matriarchal in structure, although it should always be remembered, that this does not at all connote the fulfilment of female desire. Even more significant, particularly in the broader context of the development of Russian literature, is the very prominent part played by older women. Zoya is effectively brought up by Vera Yakovlevna who, although she inadvertently colludes in the Prince's seduction of her ward, is presented as a very positive type. In turn, when they move to the provincial town to find Zoya a husband, we are introduced to Avdotya Vasilevna, the wife of the former prosecutor, who is depicted as the hub of life in the town.

Outstanding among these older women is Elena Pavlovna, aunt to Prince Evgeny, who, in certain respects, could be regarded as the moral centre of the work, its true heroine. She is introduced in the very first pages, and remains a dominant figure, and the prime mover of the plot. It is she who takes a particular interest in her favourite nephew and his fortunes, and in turn, in the brief biography given of her, is presented as the model of the woman who has married for rational reasons and has lived not to regret this.

Once it is established that Evgeny must marry to clear his debts, it is she who scours the whole city for one that will be suitable, overcoming every resistance on his part to the scheme. Once Mary is identified as a suitable partner, she makes all the necessary introductions and is on more than one occasion termed 'an excellent woman' (270). For all the ironisation of high society that permeates the work, Elena Pavlovna is consistently valorised. When we return to the main plot-line (after the extended flash-back to Zoya's childhood, education and fateful encounter at the ball), it is once again Elena Pavlovna, still 'an excellent woman' (307) who, in scenes of epic comedy, keeps the arrangements moving along, despite a sleepless night and a dreadful migraine.

In a sense, I think, she is presented as the sort of woman that Mary might one day become, a role model for the young heroine. And indeed, for all the positive attributes assigned to this matriarchal trio, the bulk of narrative interest, in the end, rests with Mary and Zoya. The pattern of *The Locket* is replicated in that this is a deeply contrasted pair, although the parameters of the duality are rather different. Nevertheless, they are presented as almost total opposites, as we have already noted. Indeed, the very fact that they have a relationship at all, given their differences, is a matter of some wonderment to their acquaintances and, to a lesser extent, to the reader. Despite this, the simple fact that two young women are presented as having a close bond of friendship should be noted, given the rarity of such a relationship in Russian fiction (before Chernyshevsky), even if in the end, one (Mary) sacrifices the interests of the other for her own selfish ends.

As in *The Locket* almost the first thing we learn about them is their appearance and in the same way as in the earlier story, we are first introduced to the more conventionally pretty woman, the one who will triumph socially, even if, again, more narrative attention will actually be paid to the victim of social exigencies. Mary, like Evgeny shortly before this, is deliberately presented almost as a lexicon of stereotypes of the typical young woman of fashion (and of literature):

> One, not very tall, with round little shoulders, a slim waist, a little foot, dressed in fashionable half-boots, with a little white hand always wearing a close-fitting French glove, dressed in the latest fashion. . . . (260)

We note the repeated use of diminutives, the implicit reference to both *Onegin* (the little foot, the French glove (rather than Tatyana's French book)) as well as to *Princess Mary* (the boots). The same slightly mocking tone is employed as in the semi-caricature of Evgeny. But Zhukova's narrator also immediately undercuts her own stereotype: although Mary is blonde and seems the empty-headed type of the vacuous fair-headed society princess, the interpretation of her appearance which follows shows that Mary is very much an independent young woman who will certainly be nobody's victim:

> with long, fair ringlets, with a ready joke on her lips and, perhaps, with a ready mockery, which was confirmed by her vivacious and slightly cunning gaze and a smile which expressed contempt more often than benevolence. (260)

And, indeed, this Princess Mary turns out to be a very determined, and self-determined young woman who does exactly what *she* wants (although, again, within the confines of accepted, patriarchal values).

Mary, up to a point, plays at life, modulates herself within the limited, available roles, offered by society, and literary predecessors. On the one hand, she has adopted the persona of the Tatyana-esque young woman, wandering in the Russian countryside, seeking solitude, surrounding herself with flowers, playing the piano (very well), reading and so on. But much more characteristic of her behaviour is the whole-hearted adoption and absorption of the ways of a typical young woman of society. It is the rules of society's game that she has learned, and will play to perfection. Thus, when she and Zoya first meet, Mary is not so much impressed by the dramatic appearance and behaviour of the other woman, but rather flattered by the effect her music-making has had. Zoya wanders in like a creature from another world (and genre) and 'Like a society girl Mary welcomed the unexpected guests with the most refined politeness and in a friendly way offered her hand to her sensitive listener' (265). Mary is intrigued, even touched by Zoya's melodrama, but the ways of breeding come first. She is attracted to Zoya because the latter is a 'novelty' (269) after the rather dull social round.

Zoya, on the other hand, has not learned society's rules, but follows the path of Romantic literature to its tragic end. In line with the axiomatic tendency of *The Locket* ('appearance is destiny') this is reflected in the physical sketch with which she is introduced. Almost every detail of this portrait (and, indeed, her later plot) is saturated with the iconography of the victim figure of Gothic Romanticism-cum-neo-Sentimentalism:

> The other girl was tall, graceful, with dark chestnut hair . . . with large, black, pensive eyes, pale and sad so that, in truth, if anyone suddenly caught sight of her, when on the sea shore in her white dress and white muslin mantilla, leaning on the stump of a storm-blasted oak, and staring fixedly into the distance, this anyone would take her for a splendid sculpture of lamentation. (260)

We should note not only the complete contrast with Mary's appearance but also the laying bare of the device in the last lines: Zoya has so fully adopted the part suggested by her iconography, that she has become an icon – of suffering and tragedy. As the plot unfolds this first vision will remain as a stern warning to young women who believe too implicitly in the Romantic fiction they are wont to read. Zoya, then, who always wears white, with a crimson fuchsia at her waist, is the very emblem of modesty and fragility.

Zoya's icon is not, however, unitary but a composite of other stereotypes from the Gothic and Sentimentalist traditions she inhabits. Both when we meet her, in the flashback to her tragedy, and at the end of the tale, she is prone to madness (often expressed in a wild laugh or semi-raving conversation). She is particularly susceptible to the power of music (a detail borrowed from Gan's *A Futile Gift*), which has an almost magical effect on her. Her behaviour, though, in both the introductory and final sections, conforms almost entirely to the dictates of the genres she has imbibed. In particular, she is very prone to the mechanistic, *physical* displays of emotionalism so prevalent in the depiction of the tragic heroines of the period.[19] Her very first appearance at Mary's door is described in semi-parodic terms:

> In the doorway, coming from behind the thick greenery of a rhododendron, by the very threshold, stood a girl in a white dress. Her hands were folded at her waist, a tear rolled down her pale cheek. (265)

After Mary's studiedly polite welcome, Zoya nevertheless proceeds her iconic way:

she looked at her with her large black eyes and entered the room in silence. Her face was strangely inspired; a light trembling caused her pale lips to move; her breast was agitated. (ibid.)

Zhukova's purpose in such passages is, I think, twofold. As already noted, she shows Zoya's dreadful state as a warning against Romanticism. At the same time, by piling on the clichés and stereotypes (and laying them bare), she is parodying the artificially elevated language employed in the period to denote the suffering of such heroines.

In this sense, much of *Dacha* can be read as a literary polemic (just as *What Is to Be Done?* was to play a similar game with such stereotypes, although in a much more obvious and sustained way[20]). And so, although the plot begins by seeming to be about the trials and tribulations of a young man of society, and ends with Mary's dominance, the main body and longest section of the narrative are taken up with the extended flashbacks to explain how Zoya had been brought to such a state. This dislocation of the *syuzhet* foregrounds this retrospective section and, thereby, reveals the author's central purposes: an attack on Romanticism and the dangers of living 'by the book'.[21]

The delineation of much of Zoya's background employs the same quasi-Gogolian style we have already seen in the setting of scene for the ball. That is, great emphasis is placed on the banality of it to highlight, by way of contrast, the wildness and inexplicable nature of Zoya's behaviour and beliefs. In other words, these are not based in or on reality. In this there is a marked contrast with Gan, whose Romantic young women often emerge from (over-) protective maternal enclaves ill-prepared and ill-fitted for the harsh realities of society.

Zoya's upbringing has been in the remote Russian provinces, where her Swiss governess mother had married a retired colonel, and had soon learned to forget her homeland. On the death of both parents (both Mary and Zoya are orphaned), Zoya had become the ward of Vera Yakovlevna, the provincial equivalent of Elena Pavlovna. Much of this background, in fact, details not so much Zoya herself, but the other inhabitants and their way of life in a very mundane routine of activities, based on social visits, drinking tea, playing cards and gossip. But one fact of her upbringing is highlighted and this is to prove her undoing. From her mother Zoya had inherited a collection of books which the girl had devoured:

> Blissful time! What did Zoya at that time not read and re-read? All her mother's small library was almost learned by heart. Chateaubriand, and Lessing and Iffland and Mme de Cattin and even Byron in the original, but the poor girl understood little of this. (277)

Again, the deliberate echoes of Tatyana and Princess Mary (who also read Byron in the original) suggest the fateful joys of the 'forbidden fruit' (as Gan calls it) of secret reading of Romantic books by impressionable young girls, who *believe what they read*. Coupled to this are Zoya's music lessons with the comical Karl Adamovich, which, for all the caricature attached to the 60-year-old German, become for young Zoya a quasi-mystical encounter:

> Zoya with a quiet smile greets these hours [her lessons], which arise from the depths of the past, sacred hours when her pure soul submissively accepted the mysterious teaching of art and she waited with fluttering heart for the curtain to rise for the newly consecrated. (281)

And so, when the great day of the ball arrives Zoya, although already all but, and willingly, betrothed to Councillor Il'in, is ready to fall in love, ready to fall like the trembling flowers with which she is so closely associated. The reader has been told that this provincial ball is a chronotope of Gogolian banality, but Zoya enters resolutely determined to play out the script she has read of: 'Zoya was dressed in a white dress, with a crimson camellia in her hair . . . Zoya was in a state of rare ecstasy, happy like a dweller in paradise' (290). She marvels at the magnificent set (which we already know the reality of) and at once we see her dangerously distorted, Romanticised perception of the world. And so, *as soon as* she hears Evgeny's voice, she responds, mechanistically: 'Zoya started and looked up' (ibid.). She answers his question 'crimsoning to her ears' (ibid.). And when she hears that he too is passionate about music. . . . Zoya falls, that is, without any resistance; indeed, she is not even seduced, but willingly falls in love, because Evgeny conforms to the image of her Romantic hero. The next day, as we know, she decides she must marry Prince Evgeny because 'everywhere and everywhere he is'. Equally, when she is so swiftly abandoned, Zoya sticks to her script, immediately entering the familiar decline of tears, insomnia, illness and so on.

When we read these scenes they are deprived of any suspense or excitement because we already know the end result of this sequence, in the sense that we have already encountered Zoya at a chronologically later stage. What is even more alarming, in terms of the underlying values of the work, is that she *still* clings not only to her iconographic dressing and behaviour but also to her ultra-Romantic views on love. Again, there is a stark contrast between the two women. For Mary the arrangements for marriage and her eventual betrothal and wedding are a matter which she approaches with a sense of the pragmatic which verges on the cynical. She even rejects love itself: 'I don't want to love. I will marry because it is necessary' (273). She is perfectly aware that Evgeny will marry her for her money but this seems to be eminently sensible and, moreover, the arrangement will suit her perfectly well. She has money, he has breeding: 'In truth, it seems to me, we are made for each other' (ibid.). For poor Zoya 'this is terrible' (ibid.) because she still holds to the picture of love she has read about – despite the pain such beliefs had caused her. Earlier she had raved on about her kind of love:

> I have in mind the sort of love which is higher than any other feeling, which allows for no calculation, which exclusively possesses our soul, – the sort of love which forgets poverty, insignificance . . . the sort of love, Mary, which is everything to us and without which life is a dream, a heavy long dream. . . . (271)

Mary almost bursts out laughing at this, but she should not have been surprised having earlier in the scene addressed her friend thus: 'You're an ante-deluvian girl, Zoya, my incomparable Zoya' (ibid.).

In the overall framework of *Dacha* the point is repeatedly made, and it is the same point as in Zhukova's other work. A marriage based on love is a dangerous liaison: an arranged match, of mutual benefit, is the only way a woman may find happiness. Her work, that is, is profoundly anti-Romantic. In the present case, we see in Zoya's tragedy the dangers of such love and such beliefs and receive the stern and clear warning that Zoya's views and behaviour either are, in themselves, a form of madness, or else, will certainly lead to madness. As Mary says to Zoya towards the end of this scene 'You must only forget . . . these childish ravings, Zoya' (274). And, indeed, Zoya soon has another of her recurrent fits. . . .

These ideas are returned to towards the end of the section detailing Zoya's background, where the three wise old women (Vera, Avdotya and Evgeny's aunt) gather to discuss how to prevent such an unsuitable match as that between the Prince and poor provincial Zoya. Their tactical plans develop into a commentary on contemporary morals which indirectly also become a gloss on Mary, Zoya, education and Romanticism. Vera Yakovlevna laments the passing of the old ways: nowadays there is

> A different education, everything foreign; whereas in our time it was simple. We didn't know corsets, or bouillon, or mazurkas; but for all that we were a bit stronger. (303)

The tone of the scene is deliberately rather comical but a very serious point is being made. To paraphrase these remarks, the reader is told that if she reads the likes of Byron, dances long complicated dances with strange men (and so on), a young woman is liable to fall in love with a complete stranger, and all the traditions of society (which kept morals firm) are threatened.

These points are soon developed. The young 'play with their feelings, their peace, the happiness of their whole lives, like a child with its toy' (309). Soon a conclusion is reached, which reverberates not only through the whole story but, indeed, also throughout Zhukova's whole *œuvre* and beyond that, back through *Evgeny Onegin* to *Poor Liza*.

> Eternal love is only found in novels. Only these little foolish girls think that as soon as they like someone, then its ah and alas, and forever . . . But it's all rubbish. (303)

Yet Zoya still wants to love and to suffer, to relive the fate of Poor Liza, of Tatyana and countless others. And for this she, like Baroness Reykhman, will be ruthlessly punished by the text and its author.

On the other hand, Mary, from beginning to end, inhabits another world, another genre. We see this collision between the two literary traditions which the women come to represent at its starkest in the story's dénouement, a recapitulation in a sense of the earlier ball-scene. Elena Pavlovna, Evgeny and many others are gathered at Mary's house for a social confirmation of the engagement. It is a scene of the utmost social propriety and decorum, and the quintessence of the society tale. Music is played and at this moment Zoya irrupts almost literally like a creature from another world, or rather, like a character from another genre. She is in full iconographic glory:

> Suddenly at the doors which were opened wide onto the garden, there appeared a white figure. It was a girl in a white dress, pale, like a marble carving; her eyes were full of unusual fire and were fixed on the people singing, her lips half open, her hands pressed to her breast. (313)

The narrator deliberately, I feel, uses the full Gothic palette to show how inappropriate ('antediluvian') such behaviour, and such iconography now are. It is a valediction to Romanticism. Soon, the new style and the new (in one sense) woman, Mary, takes over and order is restored. And although, for the last ten pages or so, there remains a certain moral debate in Mary's mind, she, in the end, abandons Zoya, who dies, and marries Evgeny to become Princess Mary, having learned never to make the same mistakes as her namesake, or any of her other predecessors.

In this resolution, the same ambivalence as I have noted throughout Zhukova's work still lingers. The story is almost entirely about women and they are deeply valorised. The old, Romantic stereotypes which still persisted (even in Gan) are mocked and banished, to make way for the tough, independent, self-determining Mary. And yet, and yet. For all Zhukova's endorsement of the development of female desire, she allows it to be expressed only within very narrow confines. Complete freedom of expression through passionate love leads to textual banishment and even insanity and death. Happiness is only to be found if female desire is expressed within the existing rules of society, that is, within 'patriarchal power'.

6

Alexander Herzen: *Who Is To Blame?*

Sir Isaiah Berlin has commented: 'At the heart of Herzen's outlook (and of Turgenev's too) is the notion of the complexity and insolubility of the central problems'.[1] In his major work of fiction, *Who Is To Blame?*[2] (1846), completed, appropriately enough, one year before he was to leave Russia forever,[3] Alexander Herzen, the leading Russian philosopher of his generation,[4] addressed himself to several of these 'central problems'. Beltov, the principal male protagonist, is an heir of Onegin, Chatsky and Pechorin, yet another 'superfluous man'; Lyubov Krutsiferskaya is yet another daughter of Tatyana and her character can be regarded as an investigation, ostensibly from a quasi-feminist perspective,[5] of the fate of the so-called strong woman in the depths of the Russian provinces, 'the kingdom of darkness', to which the novel pays great attention. The central plot, the love triangle between Lyubov, her husband, Krutsifersky and Beltov, is one of the first investigations in Russian fiction of the theme of adulterous love.[6] In many respects, then, *Who Is To Blame?* while being deeply flawed as an artistic whole, can be regarded both as a summation of the debates in literature in the 1820s and 1830s,[7] and as an anticipation of the novels of Turgenev, a life-long associate and sometime friend of Herzen.[8] As the title of the novel suggests, it is a 'problem piece', although, in accordance with the view of Berlin, no obvious solutions to these problems can be readily deduced. One particular reason for the seeming intractability of the difficulties with which the author confronts his characters is the stultifying effect of the benighted Russian provinces, as a consideration of the setting of the novel will reveal.

1. Setting

Herzen began writing *Who Is To Blame?* in 1841, in Novgorod during his second period of internal exile. Even a superficial reading of the novel shows that he made much use of his impressions of this ancient, though provincial town, as well as of the places of his earlier exile, Vyatka and Vladimir. Indeed, one of the aesthetic problems with the novel is the exceedingly long prologue to the central plot (which strictly speaking, only begins to develop in the last quarter.) Much of this prologue (or rather prologues) is taken up with sketches of the various family backgrounds of the protagonists and the emphasis throughout is on the inertia and backwardness of the Russian provinces. All the central action takes place in and around the town of N.N., or on the various estates of the lower gentry (apart from brief excursions to St Petersburg, Moscow and Switzerland as we follow *inter alia* Beltov's aborted careers and wanderings).

The novel begins very far away from the main action in the household of Aleksey Abramovich Negrov, (the father of Lyubov), where Krutsifersky will be hired as a tutor and will fall in love with Negrov's illegitimate, half-peasant daughter.[9] The opening lines of the novel, indeed, convey exactly the atmosphere in which the three central characters will play out their tragic drama: 'It was getting on towards evening. Aleksey Abramovich was standing on the balcony; he still couldn't get his senses together after his two-hour post-prandial nap; his eyes kept lazily opening wide, and from time to time he would yawn' (9). We immediately enter the milieu of the 'old-world landowners' and their indolent way of life. Much of these opening sequences, which actually occupy well over half the novel, is deliberately clichéd and ironical, a mocking account of the Larinesque lower gentry of very limited culture (in any sense of this word). Great emphasis is placed on ordinariness, typicality – and the unspeakable, endless boredom: 'It was a strange thing: in Negrov's house there was nothing striking, noting particular; but for a new person, a young man [Krutsifersky], it was somehow awkward, difficult to breathe in it. Total and utter emptiness, of the most multi-faceted kind reigned in the venerable household of Aleksey Abramovich'. (38). This is hardly the setting, then, for a great love and the fact that it is precisely against this anti-Romantic backdrop that Krutsifersky and Lyubov do fall in love goes some way to explaining the problems that were inherent in their marriage from the very outset, as we shall see.

Although we will learn much about his chequered past and its variegated setting, Beltov is first encountered in the chronotope which had by now been established as the essence of Russian hopelessness,[10] the unnamed provincial town, called here, as elsewhere,

N.N.. Again, the opening lines to this locale sum up the insignificance of it: 'In * * * , – incidentally, there is no need whatsoever to specify the time and place astronomically and geographically – in the nineteenth century . . . in the regional town N.N.' (69). There is no need to be precise because this town could be more or less anywhere in Russia; the action could be at any time over the preceding decades because, in such places, all is endlessly the same. Moreover, it is much the same as outside the town on one of the estates and, indeed, the same noun as we have already encountered is used to convey its essence: 'The town was not large, and it wasn't hard to walk through from one end to the other. The same *emptiness* everywhere' (117 – my italics). And, it should be noted, *pustota* ('emptiness') is here a metaphysical term. Once more, the narrator introduces the love-plot which will be enacted here in studiedly anti-Romantic terms. Unlike, say, Lermontov's Caucasus, this is hardly the chronotope of a grand passion. Equally, we see Beltov, who is standing (unsuccessfully it transpires) in the local elections, in a run-down hotel in this town: can this be a hero?

Apart from the pre-prologue digressions to the two metropolises and to Switzerland, then, the entire action takes place within this numbing milieu, and is thereby *vitiated* by the milieu. From the very opening lines the reader can expect no Romantic fulfilment. Yet the philosopher Herzen goes further than this, in the narrator's introduction to the most dramatic scene in the novel (in truth, almost the only dramatic scene there is!), the encounter between Beltov and Lyubov in the municipal park. In terms which exactly anticipate the pessimism of the later Turgenev he meditates: 'It has long been noted by poets that nature is to a revolting extent indifferent to what people do on its back' (169). What is more, this park, although permeated by 'indifferent nature' (170) is as run-down, as indistinguished as everything else in N.N.. So, although the meeting between the two central protagonists will result in the fateful and doom-laden kiss, once more, from this introductory setting, the 'perspicacious reader' (to borrow Chernyshevsky's phrase) should not have high expectations. Herzen's underlying purpose in his handling of setting, it seems to me, was to deflate the Romanticism both of some of his literary predecessors and of his characters. At the same time, and by the same token, he deliberately imbued the narrative with a great measure of predictability, or rather predeterminacy, as I shall now argue, in my consideration of plot and theme.

2. Plot and Theme

Martin Malia has observed: 'In the first place it is noteworthy that all the principal characters are victims of the gentry's inhumanity'.[11] Much of the first half of the novel is taken up with detailing such acts of inhumanity, as well as more explicit brutality.

Although it will take three quarters of the book to lead the patient (or exasperated?!) reader to the complication and dénouement, the novel seems to open without any prologue or introduction, but with the immediate initiation of the action, by means of the classic topos of the entry of the stranger/hero into the 'enclosed space' of the 'enclave'.[12] Added to this ancient motif is one that was to become central to Russian Realism, in both art and life,[13] in that Krutsifersky enters the Negrov household to become tutor to the son, and, thereby, meets and eventually marries the daughter, Lyubov. Krutsifersky, however, is clearly no Prince, but a rather ordinary, timid youth and son of an army doctor.[14] But this central love plot, which had already, post *Onegin* became something of a cliché, is immediately de-centred in that much of the remainder of Part One is taken up by a whole series of retrospective pre-prologues, which detail the life of Negrov, his liaison with peasant Dunya (Lyubov's mother), and eventual marriage to Glafira (and we have her family background), Krutsifersky's family circumstances and, later on, Beltov's genealogy. As a result of all this, Part One, which occupies over half the book, does not take us much further than the exposition, and therefore, the love plot is made to seem of little consequence, despite the fact that most commentators consider *only* the love plot.

Instead, we have a concentration, which anticipates Turgenev's novels, on family histories which create a determining and a seemingly predetermined sociolect. Almost all of them could be subsumed under the generic heading of 'tales of patriarchal power' – 'patriarchal' being used here not only in the feminist sense, but also in the feudal meaning. Indeed, an overall reading of the totality of the plots suggests that the novel is more of a panorama of rural backwardness than a love story and thus owes as much to *Dead Souls*[15] as to the more obvious source, *Evgeny Onegin*.

The first major section of the novel (after Chapter One which introduces us to the Negrov household) is, then, as the title of Chapter Two has it, 'The Biography of Their Excellencies'. Negrov, the father of Lyubov, is the first character to be introduced in detail as we follow his life, which is presented as entirely *typical* of his age and class. (And this is the point: no real attempt is made to individualise him but rather, he is conceived of as a representative type.) He is reasonably well-off, serves in the army, but gets bored with this way of life, so retires early to live in Moscow, to indulge in an 'endless enfilade of days and nights of a monotonous, empty, boring life' (16). Thus, the theme of 'emptiness' and boredom is immediately introduced. Similarly, like most of the other characters, he can think of nothing useful to do, takes up a typical Onegin-esque existence of the club, cards, the theatre, balls and riding. Soon bored with this latest phase of his aimless existence, he follows Onegin once more to settle on his country estate. Every detail, it seems, is culled from the preceding literary canon. This is not a result of the author's lack of imagination in my assessment. Rather, it has the deliberate purpose of typification, and of suggesting to the reader that there's absolutely nothing new in what the characters get up to.

The same pattern of banality is maintained once Negrov is ensconced on his estate and takes a peasant mistress. (Here he not so much follows Onegin but anticipates later works, such as *Fathers and Children*.) Here, however, the somewhat ironic laconicity of the narrator's tone has other implications and effects. Thus we read: 'About two months later in the windows of the master's house there appeared a splendid little female face, at first with tear-filled, but later simply with charming blue eyes' (ibid.). This, in fact, is Dunya who is to become the mother of Lyubov. The narrator passes over the undoubted cruelty and/or coercion involved in 'tear-filled', so that the woman's story (the victim's narrative) is suppressed. This is taken even further as this sub-plot progresses: 'We find in our sources little information about the conquest of the little blue eyes, about how they were encountered. I surmise that this is because these conquests are achieved very simply' (17). The striving for typicality which is one of the hallmarks of the novel consequently has the effect of silencing Dunya and we learn little of her own story – the seduction, pregnancy, sense of shame, the birth, or her experience of motherhood. The patriarchal nexus is also presented as the norm, not really worthy of comment.[16]

And these patterns continue throughout most of Part One – patriarchal relations conveyed in a rather mockingly laconic (and condescending[17]) tone. Despite the birth of the child Lyubov, Negrov does not marry Dunya, who is passed on to a valet, but Glafira, also of mixed parentage, albeit of a more acceptable social status. Their match, however, conforms entirely to patriarchal norms: he is older by seventeen years, of a higher social rank and richer. In turn, Dunya's daughter is taken from her.

Krutsifersky is now introduced. He comes, as already noted, from a rather different milieu, but, because of Lyubov's mixed parentage they are *prepared* for each other. His early life is, in a sense, a series of accidents before Dr Krupov introduces him to the Negrov home as a tutor. He is forced to take this job because of his impoverished material circumstances. Consequently, the young pair are brought together not by 'fate' but by social determinants. This anti-Romantic, 'materialist' strain is developed when they do fall in love: essentially, we are led to believe it is because they are the only available option open to each other. Their liaison, therefore, is, like much else in the novel, largely predictable.

As their love blossoms, the narrator once more deflates any Romantic possibilities, and, once more, draws attention to his deliberate recycling of literary clichés and stereotypes. He tells us that Krutsifersky 'loved as only a nervous, Romantic nature can, he loved like Werther, like Vladimir Lensky' (51). Given the eventual fate of his two prototypes, this is hardly an auspicious lineage! Like Lensky, moreover, he reads his *inamorata* poetry (Zhukovsky) and, although Lyubov is more appreciative of it than Lensky's Olga, Krutsifersky is nonetheless presented as a parody of a parody. And, consequently, we are never really able to take him seriously, nor may we expect a happy ending to a love that is mocked at its very inception.

In terms of an overall assessment of the sexual politics of this relationship there are both positive and negative auguries. Although the narrator does mock them, Lyubov's diary which is now laid before us understandably addresses their developing love in rather more serious vein. Given that the 'Rake's economy' plot of seduction and betrayal of the innocent virgin still dominated much of Russian literature throughout the 1830s (and, indeed, beyond), their relationship is refreshingly free of any such colouration. They meet as equals and there is no hint of seduction on his part, or any vulnerability on hers. This is summed up by a simple, but emblematic gesture: 'She shook his hand in such a friendly, sympathetic way'[18] (60). On the other hand, the key to their mutuality is tenderness, not passion. The depths of Lyubov's alleged 'strong nature' are not touched. Indeed, Dr Krupov, who as we shall see, can be regarded as Herzen's *alter ego* in the text, warns them against marriage. In general terms, he is opposed to marriage as such and more specifically, he counsels Krutsifersky that they are *not* equally matched: 'Your fiancée is not a match for you . . . she is a tiger-cub [*sic*!], which still does not know its own strength' (68). So, as we leave the happy couple to attend to yet another pre-prologue (Beltov's parentage and early life), we are led to regard their relationship as markedly different from the old patriarchal oppression, yet warning notes have been sounded. Is it based on reality, or is it not rather a form of Lensky-esque Romanticism which believes in literary stereotypes of 'true love' and 'happy ever after?'

The main plot, when it eventually gets under way, will answer these questions and thereby pass a verdict on Romanticism (as well as gender roles). Before any of that can come to pass, however, we have still to meet one of the three principal *dramatis personae*, namely Vladimir Beltov. (It is, indeed, one of the many curious – or unsatisfactory? – aspects of the novel's architectonics that the main hero only appears one third of the way through.)

Although Beltov is initially introduced as a man of mystery about whom many rumours circulate in N.N. upon his unexpected return to the area, his background has much in common with those of Krutsifersky and Lyubov. As in the case of their life-histories we learn first about his parentage. In itself this leads us to see him as a product of a particular environment and, as such, he too is presented as a representative type. Moreover, because his background is given first (and in the most literal sense is prioritised) he seems to be conditioned, if not *determined* by it, as were the other two. A further similarity is that Beltov, like Lyubov is the issue of yet another mésalliance in that Beltov père, a wastrel and committed womaniser, had pursued and finally won his Sophie, the governess (I shall return in more detail to her story). The senior Beltov had died when his son was only two years old, and his mother had then devoted herself utterly to her darling boy. At least partly as a result of his mother's overprotectiveness (as the narrator construes it) Beltov, like the other main characters, but to an even greater extent, has had, firstly, his life skewed by patriarchal relations, and, secondly, has been completely unprepared for the realities of life. The narrator makes this point explicitly. As he offers a summation of Beltov's upbringing he comments that his mother and tutor 'had done everything so that he would not understand reality . . .; they had prepared their own kind of moral Kaspar Hauser' (92). In Russian terms he becomes the perfect exemplar of the 'superfluous man'. Consequently, as Part Two of the novel begins and we finally will keep more or less entirely to the diegetic present and the central plot we are left with three characters, none of whom has been prepared for life. Thus, the quasi-tragic ending is largely pre-determined.

Not long after the beginning of the second of the novel's two parts, we return to the young couple, to find them already four years married and with a three-year old son. Yet again the plot rhythm is vital to our understanding of the thematic implications of the narrative. Their wedding has, narratively, been suppressed and, the narrator confesses, there is not much of interest to be said about the intervening years. In terms which anticipate the famous, lapidary opening sentence of *Anna Karenina* he remarks: 'There's nothing to be said about these four years; they were happy, their time went by brightly, quietly; the happiness of love, especially complete love . . .' (124). As a result of this narratorial silence, the value of Romantic love is once more denigrated, and the usual mocking condescension of the narrator's style adds to this impression. Moreover, although he terms their love 'complete', Krupov's warning is not scotched: both in the above quoted remarks and, elsewhere, the emphasis is on *quietness*. An additional warning note is given when the narrator does begin to comment on the intervening years. As part of the marriage settlement Lyubov had been granted a dowry (including two serfs). That is, although their 'new' mutuality (the handshake) is stressed, they remain partially within the patriarchal order and, as we shall see, old attitudes will linger to vitiate their lives, as they, like Turgenev's heroes and heroines, will be stranded 'on the eve' of 'the real day'.[19]

But for the moment due attention is paid to the idyll of 'family happiness'. This is important for a number of reasons. In thematic terms, the relationship between Lyubov and Krutsifersky is presented as truly exceptional. Part One, and later sections of Part Two show an almost unrelieved picture of marital discord or even brutality and oppression. Indeed, Dr Krupov, a cynic and opponent of Romanticism, is forced to admit that this is the first happy marriage he has seen in sixty years! In other words, this couple, *as a couple*, is the best Russia has to offer, *at this stage in its development*. In terms of the novel's architectonics this interlude acts both as a recapitulation of the somewhat diffuse and rambling progress of Part One, and simultaneously, as a prologue to the main plot which now is about to unfold. That is, the state of seeming marital bliss which is here described is the given situation which will be disturbed, indeed destroyed, by the arrival of the 'mobile' hero/stranger.

Their marriage, then, is specifically characterised as an oasis amid the surrounding patriarchal desert, an idyll. Beltov, the narrator comments, had he been wandering by their little house

> could have seen ... one of those calming, splendid family pictures which, in all its aspects, demonstrate the possibility of happiness on earth. In this picture there was something like a summer's evening in a garden when there is no wind, the pond stretches out like a metallic mirror, golden from the sun, a small hamlet can be espied in the distance amongst the trees, the dew is rising, the herd wanders home with its intermingled chorus of shouts, stamping, lowing. .... (126)

This may be somewhat clichéd, but this is quite deliberate in that an attempt is made to establish a pastoral ideal. We now have a domestic interior 'shot' of Lyubov filling Krupov's pipe, while Krutsifersky watches with peace and love, while little Yasha stumbles around. ...

As in the depiction of their courtship the message of these scenes is mixed. Yes, it is an idyll, an oasis, yet at the same time, the saccharine tone tells us that the Krutsiferskys resemble a younger version of the 'old-world landowners':[20] passion and romance are absent.

This scene is foregrounded structurally, as I have already argued. Its significance is further emphasised by the ensuing discussion between the three on the nature of love, and, especially, on the viability and desirability of marriage.[21] Krupov, as before, argues against marriage seeing it as the height of egoism. Lyubov joins her husband in defending the institution, claiming that she herself feels free, unburdened by marriage. Indeed, the young couple seem to win the argument, or at least Krupov suspends his cynicism, admitting that their domestic bliss has somewhat reconciled him to the idea of marriage. Yet, as in the earlier stages of their relationship, ominous warning notes are sounded. Quite apart from the *stasis* evoked by the pastoral and domestic idylls, Krupov reminds them of the role of the fortuitous in their lives: 'Chance and you yourselves have arranged your happiness, ... Of course, the same chance, irrational, irresistible chance may destroy your happiness' (130).

Krupov, the *raisonneur* of the novel, is proved to be tragically prophetic. He also plays the unwitting role of the agent of chance in that the very next day he introduces Beltov into their charmed circle and the idyll soon begins to collapse. Moreover, as we shall see, it is largely chance, or whim, that has brought the aimless Beltov to N.N. in the first place, and it is chance, in the form of the death of his mentor Joseph, which leads him to become involved with Lyubov.

Although Beltov has now met Lyubov, the reader has to remain patient, in that yet another sub-plot is placed before us in the shape of Karp Kondratych, his ghastly wife Marya and their attempts to marry their pathetic daughter Varvara to Beltov. This fifteen-page interlude serves a number of functions. In Formalist terms it is yet another retardation device, delaying once more the complication and dénouement. Coming as it does immediately after the idyll, it reminds us (if we needed reminding!) of the encircling kingdom of darkness: indeed, it intensifies the gloom as this provincial family is one of the most oppressive and brutal (particularly in the mother-daughter relationship, to which I will return). At the same time, it both mocks and highlights the 'exceptional' status of the three Romantics. They are presented, and see themselves, as creatures from another world, yet, in the end, they will prove to be trapped and enfeebled by the world from which they have sprung and, although they are the 'new people' they will not be able to step into the future.

After this grotesque interlude we return to Beltov who is even more plunged in gloom, having received news of Joseph's death. For Beltov this signals the passing of his youth and his hopes, which he now recalls. He finds himself at a cross-roads, as he looks at his own portrait taken nearly twenty years before, at the age of fourteen. What lies before him, he wonders:

> Nothing but grey gloom, a tedious, monotonous continuation into the future; it's too late to begin a new life, it's impossible to continue with the old. How many beginnings, how many encounters ... and everything has ended up with idleness and loneliness. ... (153)

Krupov arrives and attempts to dispel his gloom, but Beltov's self-pity is inconsolable: 'Who needs my life, apart from my mother?' (154) he demands.

Like the 'oasis' of family happiness these reflections also play an important (and similar) structural role. They sum up all we know about Beltov and provide an explanation of what has drawn him to the Krutsifersky household. However, his precise motivation remains unclear: 'what had drawn Beltov into the modest home of the teacher? Had he found a sympathetic man in him, or, indeed, was he not in love with his wife? It would have been difficult for him to have answered these questions himself' (156). Although certain explanations are then offered, reading between the lines, it would appear that Beltov is drawn to Lyubov from a desire to prove to himself that his life and all its potential have not been wasted: it is an attempt to render his existence meaningful.

Finally we arrive at the complication of the plot, almost three-quarters of the way through the novel. In essence, the plot situation echoes that of *Evgeny Onegin* and anticipates *Rudin*. The aimless 'superfluous man' arrives in a provincial back-water and the young heroine falls in love with him, because he is the first unusual man she has met. It should be noted, of course, that Herzen puts an interesting new gloss on the situation in that the heroine is already a wife and mother. In turn Beltov, realising that the traditional mechanisms of flirting and seduction would be inappropriate for such a woman as Lyubov, abandons such schemes in favour of a more 'modern' approach: 'another relationship, a more human one, quickly brought Krutsiferskaya and Beltov close to each other' (159). This, of course, is an important polemical point for Herzen who, influenced by George Sand,[22] sought to explore relationships between equals, as well as to investigate the possibility of loving two people simultaneously. Consequently, he seeks to stress the naturalness of their relationship, the absence of guile or seduction. Their friendship and mutuality seem to develop *of themselves*: 'Sympathies of this kind cannot be either developed or suppressed; they simply express the fact of brotherly development in two people' (160). Equally, Herzen seeks to de-eroticise the presentation of sexual relationships, to show their development to be natural and innocent. Thus, when we first see Lyubov and Beltov together, they are not apprehended in a forbidden, guilty encounter *à deux*, but in the domestic setting with Krutsifersky and Krupov present, as the four of them sit discussing friendship, death and other abstract matters. It is in the course of this discussion that Beltov recounts his meeting with Joseph in Switzerland that had led to his return to the elections in N.N.: this chance encounter will precipitate the events which now unfold.

This scene ends with Beltov suggesting that Lyubov alone can save him and we immediately switch to the scene in the park, in the

Alexander Herzen: Who Is To Blame? 195

lap of 'indifferent nature'. This will be the only scene in which we see the two protagonists alone together and, from many perspectives, it has enormous significance.

Despite the gloominess of the desolate park, certain Romantic notes are also struck. It is a day in April, a new beginning perhaps; she is dressed in white, while he is in black. As in the previous scene, their mutuality and equality are emphasised as they engage in another of the abstract discussions with which the novel abounds. Gradually, however, the generalities on love and friendship are particularised as Beltov takes the lead, declaring that he had loved her from the first. Significantly, he reveals that his love is based on egoism: 'I looked on you as my last *consolation*' (173 – my italics). Their feelings for each other at last find expression, as Beltov takes her hand. He attempts to persuade her of the possibility of loving both her husband and another, but Lyubov cannot understand this new morality: 'I do not understand love for two people. My husband, quite apart from anything else, by his unbounded love alone, has obtained enormous, *sacred rights* to my love' (174 – my italics). Beltov persists to argue for his rights as well, but Lyubov becomes increasingly distraught, and, finally, begins to break down into the same physical displays of feminine emotionalism that had characterised scores of heroines before her:

> With tears, with horror a frightened woman looked at him . . . her black hair, loosened by the raw evening air, became dishevelled . . . her trembling hand [now] squeezed her kerchief, . . . her breast intermittently heaved but, it seemed, the air could not reach her lungs. (175)

This is a critical moment. Although the novel has stressed the 'new' elements of this woman and her relationships with both Krutsifersky and now Beltov, in the end she is mastered, first by Beltov's insistence that she declare her love, and then by her welling femininity. As she tells him, ' "I am a simple, weak woman", – and tears flowed from her eyes' (ibid.). It should be noted, that Beltov is not entirely a rake of the old school: he too is moved to tears as they embrace.

Yet their reactions to this peripatetic scene are profoundly different. Immediately, after the bathos of Krupov interrupting their passion, we cut away to Beltov's emotions. Despite all the anguish manifested in Lyubov's unwilling submission to him, 'Beltov was intoxicated by his happiness; his slumbering soul was suddenly resurrected with all its powers' (176). In this we see another old paradigm reworked – the jaded Rake (of sorts) is renewed by the love of a pure woman.[23] This quasi-vampiric motif is made explicit: 'he was surprised that he had found both so much youthfulness and so much freshness within himself' (ibid).

While he goes off to his hotel to drink celebratory champagne, Lyubov's reaction is profoundly different. Although she has been proclaimed by Krupov and Krutsifersky as a strong nature, she *immediately* enters the traditional dysphoric decline of suffering, actual illness and eventual death. As she bids farewell to Beltov she is, in fact, already 'pale as death' (176). She cannot forget the 'hot, fiery, prolonged kiss on her lips' (ibid.). She is, of course, already a mother but this is the moment her sexuality and desire have been awoken. Female desire, in this novel as before, leads not to fulfilment but to guilt and anguish – and death.

Rather incredibly, indeed, she is already ill and will never recover. Shortly afterwards, for the second time in the novel, we are able to read her diary. While the woman's word is thus, in a sense, privileged, it conveys not strength but weakness and distress. More generally, her writing concerns itself more with others rather than with her own feelings. From her account, and subsequent events, we at last see the final stages of the plot, and the ultimate view that is taken of these half-new people and their domestic arrangements.

The most striking aspect of the plot's dénouement and resolution is that love brings no-one happiness. One kiss (however 'hot' and 'passionate' it may have been) destroys the lives of all three protagonists. Lyubov rapidly declines, Beltov's last hope in life is gone, while Krutsifersky takes to drink. All three are destroyed by the events in the park and the idyll that opened Part Two has gone forever, or, rather, it is proved to have been an insubstantial chimera, blown away at the first contact with reality.

The novel, of course, in its very title poses a question and in the final pages the narrator addresses this problem directly. In one sense, it is all a matter of chance: 'If Beltov had not come to N.N. many happy and peaceful days would have passed in the quiet family of Dmitry Yakovlevich [Krutsifersky], of course, – but this is no comfort' (188). Perhaps Beltov, then, is to blame? Krupov once more intervenes in the plot to ask Beltov to leave and castigates him for what he has done or, at least, for what he has caused to happen. He demands 'do you know or not that you have destroyed the happiness of a family' (200) and proceeds to itemise the disastrous effects of his intrusion into this oasis. Beltov, naturally enough, defends himself against these charges, speaking once more of the great love he has for Lyubov, of the genuine, mutual feeling between them. Krupov, in turn, recalls his warning before the marriage, that Lyubov and Krutsifersky were not equals: 'Oh, it wasn't without good cause that I always said that family life is a highly dangerous thing but I prophesied like John in the wilderness; nobody listened to me' (203). Krupov, then, returns to his former opinion and this is his conclusion, namely, that the couple should never have married in the first place, but also that Beltov was at fault for allowing his feelings to develop where he had no 'rights'. As Beltov leaves the town, and Lyubov declines to an early and tragic death (tended by Beltov's mother), should these also be our conclusions derived from an analysis of plot and theme? Is no-one in particular to blame, because all are to blame? And if no-one bears full responsibility for these tragic events, is that because each of them has been too badly maimed by the conditions which gave birth to them? In order to answer these questions, however provisionally, it is necessary to return to look in more detail at the forces at work in each of the characters, at how they have been constructed as men and as woman.

3. Images of Men

Who Is To Blame?, in fact, offers a number of different images of masculinity, ranging from the traditional paterfamilias to those who aspire to adopt the new, Sandian ideas. The first male character to be treated at any length is Negrov, whose early life history we have already traced. The authorial tone adopted towards him (and, indeed, to most of the background characters) is one of mocking irony, but beneath this rather thin veneer of aristocratic disdain lies a self-willed, vicious man of the old, patriarchal school. In the first few lines of the chapter devoted to his biography, we are told that he is 'Stern, hot-tempered, harsh in word and often cruel in deed' (15). As we have already seen, he organises his affairs entirely on his own terms, taking Dunya as his mistress and passing her onto an underling when it suits him. He rules his family and estates absolutely: later on we learn of his treatment of his serfs and the narrator wonders whether this is 'a measure by means of which he maintained the fear and obedience of his vassals or simply a patriarchal habit' (38). He is just as self-willed and harsh in his approach to those closer to home. When he learns of the romance between his daughter and Krutsifersky he hypocritically sermonises to the latter on his immoral behaviour: 'It is shameful, young man and immoral to pervert a poor girl who has no parents or protectors or estate' (61). He drones on for quite a while in these tones, although he finally admits that he was thinking of marrying Lyubov to him anyway![24]

Of course, Negrov is little more than a caricature but it is significant, I feel, that Herzen chose to devote his attention to such a type at the opening of the novel. He is the personification of the old world, the old type of masculinity against which the younger men seek to identify themselves. Indeed, from the very first pages young Krutsifersky is a diametrically opposed type. He is presented as a very ordinary individual, from humble origins, although well educated. In terms of his role in the novel everything about his initial portraiture tells us that *he* is not the hero: he owes more to the timid Gogolian type (especially Ivan Shponka) than to the Onegin-Pechorin line. At his entrance to the Negrov household he announces that he only drinks water. A little later we are also given his biography and he emerges as curiously inert, if studious: at the 'gymnasium he studied well; eternally shy, meek and quiet' (32). He is always acted upon, sent to the gymnasium, then to university, and finally introduced into the Negrov household.

This passivity will be important in the later development of the plot. As Krupov will warn, he is no match for Lyubov, and he will be powerless to prevent the tragedy. More generally Krutsifersky emerges as a failure and this is due in part to the feminisation of him. Certainly, both in the introductory sections and later, he is delineated in terms of motifs more traditionally associated with the heroines of Russian literature and, it seems to me, these are both the source of authorial satire and contributory factors to his inadequacy. Put simply Krutsifersky is presented as not manly enough. Indeed, Ivan Shponka is his most obvious literary prototype (along with Vladimir Lensky).

From his first appearance he displays aspects of feminine iconography.[25] He enters the room of his would-be employer 'timidly and confused' (10). A little later we read 'The young man all this time was silent, and was blushing' (ibid.). He can hardly think straight because he is so nervous. His excessive virginity is picked out both here and in his later biography. Thus, he becomes particularly agitated when introduced to Glafira as 'Up to now our graduate had never been in the society of ladies' (12). Consequently, like the earlier

Shponka or, later on, Turgenev's Lavretsky, he is utterly in awe of women, imagining them to be 'fairies, goddesses' (12), 'surrounded by some kind of nimbus' (ibid.). The narrator, indeed, plays with this feminised motif, turning him into a descendent not of Onegin, or even Lensky, but of Tatyana. As his feelings for Lyubov grow he shows all the signs of amorous attachment. Noting this, the governess Eliza Avgustovna addresses him in words which precisely (and deliberately) echo those of the scene between Tatyana and her *nyanya*: 'Are you really in love? you're distracted, sad' (52).[26] And just to complete the process of feminisation, Krutsifersky evinces his emotions by physical signs: he 'blushed up to his ears' (ibid.).

The point of this feminisation is, I think, to show his unfittedness for the harsh world of Russian reality (as embodied by Negrov). Krutsifersky's passivity and virginality are further compounded by his extreme Romanticism ('Lenskyism'). We have already seen this in the explicit parallel drawn between Krutsifersky and Lensky (and Werther), as well as in his weeping over Zhukovsky as he reads to Lyubov. This strain is summed up in an important conversation between him and Dr Krupov. For the latter such tendencies, and 'love' in general, are clearly inappropriate in a man of Krutsifersky's age. He insists 'stop behaving like a child, be a man!' (68). Krutsifersky responds in true Romantic style: 'I would better part with my life than renounce this angel' (ibid.).

In one of the original sources for this character, Pushkin had suggested that Vladimir Lensky's experience of marriage and life would have led to his abandoning such adolescent nonsense (had he lived long enough) and 'he would have discovered life as it really is'.[27] Krutsifersky, it would seem, is incapable of learning from life. Indeed, the negative aspect of the oasis that he and his wife build is that, precisely, they have cut themselves off from life. Indeed, although he now works as a school teacher, the couple are so mutually self-absorbed 'that it was difficult not to take them for foreigners in N.N.; they were not at all like everything that surrounded them' (125). Although now working, and despite his responsibilities as husband and father, Krutsifersky remains unchanged. As the storm of love gathers the narrator returns to Krutsifersky to offer a résumé of his character. All the old notes are recapitulated – his femininity, virginality and inability to deal with real life:

> It is difficult to define Krutsifersky's character: a tender nature, a loving one to the highest degree, a feminine and submissive na-

ture ... It would have been difficult to unearth a man who knew practical life less; everything he knew, he knew from books and consequently he knew incorrectly, romantically, rhetorically; he believed sacredly in the reality of the world as celebrated by Zhukovsky.... (156)

And a little later this theme is summed up in terms which tell us precisely that *he* has not learned the lessons that Lensky might have done: 'Weak by nature he didn't even think of entering into a struggle with reality' (157).

This struggle is now about to begin in earnest, in the shape of his wife's love for another man and Krutsifersky proves completely incapable of dealing with it. He certainly loves Lyubov devotedly, but this is not enough. As the dénouement of the plot reveals, Krutsifersky is destroyed by his first real contact with harsh reality. In the end, one is tempted to conclude, he is a feminine man and, as the novel construes it, *therefore*, weak. As he learns the truth about Lyubov's feelings he struggles to come to terms with this new situation, he strives towards a new persona and the new morality but does not have the resources and, instead, follows, paradoxically enough, that most traditional masculine path of dealing with difficulties – he gets drunk!

Part of Lyubov's tragedy is that her first love and husband is, as Krupov had predicted, no match for her. Equally, however, the central male protagonist, Vladimir Beltov proves no better fitted for dealing with Russian reality, even if for rather different reasons.

Initially Beltov *is* presented as a potential hero. His unexpected return to N.N. has given rise to all sorts of rumours and so he is constructed as a Romantic 'man of mystery'. Equally, in typological terms, as already noted, he fulfils the requirements of the hero in that he is a mobile character who has entered 'enclosed space'. Moreover, he will certainly cause a profound change in all those around him.[28] These expectations, however, are quickly dispelled as we follow his childhood development. While Krutsifersky may have been unfitted for reality because of his 'feminine nature', in Beltov's case it is more a product of nurture. His over-protective mother has deliberately isolated him from society, producing, we recall, 'a moral Kaspar Hauser'. Only when he enters Moscow University does he begin to mix with his contemporaries and peers, but, it would seem, the damage has already been done. Although he has great gifts, and enormous potential, he displays a complete inability to settle at

Alexander Herzen: Who Is To Blame?

anything. Quite deliberately, Herzen takes him through all the career possibilities open to a young man, and he is a failure at each one, not through lack of ability, but because of a lack of seriousness. He works for a while in the St Petersburg bureaucracy, travels, takes up medicine, tries painting, but soon gets bored with each and every of these pastimes or occupations. He remains a dilettante and the question is posed (although not really answered) as to whether he is blighted by his mother, or by 'mother' Russia. In sum, if Krutsifersky is a parody of a parody (Lensky), then Beltov emerges as a parody of Onegin, of whom Pushkin also asked 'is he not a parody?'.[29]

One 'career' that Beltov does not fully devote himself to is that of womanising. Although we are later led to believe that he has some experience in this area, his love relations are a curious lacuna in the passages devoted to his education. Apart from a cursory reference to a certain 'widow' (106) and a certain 'lorette' (121), there is almost no mention of women (apart from his mother, of course) in his biography. Only later do we learn that he had played the part of the Rake, but, clearly, from the way this information is presented, we are not to believe that love had played a serious part in his formation. As he ponders the best way to deal with his feelings for Krutsiferskaya, we are told:

> Many times he had been insanely in love, now with some primadonna, then with a dancer, then with an equivocating beauty, who sought solitude at the waters, then with some red-cheeked and fair-haired German with pretensions to dreaminess . . . (159)

Despite the 'insanely' the narrator would seem to set little store by these episodes. None of these 'loves', either here or earlier, is even named. No detail or discussion is offered. Clearly, then, Beltov had been no more capable of dealing with women, than with other facets of 'reality'.

And so he had returned to Russia, to the elections in N.N. because, as we have already seen, he felt his life to be in crisis, and had exhausted all other possible avenues. Soon, indeed, he realises that it had been a 'false step' (118) to return. Although this return can be construed, typologically, as the entrance onto the scene of the narrative hero, the narrator makes it patently clear that Beltov is, in this sense, an imposter: 'Beltov for the second time encountered *reality* under the same conditions as in the office – and again he proved to be a coward in the face of it' (120 – my italics). From a rather different genesis he has advanced no further then Krutsifersky. And, in a different way, he is just as lacking in masculinity. Although now over thirty, he displays immaturity in everything he does; he seems incapable of seeing anything through, of doing anything properly. Once more the narrator makes this point explicitly: 'he did not have the ability to be a good landowner, an excellent officer, a diligent official' (121). In short, 'he was *bereft of maturity*' (122 – my italics). That is, he still behaves like an adolescent while Krutsifersky acts like a child: neither man has obtained the capacity of responding properly to the mature woman we are led to believe Lyubov is. (Whether she is or not is another matter, to which I shall return.) Both male protagonists, that is, could be characterised as non-phallic.

And so, Beltov wanders aimlessly through Russian life. If Krutsifersky and Lyubov could be taken for 'foreigners' in N.N., then this is precisely the point about Beltov. Like Onegin (and other 'superfluous men') before him he is, indeed, characterised by his foreignness. Beltov follows Onegin's pattern, reading (and quoting) Byron, dabbling in Adam Smith. On one occasion he quotes Byron to the effect that 'no decent man should live past the age of thirty-five' (154). Krupov, as always the moral arbiter, takes this one stage further: 'You've read up all these sophisms from the damned German[30] philosophers' (ibid.), and shortly afterwards sums up Beltov's position: 'You, like all rich people, have not become accustomed to hard work' (155).

This, then, is the man that Lyubov falls in love with. He cannot face reality, he knows little of women, for all his previous infatuations, he does not know how to take anything seriously. Moreover, again like Krutsifersky, he is unable, firstly, to do anything to save himself, or Lyubov, once the storm breaks and, secondly, remains essentially unchanged by these dramatic events. Certainly, he is very different from the cold, bored Onegin or the dangerous seducers like Pechorin: he is genuinely involved in Lyubov's emotions and rendered deeply distraught by the events. But, as the novel closes and he prepares to leave, he is much the same as when we first encounter him, except that his condition has worsened. As he meets Lyubov for the last time, the narrator comments, with some significance, 'He looked like a dead man' (204). We last see him two weeks later as he leaves the area. We are not told where he is going, nor why, but, then, there would be no point in such information: his life is effectively over.

Alexander Herzen: Who Is To Blame? 203

In drawing the portraits of these two contrasting, although in many respects similar, portraits of failed masculinity, Herzen would seem to be suggesting that the basic problem with Russian manhood lay in men's inability to confront reality, to struggle against it or even, really, to make much sense of it. The causes for these failings lay in education and, more specifically, Romanticism. One man stands apart from these feelings, the *raisonneur* of the text, the man alone, Dr Krupov. Martin Malia has noted: 'Krupov was a very important personage to Herzen. As a man of science he was also a man of sense, the symbol of empirical, skeptical sanity in a world of sentimentalists'. Indeed, he is a kind of *alter ego*, 'Herzen himself in his Voltairian moments'.[31] Although he does not play a central role in the plot development he seems always to be on hand to act as intermediary and counsellor. It is he who introduces Krutsifersky to the Negrovs (and, therefore, to Lyubov), and Beltov to the Krutsiferskys. As we know, he tries to persuade Krutsifersky that marriage is a poor prospect in the circumstances. Later he counsels as well as tends the suffering Lyubov, while it is also Dr Krupov who upbraids Beltov over his conduct and requests that he leave. All in all, it is his blunt, bluff mature masculinity that is valorised: he is the Father that the two 'sons' signally fail to become. Equally, like Starodum in the *The Minor* or The Old Man in *The Gipsies*[32] he acts as the moral arbiter, a quasi-Olympian figure who comments on rather than participates in the action. In the end, it is true, he fails to prevent the destruction of three lives but, nevertheless, it seems to me, his presence is vital to an understanding of *Who Is To Blame?* Russia must shed its adherence to foreign models, must get down to some sober hard work, forget Romanticism and then, perhaps, the men of education and potential like Krutsifersky and Beltov can grow beyond their childish or adolescent arrest and achieve full manhood.

4. Images of Women

As I noted in the introduction to this chapter, *Who Is To Blame?* can be regarded as a transitional work, echoing *Evgeny Onegin* and other works of the 1820s and 1830s as well as anticipating the novels of Turgenev. In particular, the character of Lyubov can be considered a continuation of Tatyana and, at the same time, she looks ahead to the 'strong' heroines such as Elena in *On the Eve*. One particular feature that the present work shares with the Turgenev novel is that the central female figure is valorised (at least to a certain extent), whereas virtually every other female character is denigrated. This is certainly the case here. Lyubov, as we shall see, is markedly different from everyone else in the novel. On the other hand, the text (particularly in the extensive prologues of Part One) is populated by a whole host of other women and all are presented as either suffering feminine victims or vicious tyrants. And, all too often, it is precisely the tyrannical harridans who oppress the other women.

The first woman's story we encounter is that of Dunya, Negrov's peasant mistress and Lyubov's mother, who, as we know, is the bearer of the 'tear-filled eyes', who is the object of Negrov's 'conquest' before being passed on to the valet. Simultaneously, she is robbed of her daughter. As the narrator remarks: 'This was incidentally, an agonisingly bitter moment for poor Dunya' (19). The epithet *bednaya*, conveying 'disaster' as well as 'poverty', had long been the classic designation in Russian for the female victim of patriarchal relations.[33] And this is precisely the essence of her pathetic little story. As the narrator further comments: 'doomed to the langorous confinement of the harem, she concentrated in her child all her need for love, all her demands on life' (ibid.). Simultaneously, then, Dunya is passive ('doomed') a love slave ('harem'[34]) and, finally, her whole essence becomes synonymous with the maternal. Added to these signs of femininity in its classic stereotypical expression are others as Dunya 'sobbing, threw herself to her knees before the icon' (ibid.). Perhaps the reader is invited to pity pathetic Dunya. Given this intense and rapid imbrication of clichés of the feminine victim, such a response is difficult.

Standing as a total contrast to Lyubov's natural mother is her step-mother Glafira, who emerges as a misogynist caricature of the sexual woman. Everything about her is negative and loathsome and she is the butt for the narrator's thinly-veiled masculinist disgust. We first encounter Glafira as Krutsifersky is introduced to the household. She is resting in mid-afternoon, in her 'favourite outfit' (12), a loose blouse, because after fifteen years of indolence (she even goes mushroom picking in a carriage!), all her other clothes are too tight. As soon as she meets Krutsifersky she begins to make eyes at him and finds him 'interesting' (13), as she so rarely met young men. The narrator proceeds with studied irony: 'women of certain years look at a young man with the same incomprehensibly attracting sensation with which men usually look at girls' (13–14).

We return to this theme during the scene of mistaken identity which culminates in Krutsifersky's engagement to Lyubov. Ever since the tutor had arrived in the house Glafira had taken rather more care of her appearance than usual. As she finally tries to seduce him, the narrator makes clear his abhorrence in the face of female sexuality, which is particularly distressing to him because the woman concerned is of 'certain years', and because she is (mis)appropriating the masculine role. He writes:

> This slow-wittedness of his [Krutsifersky's], the shy distraction and lowered eyes inflamed more and more the passion of the forty-year-old woman; the strange overturning of the usual relationship of the sexes lent it a particular interest; indeed, Glafira Lvovna was playing the role of the conqueror and seducer, while Dmitry Yakovlevich that of the innocent girl, around whom a malevolent spider had begun to weave her web. (56)

After Krutsifersky escapes her clutches, she returns to her room, where, we read, 'her capacious bosom was heaving' (ibid.).

Glafira's story (to which some time is devoted) conforms, in fact, to another paradigm as well. As part of the biographical sketches which comprise much of Part One, we had heard of her miserable upbringing at the hands of her vicious aunt Mavra. In these sections Glafira plays the part of the suffering victim. The narrator presents this section of her life in a generalised fashion: 'the life of the little girl was not beautiful: she was deprived of all the joys of her years, was intimidated, frightened, oppressed' (21). She thus becomes more enticing a prize for the masterful patriarch Negrov. Before securing her escape from her dreadful aunt, Glafira had been in despair, but her dreams of liberation are mocked by the knowing, world-weary air in which our narrator presents them. Every stage in her life, that is, is represented as a cliché, and thereby, devalued. She thinks of becoming a nun, of contracting consumption, before she discovers the delights of French novels and now fantasises, most predictably, about 'a lively head, with mustachios and curls' (22). The narrator, indeed, draws attention to the fact that he is only going through the motions: 'she composed for herself entire stories: he carries her off, they're pursued . . . "You're mine forever!" he says, clutching his pistol, etc. etc.' (ibid.). As Glafira eventually wins her 'prince' the narrator humiliates her yet further, suggesting that her muslin dress 'all but burst into flames from the fire coursing through her veins' (24). It is all written, it seems to me, without the good humoured sympathy for these provincials that Pushkin, say, evinces, but from the point of view of the gentlemen's club: aren't these dreadful, grotesque women ridiculous and/or disgusting?

We see these misogynistic tendencies even more glaringly in the brief but poisonous account given of poor Glafira's aunt, Mavra, who emerges as one of the nastiest characters in Russian literature, but also as one of the grossest instances of masculinist venom. What is particularly depressing about the half dozen pages devoted to Mavra is that what is written on them is quite unnecessary. She is a background character to a background character. But precisely because this misogyny is *unmotivated*, narratively, it is all the more revealing of the overall sexual politics of the novel (written by a man proclaimed as an early Russian feminist!).

Mavra's life has been a sorry one. Countess Mavra Ilinishna had once been a society lady, even a 'coquette' (20), who had turned away a number of suitors in anticipation of a great match. Unfortunately for her, her father dies and within two years her wastrel brother has drunk and gambled away the estate. Thus, her story commences as a classic tale of patriarchy. The woman is the victim, first of the loss of paternal protection,[35] and then of male self-indulgence. However, she then becomes a victim for a third time, of the *narrator's* self-indulgence. Mavra, who has now reached the advanced age of thirty, tries desperately to get married, 'but gradually her bilious tongue and insufferable haughtiness drove almost everyone from her house' (21). Now the narrator becomes even more vicious in his demolition of the embittered spinster:

> Abandoned, cast aside by everyone, the old maid became even more replete with indignation and hatred; she surrounded herself with various parasitic old women . . . gathered gossip from all ends of the city . . . and placed a high distinction on her endless virginity. (ibid.)

Shortly afterwards Glafira enters her life and Mavra exacts her revenge against society on her own niece. She treats her almost as a slave, but more than this, 'she wished to devour all her youthfulness, suck out all the fresh juices of her soul' (22).

This brief section of the novel is, then, quite extraordinary, but it should be emphasised that it is the norm for Part One, rather than a passing solecism. *All* the women in Lyubov's background (and there are others, such as her wizened, drunken French governess, Eliza Avgustovna, or the 'impenetrably stupid' (41) priest's wife) constitute a roll-call of female grotesques. Moreover, a considerable amount of time is spent on itemising them. Even in Part Two the narrator interrupts his main plot for over ten pages to offer us yet another vignette of an older woman tryannising a younger one (this time it is mother and daughter, Marya Stepanovna and Varvara, Beltov's would-be-fiancée). Indeed, on this occasion the viciousness of the female goes even further with actual physical violence involved. Again, the narrator's misogynistic disgust is quite explicit. For example, he says of the mother: 'her face, always unattractive, became revolting' (139). Taking the novel as a whole, Lyubov emerges, therefore, as quite exceptional, to an extent that easily surpasses the similar situations of Tatyana and Elena. Equally, however, it seems to me, we are presented with an extreme case of narrative duplicity. The quasi-feminist author (who was inspired by George Sand and who dedicated the novel to his beloved wife) ostensibly seeks to depict a sympathetic, positive heroine. At the same time, he completely undermines his apparent intention by the savagery or condescension with which he portrays all other women.

Before moving on to an account of Lyubov, there is one more background female personage to be considered, namely, Sophie, Beltov's mother. In her portrait, it should be said at the outset, we see the same tendencies. Thus, the early stages of her story echo very closely the lineaments of Dunya's life. Born a peasant, she had been taken into the main house to be trained as a governess. The first encounter between Beltov's parents occurs when Beltov senior, already designated as a gambler, drinker and womaniser, attempts to embrace and kiss the twenty-year-old peasant governess. From the beginning, then, their relationship is characterised as classically patriarchal (again, in both senses of the word). To this initial motif are immediately added familiar motifs from the novel of pursuit, seduction and eventual conquest.[36] Sophie resists and escapes, so Beltov tries various other strategies, first presents and then threats. The young woman proves to be made of sterner stuff and flees to St Petersburg. Her very resistance excites the seducer, but his attempted abduction fails. He then manages to blacken her reputation to such an extent that she is dismissed from her new position and, unable to gain another domestic post, begins working as a seamstress. She is now reduced to abject misery: 'The days stretched out agonisingly, terribly; the unfortunate girl was drowning in this dirt, insulted, humiliated by everything and everybody' (84). She even contemplates suicide.

Every step thus far in her plot is a literary cliché, presented in the usual flat, rather mocking tone the narrator adopts throughout Part One. Again, one wonders what the purpose of this fairly lengthy, detailed background narrative is. On one level, perhaps, the intention is to mock the Gothick tradition that stems back at least as far as *Poor Liza* (because Sophie – the classic heroine's name of the eighteenth century – will not commit suicide and, in one sense, will win). On another level, her plot can be seen as a protest against the oppression of women, and, again, her eventual vindication fits this hypothesis. On yet another level, however, one could argue that Sophie's story, particularly because it echoes Dunya's fairly closely, is presented in such detail precisely to excite the male reader's fantasy: after all, the essence of it is female sexual innocence endangered by the rapacious appetites of the male.

Instead of committing suicide, Sophie writes an angry letter to Beltov, excoriating him for his baseness. He is touched, and six months later they are married. In a way, then, Sophie's virtue is preserved intact, but at great cost in that she emerges irrevocably scarred and, indeed, has become an icon of female vulnerability and suffering:

> She was afraid of people, was pensive, unsociable, concentrated within herself, was thin, pale, mistrustful, was always fearful of something, she liked to weep and would sit in silence for hours on end on her balcony. (86)

Her early life then reduces Sophie Beltova to a complete lexicon of femininity. Moreover, it leaves her deeply flawed as a maternal presence. If her background plot is only provisionally negative in its implications, then, the text would seem to be quite unequivocal in its assessment of her mothering. Indeed, she is introduced to the reader in the following terms: 'she was one of the main causes of all the failures in her son's career' (78). Throughout *Who Is To Blame?* there are a series of maternal (or quasi-maternal) relationships and almost all of them are treated very negatively, although rarely is the judgement quite as bald or as unequivocal as the words which present poor Sophie to us. Much of the rest of Part One (about thirty pages) is taken up with detailing her 'crimes' against the talented young

Vladimir. And, of course, if we take this opening *dictum* at face value, then her presence is also to blight the main plot in that it is Sophie who has rendered Beltov incapable of acting decisively or of realising his potential in any other way. Thus, even when this 'moral Kaspar Hauser' (which she, we recall, was instrumental in creating) has grown up she continues to vitiate his life. He wishes to become a doctor, but she seeks to thwart this, fearful lest he come into contact with any contagious diseases. Certainly, she is utterly devoted to him but this blanket of maternal love is seen to be ultimately suffocating or, rather, *emasculating*. In turn, she is presented as a pathetic figure, waiting anxiously at White Fields for news of him. A particularly cruel detail in this aspect of the narrator's portrayal of this unvalorised Mater Dolorosa is on her name-day when the postmaster arrives with two letters from her beloved son – which had been deliberately held back so that there would be something for her on this special occasion . . . Sophie Beltova is the only maternal figure in the novel given extended treatment, but the picture is almost entirely negative. She starts out as a persecuted virgin and ends as leading a half-life, living only for her son. As in the earlier instance of Lyubov's mother, Dunya, there is no real attempt by the author to see the realities of a woman's life, but, rather, both are presented as pathetic, pitiable creatures. Even at the very end of the novel when Sophie makes a brief reappearance to tend the dying Lyubov, the picture remains the same. The story ends with cloying sentimentality, as Lyubov 'listened to the endless stories of the old mother about her son – about their Waldemar who was now so far from them . . .' (209).

It could be argued that the almost completely negative (and largely misogynistic) presentation of the secondary female characters in this novel is intended primarily to highlight the outstanding qualities of the 'strong heroine'. Whether Lyubov Krutsiferskaya really deserves this appellation is something we may now consider.

Lyubov, we should first recall, both anticipates Beltov's origins and recalls that of her author, the man of the heart, Alexander Herzen, in that she is the issue of a peasant mother and gentry father. This detail is significant in a number of ways. As we have already seen, *Who Is To Blame?*, while being a post-Onegin and pre-Turgenevan love story between the spiritual heroine and superfluous man is also an 'encyclopedia of Russian (patriarchal) life'. That the two principal protagonists should be the products of such traditional mésalliances is therefore important. On the whole, Herzen would seem to have considered such off-spring as fatally flawed. The children of relationships based on oppression and exploitation could not flourish. As such the lives of Lyubov and Beltov, and their flawed, guilty love for each other, stand as metaphors for pre-emancipation Russia.

At the same time, Lyubov is very much a purely literary type in that her lineage is very clearly and explicitly traced back to Pushkin's Tatyana. The prototype of many later heroines in Russian literature is introduced in the following terms: 'Wild, sad, silent/ . . . She in her own family/seemed a stranger/ . . . And often for a whole day alone/She sat silently by her window' (2, xxv, ll. 5–14). 'Pensiveness', we are told in the following stanza, was her friend. Lyubov's introduction to the story is a virtual paraphrase of Pushkin's lines: 'But why then was she always pensive? Why did little cheer her? Why did she like to sit by herself in her room?' (43). Consequently, all her being and later life can be seen to be predetermined by pre-existing literary structures. Indeed, she is as much a 'stranger' in her own home as Tatyana had been (and as Turgenev's Elena was to be). Here, however, the reasons for this are made rather more obvious. We have already seen the somewhat brutish nature of Negrov and the sensitive girl responds accordingly: 'The harsh . . . nature of Negrov . . . deeply offended her' (43). She is alienated from her real mother, because she does not even know that Dunya *is* her mother, while Glafira constantly reminds her of her unconventional origins, suggesting that Lyubov is an 'orphan who is being raised with her own little ones' (44). Indeed, Lyubov is effectively an orphan.

Her education, which is also a deliberate echo of Tatyana's, does little to prepare her for her difficult passage through life. Eliza Avgustovna offers her some very inadequate tuition, while the main sustenance is derived, as was Tatyana's, from her mother's (Glafira's) library, which Lyubov reads more or less at random. As in the earlier text, the staple is French and English novels, to which Lyubov has unrestricted access. But from the age of twelve, the classically entitled 'poor girl' (42) is left more or less to her own devices, and displays, as she is to later on as well, many of the signs of the typical feminine heroine. Her inner spiritual life becomes her only resource: 'she thought and dreamed' (47) and over a period of five years (which brings us back to the present) she becomes 'pensive, secretly passionate' (ibid.). In her emblematic 'white dress' (49) she cares for her peasant children. This same emblem adorns her when Krutsifersky accosts her in the lime avenue on the estate and all the clichés of this type of heroine are trotted out as a symptomatic prelude to the burgeoning of their love. Lyubov 'was sitting on her favourite bench and pensively, sadly was looking into the distance . . . she felt sad and this sadness lent something magnificent to her features, which were more energetic, clearly-defined' (59).

To what extent this apprehension of the iconic heroine in an iconic setting is a deliberate play with established *topoi*, or, more simply, poor writing, is difficult to determine. Either way, the novel clearly seeks to establish Lyubov as an unusual, spiritual young woman. An attempt is also made to penetrate her soul through the device of extracts from her diary, a mechanism which Turgenev was also to borrow for his *On the Eve*. Indeed, anticipating Elena's outpourings the main effect of the first entries from Lyubov's journal is to emphasise her spiritual isolation and anguished femininity. Her first remarks read:

> Last night I sat for a long time under the window; it was a warm night, so lovely in the garden . . . I don't know why everything has become sadder and sadder for me; it's as if a dark cloud has arisen from the depths of my soul; it felt so heavy that I wept, wept bitterly . . . I have a father and mother – but I am an orphan; I'm utterly alone in the great wide world and I feel with terror that *I love no-one*. (47–8; italics in original)

And so it goes on in the same lugubrious tones. She feels no love for her harsh father, but also feels guilt because of this. Equally, she feels distant from her step-mother. She continues to construct herself as the lonely maiden of Sentimentalism (of which Tatyana, initially at least, is the supreme exemplar), speaking of her love of sitting alone, in the lap of nature. Thus, although this direct reflection of her inner life is in one way an important step towards creating Lyubov as the moral and sentient centre of the novel, the actual image created is, firstly, merely a collection of established literary stereotypes and, secondly, does nothing to build an impression of the 'strong heroine'.

We see very little of Lyubov after these images are created and we only return to her sixty odd pages (and four years) later to find a fairly substantial transformation. The very fact that the novel does not end with the marriage of the young couple is in itself significant,[37] as is the consequent fact that the wife and mother is still of narrative interest. Although there are few actual scenes of Lyubov as a mother she is clearly intended to be seen as a devoted parent – and this too in the overall context of the novel sets her apart. Equally, she has not undergone the same sort of transformation as some of Tolstoy's heroines (most notably Natasha Rostova in *War and Peace*), in the sense that Lyubov is very far from being identified exclusively with the maternal. Thus, as part of the scene which presents the Krutsiferskys as an idyllic ménage, they, in conjunction with Dr Krupov, engage in an extended discussion on love and marriage, in the course of which Lyubov is presented as at least the equal of her husband. Indeed, she herself presents their marriage as a partnership:

> I do not know, Semyon Ivanovich [Krupov] what so frightens you in family life; I've now been married for exactly four years, I feel free, I do not see at all either from my side, nor his, any sacrifices, any burden. (128)

More generally, there is a marked effort to show her precisely as a strong woman. In reality, as de Maegd-Soëp has pointed out,[38] this only amounts to a number of *assertions* rather than dramatically illustrated 'evidence', but there is no mistaking the author's intention in this regard. We have already noted Krupov's warning to Krutsifersky before the marriage ('she is a tiger-cub which still does not know its own strength'), and the narrator reminds us of this point shortly before the flowering of her relationship with Beltov, commenting that 'in the strong nature of his wife he [Krutsifersky] found everything' (158). Beltov is of the same view. He rejects the idea of flirting or seduction because Lyubov is 'so straightforward, so naively natural and so full of strength and intelligence' (159). Even after the catastrophe Beltov and Krupov concur that Krutsifersky's mistake was 'to join his life to a woman of such strength' (203)

But that really is about it. The three male characters and the narrator all agree that Lyubov has great strength but the reader, on the balance of the novel as a whole, is left with rather the opposite impression. As we have already seen, her reaction to the love of Beltov is immediate and utterly (and comically!) dysphoric. Much of the last quarter of the novel (and this is mainly when we see her) is taken up with her displays of femininity and emotional anguish, both in the narrator's account and in the second incursion into her diary, which reveals her to be wracked with guilt and anxiety. Love brings not ecstasy but a crushing sense of her own weakness. More or less every page is taken up with her self-laceration, and images of her suffering. In no sense can it be read as the journal of a strong heroine.

When we return to the narrator's account at the end of the novel, Lyubov has entered completely into the iconography of the woman destroyed: 'Pale, emaciated, with tear-filled eyes, the unhappy Lyubov Aleksandrovna walked on the arm of Krupov; she was feverish, the expression of her eyes was terrible' (204). The final scene shows her now as an invalid, and although the conclusion is for some reason rather vague, it is almost certain that she will shortly die.

A character in Herzen's *The Thieving Magpie* (1848) remarks: 'Everyone has seen with his own eyes that the women of our educated classes are incomparably superior to their husbands'.[39] It would certainly seem to have been his intention in *Who Is To Blame?* to demonstrate the validity of this thesis. Taking the character of Lyubov as a whole, however, it must be said that, while she is superior to Krutsifersky, she cannot be considered the 'strong nature' that she seems to the other characters and to her creator. Far too much of the traditional, vulnerable, weak heroine remains for such a conclusion. Moreover, bearing in mind the misogyny, at times of the most savage intensity, that vitiates almost all other female characters in the book, Alexander Herzen, on this evidence, did little to advance the cause of feminism in Russia, whatever his intentions may have been.

7
The Law of the Father and *Netochka Nezvanova*

In this final chapter I wish to pursue two main strands. Firstly, by way of conclusion, I will draw out some of the principal themes and arguments presented in the earlier chapters, and, secondly, I will offer an analysis of certain aspects of Dostoevsky's *Netochka Nezvanova* (1849) which illuminate these themes in a dramatic and peculiarly intense fashion.

Two quotations could serve as delayed epigraphs for this whole book. Roland Barthes has written:

> The pleasure of the text is . . . an Oedipal pleasure (to denude, to learn the origin and the end), if it is true that every narrative (every unveiling of the truth) is a staging of the (absent, hidden, or hypostatised) father.[1]

Barthes's contention has underlain my plot analyses, as well as the consideration of gender presentation, the images of masculinity and femininity in the works discussed in earlier chapters. In a sense, everything goes back to establishing the 'Law of the Father' and how this is mediated through the stages of the narrative.

In literature which is permeated by this Law, the law of patriarchy, the choices on offer for the female characters (or readers) are strictly limited by both social and literary exigencies (the power of the sociolect as manifested in literature). Elaine Showalter has encapsulated well these limitations as they found expression in nineteenth century literature:

> To waken from the drugged sleep of Victorian womanhood was agonising; in fiction it is much more likely to end in drowning than in discovery . . . [heroines] wake to worlds which offer no places for the women they wish to become; and rather than struggling they die. Female suffering thus becomes a kind of literary commodity which both men and women consume.[2]

The Law of the Father and Netochka Nezvanova 215

Central to my concerns throughout this book have been the ideas and implications suggested by these two statements. More generally, this can be reduced to the twin poles of the book's title: 'narrative' and 'desire'. That is, in analysing the narratives of Russian fiction over a formative thirty-year period, I have endeavoured, whether explicitly or implicitly, to identify whose desire speaks in narrative, while remembering that, in some senses, at least, all desire emanates from the Father. Underpinning this approach is Teresa de Lauretis' magisterial account (from which I have borrowed my title), 'Desire in Narrative'. Near the beginning of this piece de Lauretis puts forward a proposition which I have adopted. She argues that

> subjectivity is engaged in the cogs of narrative and indeed constituted in the relation of narrative, meaning, and desire; so that in the very work of narrativity is the engagement of the subject in certain positionalities of meaning and desire.[3]

These issues are, I would argue, central to any consideration of the narrative process, but are perhaps particularly relevant to the period under review. The 1820s–40s saw in Russian literature a fairly rapid expression of the literary market, great generic experimentation and, most important of all from the present perspective, the first formulations of what became known (from the 1850s) as the 'woman question'. Virtually all the narratives discussed here deal either directly or indirectly with the early phases of this question, while also exploring and expanding the most suitable forms of genres for the investigation of this and other issues.

In the period before Chernyshevsky's *What Is To Be Done?*[4] (1863), or Mikhailov's articles of the late 1850s,[5] the 'woman question' was approached in a somewhat tentative way. That is, mechanisms were explored by means of which women could *adapt to* 'patriarchal power' rather than attempt to go beyond or outside it. In no writer before Chernyshevsky is there any real sense of how this power might be overcome. Indeed, there is no real evidence of a sense that it *could* be overcome. A brief review of the works already discussed will illustrate these propositions, while also illuminating the power of the 'Father' within these texts. (This review will also stand as a concluding résumé for the preceding chapters.)

Thus, in Pushkin we have seen that, firstly, the Circassian Woman *must* commit suicide (quite apart from the typological, narrative reasons) because she has breached the tribal prohibitions, enforced by her father and brother. In turn, the 'Stern Father' of Bakhchisaray, Khan Girey dominates the text (from which he personally is largely absent) and his looming presence leads to the death of both virginal Mariya and passionate Zarema. In *The Gipsies* The Old Man acts as the *raisonneur* and moral arbiter of the discussions of love and sexuality. (It should also be remembered that all four heroines in the three poems die, one by the very drowning of which Showalter speaks.)

In Odoevsky we see a different variation on these themes. *New Year*, from which women are almost completely absent, begins by celebrating all-male camaraderie before providing an elegy for its collapse. *Princess Mimi* dramatises precisely the strategies of the patriarchal sociolect. Ostensibly the account of the life of the eponymous heroine, the tale depicts all too clearly the way women collude with established values (as the 'guardians of morality') to suppress the desires and aspirations of other women. Finally, *Princess Zizi* reveals another common tendency of the period, namely narratorial duplicity. While appearing to valorise the heroic princess who first resists the blandishments of the seducer before defeating him in the law courts, the story equally creates her as one of the many 'identikit' women of the time, that is, an impossible collage of conflicting and irreconcilable stereotypes.

The two women writers included here, Gan and Zhukova, as one might expect, tackle the 'woman question' more courageously and directly. The proto-feminist Elena Gan discovers a female voice in Russian literature, both by her ingenious table-turning and revitalising of plot clichés (especially in *The Locket*) and by allowing women to speak and write: for once we hear the woman's side of the story and it is highly significant that each of the three society tales discussed in Chapter Four ends with a piece of writing by a woman. (And, of course, in two of the stories, *Society's Judgement* and *A Futile Gift* she deals directly with the problems, indeed, the agony, of being a woman writer.) All this said, however, she offers no naive happy endings in this life at least: all her heroines are able to find fulfilment and solace only in the arms of their Saviour.

Mariya Zhukova could be termed more of a 'collaborationist'. Each of the three stories considered certainly does place a woman in the very centre of the narrative. What happiness they do find, however, is entirely within the limits and rules of 'patriarchal power' and is often at the expense of another woman. Baroness Reykhman seeks to find herself in an illicit liaison but her lover Levin colludes with the Baroness's husband (who is also Levin's commanding officer) to defeat her and, in the end, she loses her beloved son as well as unloved husband. (The story is, indeed, an early, miniature version of *Anna Karenina*.) In Zhukova's *The Locket* the two contrasting heroines present different female destinies, the worldly and the spiritual. (As in nearly every text considered, the influence of *Evgeny Onegin* is profound.) Yet both share the same fate, a society marriage of convenience. *The Dacha on the Peterhof Road* has another variation on the theme of contrastive friends. Here Princess Mary (as she becomes) learns the lessons of her more famous name-sake, while callously sacrificing her half-mad friend Zoya on the altar of self-interest and convenience.

Herzen's *Who Is To Blame?* could, perhaps, be retitled as 'On The Eve of the Eve'. The novel depicts three young Russians, the spiritual heroine Lyubov, her Lenskyesque husband Krutsifersky and the superfluous man *sans pareil*, Vladimir Beltov who all vaguely try to anticipate Chernyshevsky's 'new people' by a couple of decades. Each, however, is fatally crippled by their patriarchal (in both senses) background and the story ends tragically. Organising their lives and commenting upon it, Dr Krupov traces his heritage back to the eighteenth-century *raisonneurs*, such as Fonvizin's Starodum, by way of Pushkin's Old Man. But this valorised father (Herzen's *alter ego*) is unable to avert the catastrophe. The old ways, the Law of the Fathers are still too strong.

Given all these considerations, it seems to me highly appropriate to conclude with an account of Dostoevsky's extraordinary early work, *Netochka Nezvanova*.[6] It is a remarkable work in a number of ways. Most obviously, it is one of the very few works in Russian literature in which a male author attempts to write as a woman.[7] The overall plan of the unfinished novel[8] was to have been a *Bildungsroman* (and as such the only work of this type by Dostoevsky ever to reach the printed page[9]), written in maturity or old age by a woman from extremely deprived origins who became a famous artist. (What was completed takes Netochka only to her late teens.) As it stands, the work provides an extremely detailed account of precisely the issues I have been touching upon, namely, how a girl enters the world and attempts to come to terms with it. Even more significantly, the first sections, in particular, offer an analysis (in proto-psychoanalytical terms) of the relationship between the young girl and her 'father' (in reality, her stepfather[10]). This analysis makes the work particularly remarkable, for, although the works already discussed in this volume do show how young women enter the world of the 'fathers', actual accounts of father–daughter relationships are almost entirely missing. Looking at *Netochka Nezvanova* more broadly it also offers a fascinating study of another, more symbolic aspect of the same dynamics, namely, how the young woman enters, precisely, the 'symbolic order', through education and, in particular, reading.

That the work will conform to Barthes's model, and will also deal with the daughter's positionality within paternal presences and absences, is made startlingly apparent in the opening lines:

> I do not remember my father. He died when I was two years old. My mother married for a second time. This second marriage brought her much grief, although she married for love. My stepfather was a musician. (142)

Although the overall project may have been conceived as a female *Bildungsroman* what we have concerns not so much Netochka herself, but the power others had over her. And, to begin with at least, the story is conceived of as an Oedipal quest, both for the lost father and 'to learn the origin and the end' of the (second) father.[11] Other details demand our attention. The first ('true') father died when his daughter was too young to remember him: in that sense, he is lost forever, beyond recall and his existence leaves no trace in the writer's memory. He is never mentioned again and this solitary reference to him, which is the very first word of the Russian text stands as an emblematic sign. He is the first person to be spoken of, but then disappears. On the other hand, his death is of significance, in that this event had led to Netochka becoming fatherless and this in turn led to the initiation of the action.[12] Equally significant is the relative absence of the autobiographical 'I'. Apart from noting her age at her father's death (and the indirect self reference in 'my') the writer does not play a part in these lapidary, agenda-setting three sentences, surely a curiously oblique way to begin an autobiography.[13] And, indeed, this is the point. In order to know the daughter, we must first learn about the father(s). Finally, we should note that *family relations* are the key to this brief prologue: as Mochulsky has remarked, *Netochka Nezvanova* is the first treatment in Russian literature of 'the problem of the Russian family'[14] and, as such, this early, unfinished work anticipates one of Dostoevsky's central concerns which was to receive its culminating treatment thirty years later in *The Brothers Karamazov*.

The fourth sentence of the work is also striking. As we shall see, the first section of the work (Chapters I–III) reveal Efimov, Netochka's step-father, to be an almost completely loathesome, sadistic, megalomaniac drunkard (and more). Yet the autobiographer, a person described by Victor Terras as 'a kindly, mature, cultured lady of great understanding and tolerance for the foibles of the people around her',[15] is still, after several decades, able to state: 'His fate is very remarkable: he was the strangest, the most *wonderful* man of all those I have known' (142 – my italics). As a child the girl had fallen in love with (or rather, been seduced by[16]) her father and the impression of this childhood passion has remained all her life.

The first few pages of the narrative then concentrate almost exclusively on the early life of Efimov and the disreputable events that had led him to penury in St Petersburg, and to marry Netochka's widowed mother (who is to remain unnamed). Nearly all of Chapter I is, in fact, taken up with recounting the story of Efimov's fall from grace into degenerate despair and drunkenness. There is no need for us to go into details here. The central point is that the writer of these notes makes it patently clear that Efimov *is* a scoundrel and wastrel *before* we learn of Netochka's love for him: this renders her passion all the more remarkable, his powers of seduction all the more striking.

After his arrival in St Petersburg several years are skipped before a fellow musician B. (who had related the earlier events to Netochka) meets up with Efimov once more, by chance. Efimov's decline had become even more marked and he regales B. with an account of his marriage to 'an old bag, a cook, uneducated, a coarse woman' (153). He claims that his 'wife constituted all his misfortune and grief and that marriage had completely killed all his talent' (ibid.). These notes of abuse and recrimination are to be often repeated, and echoed by Netochka. When B. visits Efimov he finds all three living in a single garret-room and he learns the story of Netochka's mother. This story, significantly, is passed over in a single page, as opposed to the dozen or so devoted to Efimov. The very structure of the tale, then, privileges the father and marginalises the mother, quite apart from the denigration of her from both Efimov and her own daughter (who introduces her by stating that 'she was an unhappy woman' (154), a statement, it seems to me, of reproach rather than compassion). This differential focus is important. By this I mean that the older Netochka (or rather Dostoevsky) *could have* told the mother's story, rather than the father's, or at least given them equal weight. That she chooses not to reveals, I think, both the author's sleight-of-hand (even daughters think mothers are unimportant), as well as the power of the father's seduction of the daughter. Even many years later, she still sees the world, remembers the past through *his* eyes: she has been seduced into the patriarchal discourse. Thus, at this point and for much of this first section, Netochka's mother remains a shadowy, dull figure, completely overshadowed (in the narrator's presentation of the 'facts') by her sadistic husband. In this way the text is structured in classically Oedipal terms in that the girl identifies with and privileges the phallus, at the expense of the mother's body.[17] (It is worth recalling that in Gan and Zhukova the valorised relationship is with the mother: their daughters' fathers are usually completely absent or shadowy, background figures. Which version is closer to the 'truth' is for the reader to judge.)

Despite all her torments, we are led to believe, the mother 'loved him passionately right up to her death' (155). But we see little evidence of love on either side, and most of the remaining pages of this first section of *Netochka Nezvanova* are taken up with sadomasochistic rituals. The mother slaves to support them all, while Efimov drinks, complains and taunts his wife. Even when the kindly and magnanimous B. gets some work for him he gives not a copeck to the 'eternally ill, eternally suffering' (ibid.) woman. On the contrary, in fact: he steals his wife's earnings to pay for his drink. Two more years pass (Netochka is now six); Efimov has lost his job and continues his revolting behaviour. Finally Chapter I comes to an end, and, in line with the opening sentences, nearly all of its sixteen pages have been focused on Efimov, the wicked but much-loved stepfather. The last sentence of the chapter tells us that 'this most wonderful man' 'was the cause of the death of my poor mother' (158).

Chapter II also begins with a remarkable statement: 'I began to remember myself very late, only from my ninth year' (ibid.). In part, perhaps, this is by way of an explanation, even an apology, for the first chapter, for writing so much *not* about herself. At the same time, much potentially invaluable material has been lost, or rather *repressed*. Presumably, or at least arguably, these omitted years were precisely the years when Netochka would have been close to her mother, yet because this material is withheld (either because of her faulty memory or because of Dostoevsky's trickery) we will scarcely ever see the power of maternal love. Like the first, 'true' father, it is lost forever, almost without trace.

That repression is at work is also evidenced by some dim memories of earlier years that she is able to dredge up. Significantly, given the strikingly pre-Freudian ambience of the whole story, Netochka remarks: 'It's true, I can remember something from even earlier times, *as if in a dream*' (ibid. – my italics). She then goes on to recall a time when she had been unwell, injured on the street by a horse. (More Freudian resonances!) She then details her childish anxieties, but adds that she had not dared 'to wake mummy, from which I conclude that I feared her more than any fear' (159). Because no etiology is advanced for this dread of the mother (the past and any explicatory circumstances are repressed) we are left with a primal, unexplained (and inexplicable) dread and rejection of the mother, and indeed, of her body, given that the scene touched upon here has the mother and child actually sharing the same bed. This primal dread, without any explanation or motivation, is to be returned to again and again.

From this age, of about eight or nine, Netochka begins to develop fast. Quite apart from this 'unnatural' terror of her mother (which is repeated three times on one page as part of her earliest conscious memories (159)), the girl becomes exposed to other strange experiences. As Terras notes,[18] the later erotic passion between Netochka and Katya (both pre-teens) is described entirely as an adult relationship. Netochka herself anticipates this reaction as she begins to introduce her developing relationship with her father: 'I was developing rapidly, unexpectedly and many completely unchildish impressions became terribly accessible to me' (159). The rest of this first section will indeed introduce one of Dostoevsky's central themes of his later years – the sadistic torture, perversion and corruption of childish innocence. Very soon Efimov, thought by Netochka to be her real father at this stage of her life, and persistently termed *batyushka* ('little father'/'daddy'),[19] begins his seduction of his step-daughter: 'Here *batyushka* called me over, kissed me, stroked my hair, sat me on his lap, and I firmly, sweetly pressed myself to his breast' (159–60). The eroticism here (and on many subsequent occasions) is unmistakable[20] (particularly in the child's willing, passionate response). These scenes certainly teeter on the brink of child pornography.[21] Equally significant is the narrator's commentary on the scene: 'This was, perhaps, the first parental[22] caress, perhaps, precisely because I began to remember everything so distinctly from that time' (160). Even taking into account the caveats in the last clause, I feel this is another instance of authorial duplicitly. Is it really likely that she would have received no caresses from her mother? Leaving this aside, the effect of this statement is yet again to repress the mother ('she never loved me') and to privilege the (worthless) father. We should also note Netochka's next remark:

> I also noticed that I deserved father's kindness because I had stood up for him, and now for the first time, I think, the idea struck me that he endured much and bore a lot of grief from mummy. (ibid.)

This seems to me an evocation of the classic Oedipal situation from the girl's perspective. She protects the father against the mother and, thereby, she seeks to replace the mother in her father's affections. As Julia Kristeva puts it:

> But the daughter, on the other hand, *is rewarded* by the symbolic order when *she identifies with the father*: only here is she recognised not as herself but in opposition to her rival, the other with a vagina who experiences jouissance.[23] (My italics)

And, indeed, Netochka is rewarded by her father who behaves revoltingly to everyone (especially the mother) but lavishes his erotic love on his (step) daughter. She, in turn, rewards him by offering him *maternal* protection. As she puts it herself: 'there began in me a kind of boundless love for my father . . . a kind of compassionate *maternal* feeling' (160 – italics in original).

The seduction of the daughter, then, takes place. But it is not only physical conquest, for her mind too is shaped by Efimov so that she identifies completely with his view of the 'strict', unloving mother, and of the world more generally. She takes, as she puts it, 'the wondrous fairy-tale' that her father frequently recounts 'for the pure truth' (ibid.). This, in a sense, would be a natural, 'normal' childhood development, without particular consequences. However, and again Netochka is explicit about this, this is the source of her rejection of her mother: 'And as much as I became attached to my father, to the same extent I came to hate my poor mother' (161). Presumably, indeed, this is also the mechanism that has led to her repression of earlier memories, of her infantile love for her mother and her mother's body. The later Netochka, the actual autobiographer, wonders where such feelings came from and regrets these feelings for her mother, but this seems to me another piece of authorial duplicitly. If the later version of Netochka now sees the truth of her childhood situation, why does she continue to repress and marginalise her mother? What arises as a result of these machinations, however, is a perfect case-study of the girl's identification with the father and the (patriarchal) symbolic order. That is, her paltry apology aside, the mature woman narrator remains faithful to her seduction by the father: she remains identified with the phallus.

Soon, more notes are sounded, more stages of the seduction take place. Her father tells her he is an artiste, and this word takes on a magical resonance. Moreover, he tells her that he will at last become a *great* artist once the mother is dead. At first Netochka is horrified at such ideas, but soon comes to share Efimov's fantasy. The power of this proto-Freudian fantasy goes one stage further. When the mother is dead, daughter and father will go away together and she will therefore replace/become the mother. Frequently, Netochka does express sorrow, regret and guilt over her feelings for her mother. Even as a child guilt had oppressed her, she had felt the injustice of her feelings towards her, but, nevertheless, she can recall no scenes of affection between them. Once again, the power of the paternal seduction, and the consequent repression is evident. Occasionally, indeed, she is aware of this. One particular incident is recalled when her mother does caress her, calling her by the affectionate diminutive that she had invented (Netochka from Anna) but Netochka the child stubbornly will not reciprocate. A flash of insight is recorded:

> Yes, this could not have been a natural hardening within me. She could not have so aroused me against her entirely by her severity towards me. No! *I had been corrupted by my fantastic, exclusive love for my father.* (169 – my italics)

This leads on to another memory, of times when she had slept with her mother and clung to her for reassurance. But such moments, such memories of tenderness are rare, and greatly overshadowed by scenes of love and passion with her father, who is not, it should be noted, blamed for creating this 'corruption' in his stepdaughter.

On the contrary, the mature narrator persists in invoking scenes of ecstasy with the father. When she is about nine years old, Efimov introduces her to the 'symbolic order' more literally by teaching her to read. (Again, one asks, is it not more likely that such education would have happened earlier, at the hands of the mother, who, after all, had worked precisely as a governess?) In the learning process, the girl strives once more to win his love and is rewarded with ecstatic *jouissance*:[24]

> This was the happiest period of my life at that time. When he praised me for my comprehension, stroked my hair and kissed me, I would immediately begin *to cry from ecstasy*.
>
> (165 – my italics)

This liquefaction is surely significant! Indeed, the fairly obvious orgasmic significance of the child's reaction becomes even more apparent in a later scene of intimacy between the two. Netochka has been ill (as a result of stealing money from her mother to pay for Efimov's drink). She again stubbornly refuses to accept her mother's compassionate affection and when she finally leaves, Efimov feels free to indulge himself: 'he no longer restrained himself. He began to kiss me in such a way that I was in some kind of hysterical ecstasy, I laughed and cried at the same time' (171). This in turn leads on to another climactic (if I may so put it) moment, when Efimov shows her, for the first time, his instrument, the violin which he reverentially takes in his own hands before allowing Netochka to touch and kiss it. A very curious detail surely makes the significance of this instrument apparent: 'Seeing that I wanted to examine it [the violin] more closely he led me to *mother's bed* and put the violin in my hands' (172 – my italics). Once more, Netochka has become the mother, as she holds her father's instrument by her mother's bed. As this second chapter closes, Netochka recapitulates her growing 'passion' (as she calls it) for Efimov, before leading on, in Chapter III, (which will close this period in her life), to the 'terrible catastrophe' of her mother's death and stepfather's disappearance and death.

This third and final section of Part One of *Netochka Nezvanova* largely replicates the dynamics of the first two chapters. Firstly, it should be noted again that, although this is supposed to be *her Bildungsroman* autobiography, and is now written from her point of view, the narrative is, in fact, largely structured by and around events in Efimov's life, on this occasion, his final disastrous attempts to prove himself a great artiste. Again, even though she notes in passing that her mother is so ill she can hardly walk, the action and attention (and love) are focused on the father. There are more scenes of physical intimacy between the man and child, again she steals from her mother for her father. On the other hand she does finally begin to see through him, to realise that he is only using her and his power over her. This realisation, however, had not prevented the later recorder of these scenes calling him 'the most wonderful man' she had ever known: the past has not been reinterpreted in the light of this realisation. And it does not prevent her either from committing the crime of robbery from her sick mother. All of this may be psychologically accurate. What does strain credulity, however, is the mother's delighted reaction when there is a sudden, if short-lived turn in Efimov's fortunes. Netochka notes: 'Even now, despite eight whole years of uninterrupted agony and sufferings, her heart had still not altered: she could still love him!' (181). And even though she is grievously ill she gets up to iron his shirt-front, tie his tie for him and generally fuss over him. To the end she is presented as a perfect masochist. After Efimov leaves, at long last there is a scene of real physical affection between mother and daughter: 'Then she would come up to me and with insane love kiss me, kiss my hands, drench them with her tears, beg forgiveness . . .' (182). But it is too late.

The mother soon dies, whether murdered or by suicide is unclear, Efimov returns, a broken man. After some grisly scenes around the mother's body, Netochka and Efimov finally do leave together, only for Efimov to abandon her. She collapses and is taken in by a kindly family, amidst which Part Two of her life will unfold. Before this, however, the adult Netochka offers a page-long summary of this period of her life. And this is entirely in keeping with the forty-odd pages which had preceded it. Nearly the entire recapitulation is devoted to an intense valediction to her stepfather, in which he is constructed as a tragic hero. No mention is made of herself or of the corruption of her innocence he had enacted. Almost no mention is made of her poor mother either, except *en passant*, where she is dismissed as 'she whose life hung over him for so many years, who did not let him live, she, on whose death, according to his own blind belief, he was, suddenly, in a flash, to be resurrected, – she died' (188). This really is quite astonishing! What it does appear to show, however, is that the seduction of the daughter's body and, especially, her mind, has worked, for the mature author of this autobiography remains faithful to the memory of the father and to his view of reality.

For all the implausibility of certain aspects of the tale (and for all the unpleasant perversity of this and the remaining two sections) *Netochka Nezvanova* is a remarkable piece of writing, especially in its emotional intensity and its anticipation of Freudian (and post-Freudian) thinking. Certainly it does convey, in a highly dramatic way, the procrustean agonies of a girl as she seeks to become a woman in a patriarchal world. Moreover, it reveals the way the fathers, who organise this world to their own advantage, seduce their daughters into their symbolic order. And this is without doubt one of the overriding themes of the literature of the period. Other writers address this theme much more obliquely; some show rather more optimism. But none, and this is perhaps realistic, was able to show a way out of the hegemonic order that surrounded and ensnared women. The Real Day was not yet dawning.

Notes

1 INTRODUCTION

1. Other works which deserve mention (and which predate mine) are Barbara Heldt, *Terrible Perfection. Women and Russian Literature* (Indiana University Press, Bloomington and Indianapolis, 1987) and Carolina de Maegd-Soëp, *The Emancipation of Women in Russian Literature and Society* (Slavica Gandensia Analecta I, Ghent State University, Ghent, 1978).
2. I should, of course, mention that Pushkin is rightly seen as much as an ending as a beginning, the culminating zenith of the literary and cultural development of eighteenth-century Russia.
3. In the work of the Russian Formalists (especially that of Tynyanov) it has been argued that each generation of writers returns to the 'grandfathers' to oust its immediately preceding 'fathers'. Certainly it is the case for Russian literature of the 1830s and 1840s that writers attempted to 'dethrone' Pushkin, as well as paying their dues to him, by a return to the Sentimentalist and Gothic traditions which Pushkin himself had parodied.
4. The claim of Carolina de Maegd-Soëp: see her *Emancipation*, p. 124. In fact, she states: 'Not without reason he is called "the first Russian feminist"!' Regrettably, she gives no reference for this declaration.
5. For an analysis of this period see, amongst many other works, my *Writers and Society During the Rise of Russian Realism* (Macmillan, London, 1980) and William Mills Todd III, *Fiction and Society in the Age of Pushkin. Ideology, Institutions, and Narrative* (Harvard University Press, Cambridge, Mass. and London, England, 1986).
6. This terms derives, of course, from the memoirs of Pavel Annenkov, *The Remarkable Decade* (Ann Arbor, 1968). There are innumerable works which discuss this period: see, for example, Isaiah Berlin, *Russian Thinkers* (Penguin, Harmondsworth, 1978), especially pp. 114–209; Eugene Lampert, *Studies in Rebellion* (London, 1957); T.G. Masaryk, *The Spirit of Russia* vol. I (London, 1919) and Martin Malia, *Alexander Herzen and The Birth of Russian Socialism* (The Universal Library, Grosset and Dunlap, New York, 1965).
7. For an account of this see H.A. Aplin, *M.S. Zhukova and E.A. Gan. Women Writers and Female Protagonists, 1837–1843* (Unpublished PhD Dissertation, U.E.A., 1988).
8. For discussions of this, see the works cited in note 5 above.
9. There are, of course, discussions of this later in the book: see especially Chapters 4 and 5. For an excellent account of the background, see Richard Stites, *The Women's Liberation Movement in Russia. Feminism, Nihilism and Bolshevism 1860–1930* (Princeton University Press, Princeton, New Jersey, 1978), especially pp. 3–28.
10. The following section is based on the Introduction to my earlier *Women in Russian Literature: 1780–1863*. I have taken the liberty of partially

repeating this material because what I said there is still relevant to my considerations in the present volume.
11. See Judith Fetterley, *The Resisting Reader. A Feminist Approach to American Fiction* (Bloomington and London, 1978), pp. 28–9.
12. See Teresa de Lauretis, 'Desire in Narrative' in *Alice Doesn't. Feminism, Semiotics, Cinema* (Macmillan, London, 1984), pp. 103–57 (p. 111).
13. See Michel Foucault, *The History of Sexuality*, vol. I, *An Introduction* (London, 1979), p. 69.
14. See Nancy K. Miller, *The Heroine's Text: Readings in the French and English Novel 1722–1782* (New York, 1980), p. 159.
15. See Teresa de Lauretis, *Technologies of Gender. Essays on Theory, Film, and Fiction* (Macmillan, London, 1987).
16. Ibid., pp. 1–30.
17. Ibid., p. 3.
18. Quoted ibid., p. 14 (See Foucault, op. cit., p. 104).
19. Ibid., p. 4.
20. Ibid., p. 5.
21. For a discussion of the similar concept of 'hegemony', derived from Gramsci, see Andrew (1988), pp. 3–4.
22. See de Lauretis (1987), p. 6.
23. For a discussion of woman as Other, see Andrew (1988) especially pp. 4–5. (This concept is, of course, derived from the work of Simone de Beauvoir.)
24. See de Lauretis (1987), pp. 19–20. The reader will find further discussion of de Lauretis's work, especially the interconnections between narrative, gender and desire, in Section 1 of Chapter 2. This discussion is placed there because it is of particular relevance to the work discussed (*The Prisoner of the Caucasus*) but I will also be returning to de Lauretis's seminal work throughout the present volume.
25. These ideas are most clearly illustrated in Section 1 of Chapter 2 of the present work: see also Andrew (1988), pp. 113–22 and my '"The Blind Will See": Narrative and Gender in *Taman*', in *Russian Literature* (1992).
26. For further illustration of this theme, see Andrew (1988) *passim*.
27. For an illuminating discussion of gossip and gossips see John Forrester, *The Seductions of Psychoanalysis. Freud, Lacan and Derrida* (Cambridge University Press, Cambridge, New York, Port Chester, Melbourne, Sydney, 1990), pp. 243–59, especially pp. 258–9.
28. For discussion of this methodological framework, see Joe Andrew (ed.), *The Structural Analysis of Russian Narrative Fiction* (Essays in Poetics Publications, Keele, 1984), especially pp. i–xxix and L. Michael O'Toole, *Structure, Style and Interpretation in the Russian Short Story* (New Haven and London, 1982).
29. Andrew, *Women in Russian Literature*, p. 11.

2 PUSHKIN'S SOUTHERN POEMS

1. See Stephanie Sandler, *Distant Pleasures, Alexander Pushkin and the Writing of Exile* (Stanford: Stanford University Press, 1989), p. 141.

2. All references to the work are to the following edition: A.S. Pushkin, *Sobranie Sochinenii v desyati tomakh* (Moscow, 1959–62), t. 3: pp. 87–120. All translations throughout the present work are my own, and line references will be given in the text. (For later prose works page references will also be given in the text.) I am grateful to the editors of *Studies in Poetics. A Commemorative Volume for Krystyna Pomorska (1928–1986)*, edited by Elena Semeka-Pankratov (Slavika, forthcoming), for permission to reproduce material from an earlier version of this section.
3. Sandler (op. cit., p. 148) also remarks on 'captives', observing that 'That women enter the narrative as captured cannot be unimportant in this tale about a Russian captive'.
4. See V.M. Zhirmunsky, *Bayron i Pushkin* (Leningrad, 1924, reprinted München, 1970), p. 143.
5. See Ju. Lotman, 'The Origin of Plot in the Light of Typology', in *Poetics Today*, vol. 1, nos 1–2 (Autumn 1979), pp. 161–84 and T. de Lauretis, 'Desire in Narrative', in *Alice Doesn't: Feminism, Semiotics, Cinema* (London, 1984), pp. 103–57 and T. de Lauretis, *Technologies of Gender: Essays on Theory, Film and Fiction* (London, 1989). See also the Introduction of the present work.
6. See Lotman, p. 167.
7. Ibid., p. 168.
8. Ibid., p. 173.
9. See de Lauretis (1984), pp. 104–5.
10. Ibid., p. 106.
11. Ibid., p. 111. At this point de Lauretis' argument is influenced by S. Felman, 'Rereading Femininity', *Yale French Studies*, no. 62 (1981), pp. 19 and 21.
12. For a discussion of similar points, see Sandler, p. 154.
13. See de Lauretis (1984), p. 115 and A. Shukman, 'The Short Story, Theory, Analysis, Interpretation' in *Essays in Poetics*, 2, 2 (1977), p. 77. Each writer derives her argument from Propp.
14. See de Lauretis (1984), p. 119.
15. Quoted ibid., p. 103.
16. Sandler sees the Southern Poems in remarkably similar terms (although her approach is not typological): 'The plots of sexual involvement become contests for authority, games or battles in which the conclusion can only be victory or defeat' (p. 144).
17. See de Lauretis (1989), p. 19.
18. Ibid., p. 5.
19. See S. de Beauvoir, *The Second Sex* (London, 1972) *passim* for a discussion of woman as the Other, from a different perspective.
20. See de Lauretis (1989), p. 14.
21. Ibid., p. 20.
22. See Lotman, p. 183.
23. See Sandler, p. 141.
24. Ibid., p. 148.
25. Sandler writes 'for the Russian captive, these people are almost universally male' (p. 146). I would disagree that this is the Prisoner's perspective, but rather the narrator's (and, therefore, *ours*).

26. Sandler makes the same point, p. 148.
27. For a discussion of this tendency in Russian literature, see my *Women in Russian Literature, 1780–1863* (London, 1988).
28. See Sandler, p. 148.
29. Ibid., p. 149. These actions have other associations which will be discussed later.
30. Sandler writes: 'The Circassian woman is represented as a creature of sexual passion, and that alone' (p. 149). I would not agree with the last point, as I argue in the main text. Pushkin's friend, Vyazemsky seems to concur with Sandler's judgment: 'We know only one thing about her, that she has loved, and we are satisfied.' Quoted in Sandler, p. 235, n. 7.
31. Line 421, as a gerundive subordinate clause, could be applied either to the Prisoner or to the woman. (Sandler (p. 149) applies it to the Prisoner.) In the overall context of my reading I would argue that it is more appropriate to apply it to the woman.
32. Sandler (p. 150) also sees traces of male Byronism in the Circassian woman, although she makes a rather different point.
33. See J. Bayley, *Pushkin. A Contemporary Commentary* (Cambridge, 1971), p. 101.
34. Sandler (pp. 156–7) offers an excellent, broadly-based interpretation of this situation.
35. On this point Sandler writes: 'The assurance of previous chastity proves not that she is uninterested in sex, but that she has always thought of herself as defined by some deferred sexual involvement' (p. 149). I am not sure on what this latter point is based.
36. Sandler (p. 153) also discusses her initial silence, although she makes a rather different point.
37. Ibid.
38. Ibid., pp. 150, 157.
39. See Zhirmunsky, p. 144.
40. See my *Women in Russian Literature, 1780–1863*, pp. 39 and 59–60.
41. See Bayley, p. 75.
42. See Andrew, *passim*.
43. See Sandler, p. 157.
44. Ibid., p. 153.
45. Ibid., p. 149 for similar, but also different points.
46. I am indebted to Sandler, pp. 154–61 for the ensuing discussion.
47. Ibid., p. 140.
48. See Sandler, p. 158.
49. For a discussion of men's friendships in this age see S. Karlinsky, *The Sexual Labyrinth of Nikolai Gogol* (Cambridge, Mass., 1976) and Sandler, p. 236, n. 16.
50. Sandler writes: 'the masculine values of friendship and war are exalted with great intensity' (p. 154). See also my *Women in Russian Literature, 1780–1863*, pp. 43–8, 70–2 for discussions of the male/male relations in *Evgeny Onegin* and *A Hero of Our Time*.
51. See de Lauretis (1984), p. 148.
52. See Sandler, p. 146 and n. 24 above.

Notes to Chapter 2

53. See Sandler, p. 153. Again I would disagree with her emphasis.
54. For a discussion of horses and other animals in *A Hero of Our Time*, see my *Women in Russian Literature, 1780–1863*, p. 63.
55. Sandler (p. 147) translates 'podruga' merely as 'companion' which, I think, misses the point.
56. See Sandler, p. 148.
57. Ibid., p. 151.
58. Pushkin wrote of his hero in 1822: 'I wanted in him to portray this indifference to life and its pleasures, this premature senility of the soul, which have become the distinguishing features of nineteenth century youth' (Works, vol. 3, p. 396).
59. See Sandler, p. 151, although, again, her interpretation is somewhat different from mine.
60. Pushkin wrote in February 1823 to Vyazemsky concerning the poem's dénouement: 'Try jumping in yourself – I have swum in the rivers of the Caucasus . . . My Captive is an intelligent and sensible fellow. He is not in love with the Circassian girl and he did right not to drown himself' (Quoted in Bayley, pp. 78–9).
61. Significant thematic and structural use is also made of this word in *The Gipsies*.
62. Walter Vickery finds that 'the "Epilogue" runs counter to the spirit of the preceding narrative' (Quoted in Sandler, p. 237, n. 25). I would disagree. See Sandler, pp. 161–5 for an excellent discussion of the Epilogue.
63. Sandler's translation of this verb (p. 162) as 'plucked', again misses the force (literally!) of the Russian.
64. For a discussion of flowers as symbolic of women, see my *Women in Russian Literature, 1780–1863*, pp. 24 and 185, n. 32.
65. See Lotman, p. 171.
66. Ibid.
67. Ibid.
68. For a discussion of this see my *Women in Russian Literature, 1780–1863*, p. 65.
69. See de Lauretis (1984), p. 139.
70. Sandler (p. 150) argues that 'her fate has all along been determined by his egoism'. I would argue that it *is* determined, but rather by her narrative situation.
71. See de Lauretis (1984), p. 112.
72. Ibid., p. 133.
73. See E. Showalter, 'Towards a Feminist Poetics', in M. Jacobus (ed.), *Women Writing and Writing About Women* (London, 1979), p. 31.
74. For a discussion of this motif, see Sandler, p. 152.
75. See de Lauretis (1984), p. 110.
76. See Sandler, p. 141.
77. Ibid., p. 150.
78. All references to this work are to A.S. Pushkin, *Sobranie sochinenii v desyati tomakh* (Moscow, 1959–62), t. 3, pp. 143–58. I am grateful to the editors of *Russian Literature* for permission to re-use some material from an earlier version of this section.

79. See de Lauretis (1984), pp. 118–19.
80. See Lotman, op. cit., pp. 161–2, and M. Daly, *Gyn/Ecology* (London, 1979), pp. 107–312.
81. For Foucault's theories of the panopticon see M. Foucault, *Discipline and Punish: The Birth of the Prison* (New York, 1977), pp. 195–228.
82. For a discussion of this syndrome in Karamzin's *Poor Liza*, see Andrew, op. cit., pp. 22–6.
83. de Lauretis (1989), p. 150.
84. For discussions of the heroines in these terms, see J. Bayley, op. cit., pp. 83–5, and V.M. Zhirmunsky, op. cit., p. 143.
85. For a discussion of the *topos* of the nocturnal visit in Byron and Pushkin, see Zhirmunsky, op. cit., p. 114.
86. For a discussion of the role of the past in the characterisation of the heroines see Bayley, op. cit., p. 84. For a general discussion of this theme, see de Lauretis (1984), p. 150.
87. For a discussion of the relations between the two women, see Bayley, op. cit., p. 84.
88. For a general discussion of this, see de Lauretis (1984), pp. 139–40.
89. See Lotman, op. cit., p. 173.
90. See de Lauretis (1984), p. 110.
91. See Bayley, op. cit., p. 84, and Zhirmunsky, op. cit., p. 145 for different discussions of this.
92. For a more extended discussion of voyeurism (in Lermontov's *A Hero of Our Time*) see my *Women in Russian Literature, 1780–1863*, Chapter 4.
93. For a rather different view of this scene see Bayley, op. cit., p. 85.
94. See Zhirmunsky, op. cit., p. 143.
95. Bayley, op. cit., p. 84.
96. Zhirmunsky, op. cit., pp. 145 and 162.
97. See Zhirmunsky, op. cit., pp. 143 and 162.
98. See Bayley, op. cit., p. 84.
99. All references to this work are to the following edition: A.S. Pushkin, *Sobranie Sochinenii v desyati tomakh* (Moscow, 1959–62), t. 3, p. 159–80. I am indebted to the editors of *The Semantic Analysis of Literary Texts* for permission to use some of the material from an earlier version of this section.
100. See J.L.I. Fennell, 'Pushkin' in J.L.I. Fennell (ed.), *Nineteenth-Century Russian Literature* (London, 1973), pp. 17 and 24.
101. Ibid., p. 24.
102. See V.M. Zhirmunsky, pp. 140–5.
103. See J. Bayley, p. 101.
104. See A.D.P. Briggs, *Alexander Pushkin: A Critical Study* (London, 1983), p. 102 for a brief discussion of this poeticism in Pushkin's literary development.
105. See Zhirmunsky, p. 143 for the Byronic source of this cliché. Zarema, of course, is a similar type.
106. See Briggs, pp. 100–2.
107. See Fennell, p. 21.
108. Ibid., p. 22.

109. See ibid., pp. 23–4 for a discussion of the language used by and about Aleko.
110. See ibid., p. 24.
111. The words *lepet/lepetan'yem* are almost exclusively used in relation to children.
112. See de Lauretis (1984), p. 112. Her argument at this point is influenced by the work of Greimas.
113. See ibid., pp. 121–2 for a general discussion of these ideas.
114. See de Lauretis (1984), p. 134.
115. See Fennell, p. 23 for a brief discussion of this anthropomorphism.
116. Kristeva sums up rather better than I could the broader significance of the gender implications of these relationships:

> The economy of this system requires that women be excluded from the single true and legislating principle, namely the Word, as well as from the (always paternal) element that gives procreation a social value: they are excluded from knowledge and power. The myth of the relationship between Eve and the serpent is the best summary of this exclusion. The serpent stands for the opposite of God, since he tempts Eve to transgress His prohibition. *But he is also Adam's repressed desire to transgress, that which he dares not carry out, and which is his shame.* (My italics)

See J. Kristeva, 'About Chinese Women' in T. Moi (ed.), *The Kristeva Reader* (Oxford, 1986), pp. 138–59 (p. 143).
117. Quoted in de Lauretis (1984), p. 111, who in turn is quoting from Felman.
118. See Fennell, p. 16.
119. Ibid., p. 21.
120. See Briggs, p. 102.
121. Ibid.

3 V.F. ODOEVSKY AND THE TWO PRINCESSES

1. For a discussion of this, see my *Women in Russian Literature, 1780–1863*, pp. 112–54 and Carolina de Maëgd-Soep, *The Emancipation of Women in Russian Literature and Society*.
2. See Andrew, op. cit.
3. For details of Odoevsky's life and career, see Neil Cornwell, *V.F. Odoevsky. His life, times and milieu* (The Athlone Press: London, 1986). More particularly for his publication output, see p. 371.
4. For details of this see Chapters 4 and 5 of the present volume, as well as H.A. Aplin, *M.S. Zhukova and E.A. Gan. Women Writers and Female Protagonists, 1837–1843* (Unpublished PhD, U.E.A., 1988) and Richard Stites, *The Women's Liberation Movement in Russia: Feminism, Nihilism and Bolshevism (1860–1930)* (Princeton, 1978), pp. 23–5.
5. For the best account of this, see Stites, op. cit., *passim*.

6. The texts of these stories which I will be using are all in V.F. Odoevsky, *Sobraniye Sochinenii v Dvukh Tomakh* (Khudozhestvennaya Literatura: Moscow, 1981), ed. V.I. Sakharov. *Princess Mimi* is in vol. II, pp. 220–57; *Princess Zizi* is ibid., pp. 258–303, and *New Year* is ibid., pp. 35–42.
7. This is not as obvious as it sounds. Lermontov's *Princess Mary*, for example, is not so much the story of this young woman, but, rather, the title announces her as the object of Pechorin's quest/seduction. A similar instance is Turgenev's *Asya*.
8. Cornwell, op. cit., pp. 51–2.
9. For a discussion of the phallic implications of this implement, see my '"The Blind Will See": Narrative and Gender in Lermontov's *Taman*', forthcoming in *Russian Literature*.
10. For discussions of male friendships in this period, see Simon Karlinsky, *The Sexual Labyrinth of Nikolai Gogol* (Cambridge, Mass., 1976), Stephanie Sandler, *Distant Pleasures. Alexander Pushkin and the Writing of Exile* (Stanford: Stanford University Press, 1989), p. 236, n. 16, as well as Chapter 2 of the present work.
11. For a discussion of this phrase, and its place in a typological model of plot development, see Yury Lotman, 'The Origin of Plot in the Light of Typology' in *Poetics Today*, Vol. 1, Nos. 1–2 (Autumn, 1979), pp. 161–84, especially p. 168, as well as Section 1 of Chapter 2 of the present work.
12. See, for example, E. Ann Kaplan's remark: 'For Lacan, woman cannot enter the world of the symbolic, of language, because at the very moment of the acquisition of language, she learns that she lacks the phallus, the symbol that sets language going through a recognition of difference; her relation to language is a negative one, a lack.' See E. Ann Kaplan, 'Is the Gaze Male?' in Ann Snitow, Christine Stansell, Sharon Thompson (eds), *Desire. The Politics of Sexuality* (Virago: London, 1984), pp. 321–8 (p. 321). See also Chapter 4, pp. 131–8 of the present work for Gan's treatment of this theme in *A Futile Gift*.
13. For a definition of this term, see Maggie Humm, *The Dictionary of Feminist Theory* (Harvester Wheatsheaf: New York, London, Toronto, Sydney, Tokyo, 1989), p. 163.
14. For a discussion of this theme, see Simon Karlinsky, op. cit., and my *Women in Russian Literature*, pp. 86–101.
15. For a discussion of the changing social composition of the literary world in the 1830s, see my *Russian Writers and Society During the Rise of Russian Realism* (Macmillan: London, 1980), especially pp. 114–50, Eugene Lampert, *Studies in Rebellion* (London, 1957) and Martin Malia, *Alexander Herzen and the Birth of Russian Socialism* (Harvard University Press, 1965).
16. This poem was written in 1836 by Pushkin for the jubilee reunion of former pupils of the Tsarskoye Selo Lycée. At the gathering on October 19 1836 Pushkin was unable to complete his reading of the poem because of the emotional distress occasioned by memories of fallen and exiled comrades.
17. For references to this concept and theme, see n. 27 to Chapter 4 of the

present work. Apart from Gan's treatment the most celebrated instances of this chronotope are to be found in the work of Gogol, especially *The Government Inspector* and *Dead Souls*.
18. See Cornwell, op. cit., p. 52.
19. The phrase of Lea Melandri, quoted in Teresa de Lauretis, *Technologies of Gender. Essays on Theory, Film, and Fiction* (Macmillan: London, 1989), p. 45.
20. Cornwell, op. cit., p. 52.
21. For a discussion of this theme see my *Writers and Society During the Rise of Russian Realism*, pp. 1–2 and 152–3.
22. This theme receives a much fuller and more explicit treatment in Gan's *Society's Judgement*: see pp. 117–31 of the present work.
23. For a discussion of this see my *Women in Russian Literature, 1780–1863*, especially pp. 5–7.
24. This theme was particularly developed in the work (and, indeed, the life of Gogol). For a discussion of this, see, *inter alia*, Ruth Sobel, 'Gogol's *Rome*: A Final Draft for a Utopia', in *Essays in Poetics*, vol. 5, no. 1 (April, 1980), pp. 48–70.
25. See, for example, Boris Eykenbaum, *Lermontov. Opyt istoriko-literaturnoy otsenki* (Wilhelm Fink Verlag: Munich, 1967) (Originally, Leningrad, 1924), pp. 127–58, especially pp. 134–5 and 143.
26. Neil Cornwell notes, 'Perhaps the main weakness of *Princess Mimi* to the modern reader is its somewhat abrupt and melodramatic dénouement (as though the author had to finish it in a hurry), which seems to be heavily determined by its "instructional" motivation' (op. cit., p. 53).
27. See Eykhenbaum, op. cit., pp. 144 and 152.
28. For the origin of this usage, see n. 11, above.
29. For a discussion of this form of address in Lermontov's *A Hero of Our Time*, see my *Women in Russian Literature, 1780–1863*, p. 73.
30. For a very different treatment of all-female spaces in the literature of the period, see my discussions of Gan and Zhukova in the present work.
31. For a radical feminist interpretation of this practice see Mary Daly, *Gyn/Ecology. The Metaethics of Radical Feminism* (The Women's Press: London, 1979), pp. 134–52.
32. For Pushkin's use of the image of the harem in *The Fountain of Bakhchisaray*, see Chapter 2 of the present work.
33. My remarks are a kind of paraphrase of Elaine Showalter who has written 'the feminine heroine grows up in a world without female solidarity, where women in fact police each other on behalf of patriarchal tyranny'. See Elaine Showalter, *A Literature of their Own: British Women Novelists from Brontë to Lessing* (Virago: London, 1978), p. 117.
34. See n. 13 above.
35. In Gogol's tale *Ivan Shponka and His Auntie* the timorous hero dreads marriage and his dream is populated by wives wherever he looks. For a discussion of this dream, see my *Women in Russian Literature, 1780–1863*, p. 85.
36. See n. 13 above.

37. For a discussion of this and its wider context, see Teresa de Lauretis, *Alice Doesn't. Feminism, Semiotics, Cinema* (Macmillan: London, 1984), p. 134.
38. See n. 29 above.
39. Odoevsky, in fact, even provides a footnote to this own text (p. 244) to draw the reader's attention to this parallel. For an excellent discussion of Tatyana's letter as a form of writing, see Diana Burgin, 'Tatiana Larina's *Letter to Onegin*, or *La Plume Criminelle*' in *Essay in Poetics*, Vol. 16, No. 2 (September, 1991), pp. 12–23.
40. See Cornwell, p. 53.
41. See ibid. Cornwell comments that 'the apparent "realism" of the story . . . [is] undercut by the deliberate literariness which permeates character and text: Gorodkov the domineering "classicist" (p. 277) and Radetsky "our romantic".'
42. The theme of 'literature/life' was common in the period, stemming from *Evgeny Onegin*. For other treatments see Gan's *The Ideal* and Zhukova's *The Dacha on the Peterhof Road*, for discussions of which see Chapters 4 and 5 of the present work.
43. Cornwell, p. 53.
44. For discussions of this motif, see my *Women in Russian Literature, 1780–1863*, pp. 70, 113, 114–17, 119, 121, 122–5, 126–31, 136 and 146.
45. For a feminist reworking of Freud's celebrated question, see de Lauretis (1984), pp. 111–12.
46. This seems to me a kind of inversion of the 'found manuscript' motif. For another play on the missing ending of a crucial text see my discussion of *Ivan Shponka* in *Women in Russian Literature, 1780–1863*, p. 85.
47. Such origins can be seen in, for example, the Sleeping Beauty stories. For a structuralist approach to the arrival of the stranger in 'enclosed space' see no. 11 above. Once more Pushkin's *Evgeny Onegin* is the fountainhead for the later development of Russian literature and, as is well known, Ivan Turgenev used the basic plot situation of *Onegin* in nearly all his novels. Jane Austen's novels provide an English variation on the same *topos*.
48. Gan uses the same motif (and sometimes the same word) in many of her stories: see Chapter 4 of the present work.
49. See n. 33 above.
50. This was a common problem in this period of Russian literature, as many commentators on *A Hero of Our Time* have observed. For a general discussion see Eykhenbaum, op. cit.
51. See Terry Eagleton, *The Rape of Clarissa. Writing, Sexuality and Class Struggle in Samuel Richardson* (Basil Blackwell: Oxford, 1982).
52. See also Cornwell, op. cit., p. 53.
53. For a discussion of this see my *Women in Russian Literature, 1780–1863*, pp. 151–4.
54. In the original the word is *roman* which, significantly, can mean either 'novel' or 'romance': the double meaning would seem to be deliberate.
55. This is yet a further contrast with Gan's depiction of the world of women, on the one hand, and an anticipation of Turgenev, on the other.

56. This proposition holds, in general terms, for both Gan and Zhukova: see Chapters 4 and 5 of the present work.
57. Gan makes use of precisely the same motif in her *A Futile Gift*: see pp. 134–6 of the present work. The theme can also be seen in Dostoevsky's *Netochka Nezvanova*.
58. For feminist accounts of this compound term, see, *inter alia*, Jane Gallop, *Feminism and Psychoanalysis: The Daughter's Seduction* (London, 1982), p. 47 and 74–5 and Janet Sayers, *Sexual Contradictions: Psychology, Psychoanalysis and Feminism* (London, 1986), pp. 85–6.
59. See n. 42 above.
60. We see similar 'identikit' heroines in Pushkin's *The Prisoner of the Caucasus* and Lermontov's *Taman'*: for discussions of these characters, see Chapter 2 of the present work, and my forthcoming article on *Taman'* (see no. 9 above).
61. A similar use of 'sacrilege' can be seen in Pushkin's *The Fountain of Bakhchisaray* and Lermontov's *Demon*. See Chapter 2 of the present work and my *Women in Russian Literature, 1780–1863*, pp. 54–60.

4 ELENA GAN AND *A FUTILE GIFT*

1. See John Mersereau, 'The nineteenth century, 1820–40', in C. Moser (ed.), *The Cambridge History of Russian Literature* (Cambridge University Press, 1989), p. 163.
2. D. Mirsky, *A History of Russian Literature* (London, 1968), p. 142. The work of Elena Gan has aroused a little more attention in Russia/the Soviet Union, although only three of her works, *The Ideal*, *Society's Judgement* and *A Futile Gift*, have been republished. The fullest account of Gan's work (and life) is H.A. Aplin's *M.S. Zhukova and E.A. Gan. Women Writers and Female Protagonists, 1837–1843*. (Unpublished PhD Dissertation, U.E.A., 1988).
3. R. Stites, *The Women's Liberation Movement in Russia*, pp. 23–4.
4. For a discussion of this genre, see Aplin, pp. 49–66. The fullest treatment of the subject remains R.V. Iezuitova, 'Svetskaya Povest', in *Russkaya Povest XIX veka* (Leningrad, 1973), pp. 169–99.
5. There is no conventional translation of the Russian title *Sud Sveta*. Both terms can be rendered variously: '*sud*' can mean 'court', 'justice', 'judgement' or 'trial', while '*svet*' can mean '(high) society' or 'the world' (as well as 'light'). The Russian title, therefore, is punningly polyvalent and my own rendering only conveys some of its force although I hope it encapsulates the *central* meaning that the tale suggests.
6. All Gan's work can be found in E.A. Gan, *Polnoye Sobranie Sochinenii* (St Petersburg, 1905), edited by N.F. Mertz. *The Ideal* is more easily accessible in V.I. Sakharov (ed.), *Russkaya Romanticheskaya Povest* (Moscow, 1980), pp. 435–80 and this is the edition I have used.
7. Gan actually began writing in about 1827 (at the age of thirteen): see Aplin, p. 212.
8. For discussion of this theme in Gan's work (and life), see Aplin, especially p. 356.

9. *Dusha*, the soul, was to be a key referent for Gan's heroines and I will return frequently to this word in the following discussions.
10. Elaine Showalter describes this process: 'the feminine heroine grows up in a world without female solidarity, where women in fact police each other on behalf of patriarchal tyranny' (Showalter, 1979, p. 117. The reference is to *Jane Eyre*. Indeed, it could be said that the social alienation of Gan's heroines has parallels with Brontë's heroine although, usually, they are not poor.) For a discussion of this lack of female solidarity elsewhere in Russian literature, see Andrew (1988), p. 25 (with reference to *Poor Liza*).
11. Despite the narrator's caveat, such meetings are not uncommon in Gan's work: see, especially, *Society's Judgement*.
12. For an interesting discussion of 'a break in fictional decorum' (the term of Mary Jacobus) in the work of Mary Wollstonecraft, see Janet Todd, *Feminist Literary History*, pp. 103–17, especially 105–7.
13. In this, her first work, it seems to me, Gan deliberately attempted to counteract the dominant masculinist tradition in which women are rivals to each other and 'sisterhood' is all but absent. Her attempt is only partially successful as Vera is little more than a cypher, playing the role of the confidante of Neo-Classical tragedy. For a more successful attempt at creating a realised relationship between two women, see my later discussion of *The Locket*.
14. For a discussion of this strategy in Chernyshevsky's novel, see Andrew (1988), pp. 166–7. For a more general discussion of transformation in Chernyshevsky see Irina Paperno, *Chernyshevsky and the Age of Realism. A Study in the Semiotics of Behaviour* (Stanford, 1988), especially pp. 159–218.
15. For a description of Gan's own erudite mother, see Aplin, pp. 209–10; and pp. 326–7 for a discussion of this theme in Gan's work.
16. For a discussion of this in male-authored literature of the period, see Andrew (1988), especially pp. 90–2.
17. See Aplin, pp. 34–5 for an interesting discussion on the ambivalent evaluation of female upbringing in Gan's work.
18. Mirsky, op. cit., p. 142.
19. For discussions of this phenomenon see Andrew (1988), *passim*. For a good account of the Freudian analysis of the process that leads to fetishisation see Jacqueline Rose, '*Hamlet* – the "Mona Lisa" of Literature' in her *Sexuality in the Field of Vision*, pp. 123–40, especially p. 127.
20. Although this iconography may have originated in the eighteenth century, it was to endure until the second half of the nineteenth: see Andrew (1988) on Turgenev.
21. V. Uchenova (echoing Belinsky) comments on this phenomenon (with reference to *Society's Judgement*): 'This tale, like other works by E.A. Gan, is not free from an excess of patheticism . . . romantic phraseological clichés.' See her Introduction to *Dacha na Petergovskoy Doroge. Proza Russkikh Pisatelnits Pervoy Poloviny XIX veka* (Moscow, 1986), pp. 3–18 (p. 10).
22. The best account of the conflict between 'romanticism' and 'realism' in the 1830s is still probably M. Malia, *Alexander Herzen and The Birth of*

Russian Socialism (New York, 1965). See also Andrew (1980), Chapter 4 for a discussion of this tension in Belinsky and Paperno for its lasting legacy (the 1850s–1860s).
23. I think I am justified in seeing this literary *topos* as an anticipation of Freud's interpretation of hysteria. For an excellent feminist account of Freud on this, see Rose, op. cit., especially pp. 34–40 and 97–8.
24. Mirsky, op. cit., p. 142 has asserted 'The male characters are . . . cads who seduce women by a pretense of love.'
25. There is a nice piece of role reversal here of the general tendency of female characters being used primarily to illuminate the hero, as for example, Bela, Mary and Vera in *A Hero of Our Time*.
26. Quoted in Andrew (1980), p. 144.
27. M.M. Bakhtin, 'The Forms of Time and the Chronotopos in the Novel. From the Greek Novel to Modern Fiction', in *PTL. A Journal for Descriptive Poetics and Theory of Literature* (Vol. 3, No. 3, Oct. 1978, pp. 493–528), p. 493. (This is a translation of excerpts from 'Formy vremeni i khronotopa v romane: ocherki po istoricheskoy poetiki' in M.M. Bakhtin, *Voprosy Literatury i Estetiki* (Moscow, 1975), pp. 234–61, 391–407.) For more recent discussions and applications of the term, see J.J. van Baak, 'The House in Russian Avantgarde Prose: Chronotope and Archetype', in *Essays in Poetics* (Vol. 15, No. 1, April 1990, pp. 1–16) and J.J. van Baak, '"The Guests Gathered at the Dača . . .": The Dynamics of a Drawing Room', in E. de Haard, T. Langerak, W.G. Weststeijn (eds), *Semantic Analysis of Literary Texts. To Honour Jan van der Eng on the Occasion of his 65th Birthday* (Amsterdam, New York, Oxford, Tokyo, 1990), pp. 51–66.
28. For a discussion of generic play in the development of Russian prose in the 1830s, see B.M. Eikhenbaum, *Lermontov. A Study in Literary-Historical Evaluation* (Ann Arbor, 1981), especially pp. 147–71.
29. Famous ball scenes of this period are to be found in Pushkin's *Evgeny Onegin*, Griboedov's *Woe from Wit*, several works by Lermontov, especially *A Hero of Our Time* and *The Masquerade* as well as, in a rather different key, Gogol's *Dead Souls*.
30. See also van Baak on this topic (see note 27 above).
31. Bakhtin, op. cit., p. 519. His main point of reference is *Madame Bovary*, although he also adduces a number of Russian instances.
32. Gan herself was excited and inspired by the art and beauty of St Petersburg which she visited for the first (and only) time from Spring 1836 to May 1837. At the same time her sense of isolation grew. (See Aplin, pp. 216ff.)
33. For an excellent discussion of this theme in Russian literature, see Marshall Berman, *All That Is Solid Melts Into Air. The Experience of Modernity* (New York, 1982), pp. 173–286.
34. The motif is probably initiated in Chapter One of *Evgeny Onegin* (published February 1825). Onegin arrives (late) at the opera and 'Directs his double lorgnette askance/At the boxes of ladies he doesn't know' (stanza XXI, ll. 3–4).
35. See Aplin, pp. 213–14 for Gan's own experience of life married to the army.

36. See Andrew (1988) for various discussions of this plot. See also Nancy K. Miller, *The Heroine's Text: Readings in the French and English Novel 1722–1782* (New York, 1980), to whom I was (and remain) much indebted.
37. See Wolf Schmid, 'Nevezučij ženich i vetrenye suženye. Podteksty i razvertyvajuščiesja rečevye kliše v povesti Puškina "Metel"', in E. de Haard et al. (eds), pp. 443–66 (p. 465).
38. For an excellent discussion of 'woman as enigma' in culture, see Teresa de Lauretis, 'Desire in Narrative', in her *Alice Doesn't. Feminism, Semiotics, Cinema* (London, 1984), pp. 103–57, especially p. 110. See also Jacqueline Rose, op. cit.
39. Lermontov also used this motif in his *Princess Ligovskaya*, an earlier version of *Princess Mary*, although he abandoned it in the second variant.
40. de Lauretis puts it thus: 'In this [Lotman's] mythical-textual mechanics, then, the hero must be male, regardless of the gender of the text-image, because the obstacle, whatever its personification, is morphologically female.' For a more detailed discussion of de Lauretis, in relation to Lotman and Propp, see Chapters 1 and 2 of the present work.
41. A similar discovery is made regarding Germann in *The Queen of Spades*. See J. Doherty, 'Fictional Paradigms in Pushkin's "Pikovaya Dama"', in *Essays in Poetics* (Vol. 17, No. 1, 1992).
42. In the Russian the word is *roman* which covers both English meanings. The pun is, I think, intended.
43. For a discussion of this plot typology see de Lauretis, op. cit., and Yury Lotman, 'The Origin of Plot in the Light of Typology', in *Poetics Today* (Vol. 1, Nos 1–2 (Autumn 1979), pp. 161–84. (I will return in more detail to Gan's use of this typology in my discussion of *Society's Judgement*.)
44. Pushkin's use of the pronoun 'on' has added resonance, of course, in that it is the first syllable of On-egin.
45. I'm sure it's no accident that Gan gave her first spiritual heroine the same name as Tatyana's rather worldly and superficial sister.
46. See p. 443 of the text where we learn that the two girls had read (significantly) de Staël and Genlis.
47. Miller, *The Heroine's Text*, p. 26. See also E.A. Kaplan, 'Is the Gaze Male?', in A. Snitow, C. Stansell, S. Thompson (eds), *Desire. The Politics of Sexuality* (London, 1984), pp. 321–38.
48. This verbal possession/taking of the woman is a common feature in the literature of the period as, for example, in the cases of Aleko (*The Gipsies*) and Grushnitsky and Pechorin.
49. Martial metaphors for seduction are common in Gan's work as they were to be in *A Hero of Our Time*. Both writers derive many of the plot motifs and typologies from eighteenth century sources and the workings of these motifs have been nicely encapsulated by Nancy K. Miller: 'In a series of cruel assaults, the aggressor wreaks destruction upon his female adversary by deploying a weapon of propulsion. The response, symmetrically, is coded as a military typography: the vulner-

able territory under attack gives way to the invader' (op. cit., p. 57). It should be noted that, whereas Pechorin's assaults almost always succeed, those of Gan's 'heroes' never do, at least physically.
50. For a discussion of this in nineteenth century literature see G. Gibian, 'Love by the Book: Pushkin, Stendhal, Flaubert', in *Comparative Literature*, Vol. VIII (1956), pp. 97–105. It is also a feature of *A Hero of Our Time*: see Marie Gilroy, *Lermontov's Ironic Vision* (Birmingham Slavonic Monographs, No. 19, 1989), p. 43, where she notes 'This theatricalisation is a form of hero-worship, a conscious modelling of one's life on a literary character'. For a fascinating discussion of the interrelationships of 'Reality – Literature – Reality', see Paperno, op. cit.
51. Aplin also sees this as a central theme in Gan's work; see pp. 276–364 *passim*.
52. It remains an open question whether Gan saw women's oppression as 'natural', 'God-given' or the result of specific social conditions. I return to this question in my consideration of *A Futile Gift*. Gan herself, whatever her works may suggest, was not an emancipationist, writing:

> You hold to *l'émancipation des femmes*, would like it *à la Saint-Simon*, that women should reach equality with men and you pursue the latter for the oppression of our sex? You're not correct! I am also a woman, I suffer a lot from the conditions with which our sex has been enmeshed, but I will never agree to the opinion that woman has been placed *by nature* on an equal height with man.
> (Quoted in Aplin, p. 243 – my italics)

53. For an interesting discussion of the conflict between 'reality' and 'dream'/ideal, see Aplin, pp. 295–6.
54. For a discussion of the *dusha* as metaphor in this period, see Andrzej Dudek, 'Types and Functions of Metaphor in Russian Poetry of Late Romanticism', in *Essays in Poetics*, forthcoming.
55. All references to this work are to E.A. Gan, *Polnoye Sobraniye Sochinenii*, pp. 210–99.
56. *The Locket* and *Princess Mary*, both of which were written at the same time, although *The Locket* was published a year earlier, have many striking similarities – the initial setting in Pyatigorsk, followed by a move to Kislovodsk; the social scene, certain set pieces (the cavalcade); the basic plot typology; some of the actual dialogue between Sophia Engelsberg and Prince Yurevich anticipates that of Pechorin and Princess Mary.
57. For a fascinating discussion of Tatyana Larina as an anxious female writer, see Diana Burgin, 'Tatiana Larina's *Letter to Onegin* or *La Plume Criminelle*', in *Essays in Poetics*, Vol. 16, No. 2, 1991, pp. 12–23.
58. Russian Romanticism took an ambivalent attitude to its precursor. Pushkin is frankly mocking and parodic in *Evgeny Onegin* and *The Tales of Belkin*, amongst others. (See Wolf Schmid, note 37 *supra*). On the other hand, 'Neo-Sentimentalism' was an important factor in the

development of the 'natural school' (*The Overcoat*, *Poor Folk*, *Notes of a Hunter*, for example), where a generally positive re-evaluation of Sentimentalism featured.

59. This word ('*starukha*') also represents a difference between Gan and certain male authors of the period, especially Gogol, in which 'old woman' is virtually synonymous with 'witch'. (Here, admittedly, Gan uses the affectionate diminutive form '*starushka*'.)
60. Jane Gallop, op. cit., uses this phrase in her brilliantly witty analysis of Jacques Lacan (p. 34).
61. Given Gan's pervasive valorisation of the maternal this coded insult seems to me an instance of 'bad faith': she wants it both ways.
62. This metaphor is one of the most striking instances of Gan's anticipation of *Princess Mary* in which Pechorin remarks: 'But surely there is a boundless pleasure in the possession of a young, scarcely burgeoned soul! It is like a flower whose finest aroma evaporates at the first ray of sunlight; one must pick it at this moment, and, breathing it in to one's fill, cast it on the road: perhaps someone will pick it up.' *A Hero of Our Time* in M. Yu. Lermontov, *Sochineniya*, Vol. IV (Leningrad, 1962), p. 401. The metaphor is, of course, a common poeticism, so direct borrowing/influence is not necessarily what's happening here.
63. 'Part One' and 'Part Two' are not formally marked in what is a unitary text: I use the divisions both for my own convenience but also because the text is very clearly organised in two complementary halves.
64. Another interesting contrast: Gogol's Shponka's 'mutism' and 'femininity' in the presence of ladies is negatively encoded. See Andrew (1988), p. 85.
65. Chernyshevsky was to adopt this strategy for his 'ordinary', but heroic, heroine Vera Pavlovna, but in a much more explicit fashion.
66. For an extended and highly illuminating discussion of desire in narrative see de Lauretis (1984).
67. For discussion of 'static' and 'dynamic' characters see ibid., and Lotman (1979).
68. These last two 'cases' are enacted in, for example, *Poor Liza*, *Bela* and *Princess Mary*.
69. For the foundations of this plot motif, see Lotman (1979), especially pp. 168 and 173.
70. Famous duels in Russian literature are, of course, in *Evgeny Onegin* and *Princess Mary*. In both instances fiction tragically prefigured life.
71. The first person is being used as Olympia's letters to her sister play an important part of the narrative in Part Two.
72. A point also made by Aplin, see pp. 306ff., especially p. 316.
73. Aplin draws our attention to this point, see ibid., p. 315.
74. All references to this work are to the following edition: *Sud Sveta* in *Dacha na Petergovskoy Doroge. Proza Russkikh Pisatelnits Pervoy Poloviny XIX veka* (V. Uchenova (ed.), Moscow, 1986), pp. 147–212.
75. This remark will be tragically prophetic when Vlodinsky murders Zenaida's brother in a duel, thinking he is Zenaida's lover.
76. That this is one of the many autobiographical instances in this story hardly needs mentioning.

77. For the 'maleness' of the lorgnette, see note 34 above.
78. See note 5 above. There is a play on the double meaning of *svet* at this point.
79. See note 63 above: much the same considerations apply at this point.
80. For a discussion of this topos in *The Queen of Spades*, see Yury Lotman, 'Theme and Plot. The Theme of Cards and the Card Game in Russian Literature of the Nineteenth Century' in *PTL. A Journal for Descriptive Poetics and Theory of Literature*, Vol. 3, No. 3, Oct. 1978, pp. 455–92. (This article was first published in Russian in *Trudy po znakovym sistemam*, VII, Tartu, 1975, pp. 120–42.)
81. See note 70 above.
82. The narrator also makes the same point as the travelling narrator of *A Hero of Our Time* who also felt free to publish *Pechorin's Journal* once the protagonist was dead.
83. See Lotman (1979) *passim*.
84. See note 69 above, as well as the radical (feminist) reworking of Lotman's typologies in de Lauretis (1984).
85. For a discussion of this point, see de Lauretis (1984), especially pp. 110–12.
86. For a discussion of an earlier version of the heroine as a revivifying Christ figure see Chapter 2 of the present work. Aplin (pp. 345–6) sees Zenaida's role here as quasi-maternal.
87. See de Lauretis, op. cit.
88. It is surely no coincidence that the heroine of this story is given Gan's own pseudonymous Christian name.
89. See E.A. Kaplan, op. cit., p. 322.
90. Rose, op. cit., p. 127.
91. For another discussion of this point, see Aplin, p. 337.
92. All references to this work are to the *Polnoye Sobraniye Sochinenii*, pp. 710–837. Almost certainly Gan would have been familiar with Pushkin's famous lyric '*Dar naprasny*' (literally 'Gift futile') which had already been published twice. Gan fundamentally reworks the implications of Pushkin's lyric. *A Futile Gift* remained unfinished on Gan's death and my present discussion refers exclusively to the completed Part One, which can legitimately be read as a finished work in its own right. Indeed, what was written of Part Two bears little obvious thematic relationship to Part One.
93. This contrast is most explicitly stated by an unnamed woman in *The Locket* in the preliminary discussion leading to Sophia's narrative and bears quotation in full:

> In the life of a man there are many collateral adventures which he can communicate to all and sundry, without touching upon a single one of his sincere feelings; a woman's existence, on the contrary, is entirely comprised of tones and echoes from her inner world; we do not have external circumstances which would not be intimately linked with it: our entire life is a single harmony, and whichever string you might touch, its sound evokes an echo of the whole chord. (257)

94. See note 28 above.
95. Chernyshevsky was to repeat this motif in *What Is To Be Done?* For an illuminating discussion of the semiotic role of the tutor in Chernyshevsky's life see Paperno, op. cit., pp. 91–9.
96. E.A. Kaplan, op. cit., p. 321. See also note 12 to Chapter 3.
97. Just as Olga (in *The Ideal*) becomes Tatyana's 'real' (spiritual) sister, Anyuta here becomes Lensky's cousin, although her creator does not mock her 'misty romanticism'.
98. For once the mother (perhaps because she is still alive?) is not valorised. On the other hand, Countess Belskaya plays the fairy-tale role of the 'good' ('real') mother.
99. For a discussion of this work as a reflection of Gan's own experiences as a woman writer and of her views on the matter, see Aplin pp. 237–42 and 356–63.
100. The closing words, of course, of Lermontov's 'Foreword' to *A Hero of Our Time*.

5 MARIYA ZHUKOVA AND PATRIARCHAL POWER

1. One problem for any study of Zhukova's life is the dearth of source material. For an account of her life (and the problem of sources), see H.A. Aplin, *M.S. Zhukova and E.A. Gan. Women Writing and Female Protagonists, 1837–43*. (Unpublished PhD Dissertation, U.E.A., 1988), especially pp. 81–98.
2. See, for example, M.S. Zhukova, *Vechera na Karpovke*, ed. R.V. Iyezuitova (Moscow: Sovetskaya Rossiya, 1986) and *Dacha na Petergovskoy doroge: Proza russkikh pisatelnits pervoy poloviny XIXveka*, ed. V. Uchenova (Moscow: Sovremennik, 1986). For full details of the publication of Zhukova's work see Aplin's excellent bibliography.
3. For a discussion of this, see Aplin, op. cit., pp. 173–205 and 365–90.
4. Ibid., p. 8.
5. For a brief discussion of this, see B.M. Eykhenbaum, *Lermontov: Opyt istoriko-literaturnoy otsenki* (Munich, 1967: originally, Leningrad, 1924), p. 140.
6. See Richard Stites, *The Women's Liberation Movement in Russia*, especially pp. 23–4.
7. All references to the texts will be as follows: *Baron Reykhman* and *The Locket* in *Vechera na Karpovke*, pp. 40–73 and 75–109 respectively; *The Dacha on the Peterhof Road* in *Dacha na Petergovsky Doroge*, pp. 245–322.
8. In her notes to the recent edition of *Evenings*, Iyezuitova (p. 281) remarks on the relative inferiority of *Baron Reykhman*, vis-à-vis Tolstoy's novel. Given the relative lengths of the two works (apart from other considerations, such as the fact that Zhukova's work appeared fifty years before Tolstoy's), the comparatively primitive treatment of the subject by Zhukova is hardly surprising.
9. For a discussion of this theme in Zhukova's work, see Aplin, p. 113.
10. For an excellent discussion of this motif in Pushkin's *The Prisoner of the*

Caucasus, see Stephanie Sandler, *Distant Pleasures. Alexander Pushkin and the Writing of Exile* (California: Stanford University Press, 1989), pp. 157–8.

11. See, for example, certain details in the portrayal of Lermontov's Princess Mary and the 'undine' in *Taman'*: for a general account of this see my *Women in Russian Literature, 1780–1863*.
12. This seems to be an implicit reference to the mores outlined in the preceding (and lead) story in the cycle, *The Monk*, in which a jealous husband does, indeed, murder his wife. It is in this story that the motif of 'patriarchal power' is established.
13. For an excellent account of this chronotope in Russian literature and thought, see Marshall Berman, *All That Is Solid Melts Into Air. The Experience of Modernity* (London: Verso, 1983), pp. 173–286.
14. For a discussion of this theme in Zhukova, see Aplin, pp. 117ff.
15. For a discussion of this point see my *Women in Russian Literature, 1780–1863*, p. 22 and Chapter 2, p. 34 of the present work.
16. An interesting parallel can be drawn here with Turgenev's *On the Eve*, in which the heroine Elena is also chastised by her parents for the love of a social inferior.
17. It is important to note that 'chronotope' is not just a time/space structural mechanism, but imparts value as well. As Holquist puts it: 'Chronotope is a term, then, that brings together not just two concepts, but four: a time, plus its value; and a space, plus its value.' See Michael Holquist, *Dialogism. Bakhtin and his world* (London and New York: Routledge, 1990), p. 155.
18. For a discussion of simultaneity in Bakhtin, see ibid., especially pp. 18–20.
19. See my *Women in Russian Literature, 1780–1863*.
20. See ibid., Chapter 7.
21. See Chapter 4, n. 50.

6 ALEXANDER HERZEN: *WHO IS TO BLAME?*

1. See 'Alexander Herzen' in Isaiah Berlin, *Russian Thinkers*, edited by Henry Hardy and Aileen Kelly (Penguin, Harmondsworth, 1979), pp. 186–209 (p. 202).
2. All references will be to the following edition: *Kto Vinovat?* in A.I. Herzen, *Sobraniye Sochinenii v tridsati Tomakh* (Akademiya Nauk, Moscow, 1954–66), vol. 4 (1955), pp. 5–209.
3. For a vivid account of Herzen's life, see E.H. Carr, *The Romantic Exiles. A Nineteenth-Century Portrait Gallery* (Penguin, Harmondsworth, 1968).
4. See, for example, Berlin's observation: 'Herzen (although this has been seldom recognised even by his greatest admirers) is an original thinker, independent, honest, and unexpectedly profound'. See his article, 'Herzen and Bakunin on Individual Liberty' in *Russian Thinkers*, pp. 82–113 (p. 111).
5. For a good introduction to Herzen's socio-political views, see Martin

Malia, *Alexander Herzen and the Birth of Russian Socialism* (The Universal Library, Grosset and Dunlap, New York, 1965), especially pp. 257–77.
6. Herzen is often credited with introducing this theme to Russian literature. Both Gan and Zhukova, in fact, anticipated him by about ten years in their respective stories *The Ideal* and *Baron Reykhman* (both 1837): see my discussion of these works in Chapters 4 and 5 of the present work.
7. Malia (op. cit., p. 269) offers a good summary of the significance of the novel:

> As literature it is only partially successful; Herzen was an excellent reporter of the Russian social scene, but he could not construct a plot or draw character. Nonetheless the novel is important in the ideological, if not in the aesthetic, development of Russian literature. It is among the most notable products of the "natural school" of the forties, while it is easily one of the boldest bits of social criticism to get published under Nicholas. It made its mark at the time: Belinski raved over it and the Westerners received it as a significant contribution to the cause.[35] The chief originality of *Who Is To Blame?* is to combine the general socialist theme of the "rehabilitation of the flesh" with the particularly Russian one of the "superfluous man".

8. For an account of the sometimes close, sometimes bitter relationship between the two men, see my *Russian Writers and Society in The Second Half of The Nineteenth Century* (Macmillan, London, 1982), pp. 20–3, 28, 31, 35 and 38–9.
9. This type of 'mixed marriage' and, its progeny, is an important theme in the novel, and is, of course, an autobiographical one.
10. I touch upon this theme in several other sections of the present work. For the bibliographical sources see Chapter 4, n. 27.
11. Malia, op. cit., p. 270.
12. For a discussion of these concepts, see Jurij M. Lotman, 'The Origin of Plot in the Light of Typology' in *Poetics Today*, Vol. 1, Numbers 1–2, Autumn, 1979, pp. 161–84 and Victor Ripp, *Turgenev's Russia* (Ithaca and London, 1980).
13. For an excellent discussion of this semiological nexus, see Irina Paperno, *Chernyshevsky and the Age of Realism. A Study in the Semiotics of Behavior* (Stanford University Press, Stanford, California, 1988), especially pp. 91–9.
14. In the overall context of the social development of Russian literature Krutsifersky's background as a scion of the *raznochintsy* is of some significance, given that few members of this 'class' had yet achieved literary prominence, either in art or life. For discussions of this, see ibid. and my *Writers and Society During the Rise of Russian Realism* (Macmillan, London, 1980), especially pp. 114–50.
15. Malia notes that, to the Onegin-esque central plot 'Herzen added a setting in Russian life of the day in a manner (roughly) imitated from

Gogol's': see op. cit., p. 270.

16. It is arguable that the novel seeks, in fact, to expose and condemn patriarchal relations and, in particular, the oppression and exploitation of women. Certainly, as I will argue later on, this seems to have been Herzen's *intention*. The way he presents his 'case', however, often has the opposite effect of his apparent aim.
17. There is an important contrast here with Pushkin's approach to similar social types in, for example, *Evgeny Onegin, The Tales of Belkin* and *The Captain's Daughter*. He may tease, even mock those of an inferior social class and culture to his own, but the tone is gentle, sympathetic. Herzen's tone, for all his socialism (and, indeed, for all his own mixed social origins) is that of the *grand seigneur* looking down from his Olympian, metropolitan heights on these unspeakably backward denizens of the sticks.
18. This symbolically significant gesture is also used by Turgenev in *On the Eve* and Chernyshevsky in *What Is To Be Done?*: see my *Women in Russian Literature: 1780–1863* (Macmillan, London, 1988), pp. 171 and 202, n. 40.
19. This is a reference to Drobrolyubov's famous review of Turgenev's *On the Eve*, entitled 'When Will the Real Day Come?': see my *Women in Russian Literature, 1780–1863*, pp. 153–80.
20. A reference, of course, to Gogol's story in *Mirgorod*, which bears this title, and which depicts an elderly couple and their almost entirely static existence.
21. Once more the novel is deeply autobiographical at this point: see Malia, op. cit., especially pp. 151–80 and 257–77.
22. See ibid.
23. For discussion of this theme see my *Women in Russian Literature, 1780–1863, passim*.
24. Turgenev borrowed many motifs and situations from *Who Is To Blame?* in the composition of his *On the Eve*. Elena's father, Nikolay Stakhov is modelled on Negrov, and there are many echoes of the scene distributed here in the latter novel: see ibid., pp. 148 and 152–3.
25. For discussions of this, see ibid., *passim*.
26. See *Evgeny Onegin*, Chapter 3, stanzas xvii–xx.
27. See ibid., Chapter 6, stanzas xxxvii–xxxix. The last of these stanzas reads: 'But perhaps it would have been different: the poet/Was awaited by an ordinary fate./The years of youth would have passed:/In him the ardour of his soul would have cooled./He would have changed in many ways./He would have parted company with the muses, would have married,/In the countryside, happy and cuckolded,/He would have worn a quilted dressing gown;/He would have discovered life as it really is'. (ll. 1–9)
28. See Teresa de Lauretis' powerful and persuasive definition of narrative: 'Story demands sadism, depends on making something happen, forcing a change in another person, a battle of will and strength, victory/defeat, all occurring in a linear time with a beginning and an end'. See her 'Desire in Narrative' in *Alice Doesn't. Feminism, Semiotics,*

Cinema (Macmillan, London, 1984), pp. 103–57 (pp. 132–3). For more extended use of this model, see Chapter Two of the present work.
29. See *Evgeny Onegin*, Chapter 7, stanza xxiv, l.14.
30. For the influence of German philosophy on Russian thought in the 1830s and 1840s see, *inter alia*, Malia, op. cit., especially pp. 69–98 and 218–56, my *Writers and Society During the Rise of Russian Realism*, especially pp. 123–8, and Berlin, op. cit., especially pp. 136–49. Another valuable and still relevant resource is D. Ciževski, *Gegel' v Rossii* (Paris, 1939).
31. Malia, op. cit., p. 271.
32. For Starodum, see my *Women in Russian Literature: 1780–1883*, pp. 17–18; for The Old Man, see Chapter 2 of the present work. Another character in *Who Is To Blame?* who has a similar function and status is the Swiss tutor, Joseph, a not accidentally Rousseauesque personage.
33. For a discussion of one of the fountainheads of this motif, see my account of *Bednaya [Poor] Liza* in *Women in Russian Literature: 1780–1863*, pp. 22–6.
34. For discussion of the motif in Pushkin's *The Fountain of Bakhchisaray* and Odoevsky's *Princess Mimi*, see pp. 31–41 and 62 of the present work.
35. For other discussions of this motif, see n. 33 above.
36. The classic text of this school in Russian literature is Lermontov's *A Hero of Our Time*: for a discussion of this from these perspectives, see my *Women in Russian Literature: 1780–1863*, pp. 61–78.
37. Boris Eykhenbaum makes a similar point about Tolstoy's later (1859) *Family Happiness*, observing that 'Marriage is the starting point of the plot, rather than the dénouement (as it ordinarily is in love stories). This is an intentional deviation.' See 'On Tolstoy's Crises' in *Tolstoy. A Collection of Critical Essays*, edited by Ralph E. Matlaw (Prentice-Hall, New Jersey, 1967), pp. 52–5 (p. 53). For a more detailed account of Tolstoy's dislocation of the love plot in this work see Eric de Haard, *Narrative and Anti-Narrative Structures in Lev Tolstoj's Early Works* (Rodopi, Amsterdam-Atlanta, 1989), pp. 143–51.
38. See Carolina de Maegd-Soëp, *The Emancipation of Women in Russian Literature and Society* (Ghent, 1979), pp. 129–32.
39. See Herzen, op. cit., p. 216.

7 THE LAW OF THE FATHER AND *NETOCHKA NEZVANOVA*

1. Quoted in Teresa de Lauretis, *Alice Doesn't. Feminism, Semiotics, Cinema* (Macmillan, London, 1984, pp. 107–8). (The quotation is from Roland Barthes, *The Pleasure of the Text*, trans. Richard Miller (Hill and Wang: New York, 1975), p. 10).
2. Elaine Showalter, 'Towards a Feminist Poetics', in Mary Jacobus (ed.), *Women Writing and Writing about Women* (Croom Helm, London, 1979), pp. 22–42 (p. 31).
3. de Lauretis, op. cit., p. 106.

4. For recent discussions of the significance of Chernyshevsky's novel in the development of Russian literature and of the 'woman question', see my *Women in Russian Literature: 1780–1863* (Macmillan, London, 1988) especially pp. 155–80 and Irina Paperno, *Chernyshevsky and the Age of Realism. A Study in the Semiotics of Behavior* (Stanford University Press, Stanford, California, 1988), especially pp. 159–218.
5. For the significance of Mikhailov in these debates see Richard Stites, *The Women's Liberation Movement in Russia: Feminism, Nihilism and Bolshevism (1860–1930)*, (Princeton University Press, Princeton, 1978), especially pp. 38–48.
6. All references to this work will be to the following edition: F.M. Dostoevsky, *Polnoye Sobraniye Sochinenyy v Tridsati Tomakh* (Nauka, Leningrad, 1972–91), vol. 2 (1972), pp. 142–267.
7. For a brief discussion of this tendency in Russian and other literatures, see Eric de Haard, *Narrative and Anti-Narrative Structures in Lev Tolstoj's Early Works* (Rodopi, Amsterdam–Atlanta, 1989), pp. 144–5. Victor Terras writes somewhat disparagingly of Dostoevsky's attempts at this authorial cross-dressing. In the last part, especially, Terras claims, Dostoevsky 'shows all the traits typical of the "lady writer": emotional clichés, sentimental moralising, disorganised effusions about the inner life of a passionate, yet virtuous young lady'. See Victor Terras, *The Young Dostoevsky, 1846–1849. A Critical Study* (Mouton, The Hague, 1969), p. 54. If Dostoevsky did indeed write in this way it is not altogether surprising, given his own views on 'lady writers': 'No, our women writers simply don't know how to write; take for instance Koxanovskaja: she has talent, sensibility, even some ideas, but how she writes, how she writes . . . how can anybody write like this?!' Quoted ibid., p. 103.
8. For further details on this, see Joseph Frank, *Dostoevsky; The Seeds of Revolt 1821–1849* (Princeton University Press, Princeton, 1976), pp. 349–50.
9. See Terras, op. cit., pp. 47–8.
10. Apart from initially stating that Efimov is her stepfather, Netochka refers to him throughout as *batyushka* ('little father'/'daddy'). For the sake of simplicity I will also refer to him as her 'father'.
11. As Freud (amongst many others) has noted, both in his life and works, the father was of immense significance to Dostoevsky: see Freud's still valuable essay 'Dostoevsky and Parricide', in René Wellek (ed.), *Dostoevsky. A Collection of Critical Essays* (Prentice-Hall, New Jersey, 1962), pp. 98–111. It is perhaps also interesting to note in this connection that the primary reason that *Netochka Nezvanova* remained unfinished was Dostoevsky's arrest and mock execution, in 1849, which stemmed ultimately, of course, from Tsar Nicholas I, termed 'affectionately' *tsar-batyushka*, the latter word being precisely the one that is used about the father in the text. Returning to Freud we should remember his words on this subject:

> We can safely say that Dostoevsky never got free from the feelings of guilt arising from his intention of murdering his father. They

> also determined his attitude in two other spheres in which the father-relation is the decisive factor, his attitude towards the authority of the State and towards belief in God. In the first of these he ended up with complete submission to his Little Father, the Tsar, who had once performed with him in *reality* the comedy of killing which his attacks had so often represented in *play*.
>
> (op. cit., p. 106, italics in original)

In this light, we may say that the 'little father' has castrated Dostoevsky's text, a consequence of which is that we never will know whether Netochka overcame the drama of seduction by her 'little father'.

12. For other instances of this, see my discussion of *The Fountain of Bakchisaray* in Chapter 2 of the present volume, and of *Poor Liza* in *Women in Russian Literature: 1780–1863*, pp. 22–6.
13. For a discussion of the opposite tendency (an over-insistent concentration on the first person singular) see my discussion of Lermontov's *Taman*: '"The Blind Will See": Narrative and Gender in *Taman*,' in *Russian Literature* (1992) XXXI, pp. 449–76.
14. See Konstantin Mochulsky, *Dostoevsky. His Life and Work* (Princeton University Press, Princeton, 1967 (1971)), p. 106.
15. See Terras, op. cit., p. 266.
16. For a recent discussion of this theme, see John Forrester, *The Seductions of Psychoanalysis. Freud, Lacan and Derrida* (Cambridge University Press, Cambridge, 1990).
17. For a discussion of the psychoanalytical semiotics of the maternal body see especially Julia Kristeva's 'About Chinese Women' in Toril Moi (ed.), *The Kristeva Reader* (Basil Blackwell, Oxford, 1986), pp. 138–59.
18. Terras, p. 105.
19. See n. 11, above.
20. See Terras, op. cit.
21. In 1992 we may be particularly sensitive to such issues and see evil where it may not really exist. Even so, in my view, the scenes involving Efimov and Netochka could be termed pornographic.
22. The Russian word 'roditel'skaya' can mean either 'paternal' or 'parental'. In this context it is not entirely clear which translation is more appropriate, but the latter is certainly possible.
23. Kristeva, op. cit., p. 150.
24. For a helpfully succinct definition of this term see Maggie Humm, *The Dictionary of Feminist Theory* (Harvester Wheatsheaf, New York, London, Toronto, Sydney, Tokyo, 1989), p. 108.

Bibliography

Althusser, L., *Lenin and Philosophy and Other Essays* (London, 1977).
Andrew, J., *Writers and Society During the Rise of Russian Realism* (London, 1980)
____, *Russian Writers and Society in the Second Half of the Nineteenth Century* (London, 1982).
____, (ed.), *The Structural Analysis of Russian Narrative Fiction* (Keele, 1984).
____, *Women in Russian Literature: 1780–1863* (Macmillan, London, 1988).
Ardener, S. (ed.), *Perceiving Women* (London, 1975).
____, *Defining Females* (London, 1978).
Atkinson, D., Dollin, A. and Warshovsky, G. (eds), *Women in Russia* (Brighton, 1978).
de Beauvoir, S., *The Second Sex* (London, 1972).
Benhabib, S. and Cornell, D., (eds), *Feminism as Critique. Essays on the Politics of Gender in Late Capitalist Societies* (Polity Press, Cambridge, 1987).
Boumelha, P., *Thomas Hardy and Women: Sexual Ideology and Narrative Form* (Harvester, Brighton, 1982).
Brownmiller, S., *Femininity* (Paladin, London, 1986).
Brownstein, R.M., *Becoming a Heroine: Reading About Women in Novels* (Harmondsworth, 1984).
Brunsdon, C., (ed.), *Films For Women* (B.F.I., London, 1986).
Cameron, D.C., *Feminism and Linguistic Theory* (London, 1985).
Charvet, J., *Feminism* (London, 1982).
Colby, V., *The Singular Anomaly: Women Novelists of the Nineteenth Century* (New York, 1970).
____, *Yesterday's Woman: Domestic Realism in the English Novel* (Princeton, 1974).
Cornillon, S.K. (ed.), *Images of Women in Fiction: Feminist Perspectives* (Ohio, 1972).
Daly, M., *Gyn/Ecology* (London, 1979).
Delamont, S. and Duffin, L. (eds), *The Nineteenth Century Woman: Her Cultural and Physical World* (New York, 1978).
Diamond, A. and Edwards, L.R. (eds), *The Authority of Experience: Essays in Feminist Criticism* (Amherst, 1977).
Donovan, J. (ed.), *Feminist Literary Criticism: Explorations in Theory* (Lexington, 1975).
Eagleton, M. (ed.), *Feminist Literary Theory. A Reader* (Blackwell, Oxford, 1986).
Eagleton, T., *The Rape of Clarissa* (Oxford, 1982).
Evans, M., *Simone de Beauvoir. A Feminist Mandarin* (Tavistock, London and New York, 1985).
Femia, J.V., *Gramsci's Political Thought: Hegemony, Consciousness and the Revolutionary Process* (Oxford, 1981).
Fetterley, J., *The Resisting Reader. A Feminist Approach to American Fiction* (Bloomington and London, 1978).

Figes, E., *Sex and Subterfuge: Women Writers to 1850* (London, 1982).
Foucault, M., *The History of Sexuality. vol. I. An Introduction* (London, 1979).
Freud, S., *Totem and Taboo* (London, 1950).
―――, *Civilisation and Its Discontents* (London, 1957).
Gallop, J., *Feminism and Psychoanalysis. The Daughter's Seduction* (London, 1982).
Golitsyn, N.N., *A Bibliographical Dictionary of Russian Women Writers* (St Petersburg, 1889).
Gornick, V. and Moran, B.K. (eds), *Women in Sexist Society* (New York, 1971).
Greene, G. and Kahn, C. (eds), *Making a Difference: Feminist Literary Criticism* (London and New York, 1985).
Hays, H.R., *The Dangerous Sex: The Myth of Feminine Evil* (London, 1966).
Heilbrunn, C.C., *Reinventing Womanhood* (London, 1979).
Heldt, B., '*Rassvet* (1859–1862) and the Woman Question', *Slavic Review* (March 1977), pp. 76–85.
―――, 'Tolstoy's Path Towards Feminism', in V. Terras (ed.), *American Contributions to the Eighth International Congress of Slavists. vol. II. Literature* (Ohio, 1978), pp. 523–35.
―――, *Terrible Perfection. Women and Russian Literature* (Indiana University Press, Bloomington and Indianapolis, 1987).
Humm, M., *Feminist Criticism. Women as Contemporary Critics* (Harvester, Brighton, 1986).
―――, *The Dictionary of Feminist Theory* (Harvester Wheatsheaf, New York, London, Toronto, Sydney, Tokyo, 1989).
Jacobus, M., *Women Writing and Writing about Women* (London, 1979).
Jardine, A. and Smith P. (eds), *Men in Feminism* (Methuen, New York and London, 1987).
Joll, J., *Gramsci* (London, 1977).
Kaplan, E.A. (ed.), *Women in Film Noir* (London, 1980).
―――, *Women and Film: Both Sides of the Camera* (New York and London, 1983).
Kauffman, L. (ed.), *Gender and Theory. Dialogues on Feminist Criticism* (Blackwell, Oxford, 1989).
Kirkham, M., *Jane Austen, Feminism and Fiction* (Harvester, Brighton, 1983).
Kristeva, J., *Desire in Language. A Semiotic Approach to Literature and Art*. Edited by Leon S. Roudiez. Translated by Thomas Gora, Alice Jardine and Leon S. Roudiez (Blackwell, Oxford, 1981).
de Lauretis, T., *Alice Doesn't. Feminism, Semiotics, Cinema* (Macmillan, London, 1984).
―――, *Technologies of Gender. Essays on Theory, Film and Fiction* (Macmillan, London, 1989).
McCabe, C., *Godard: Images, Sounds, Politics* (London, 1980).
de Maegd-Soëp, C., *The Emancipation of Women in Russian Literature and Society* (Ghent, 1978).
Marks, E. and de Courtivron, I. (eds and intros), *New French Feminism. An Anthology* (Harvester, Brighton, 1981).
Mill, J.S., *On The Subjugation of Women* (London, 1861).
Miller, J., *Women Writing about Men* (London, 1986).

Miller, N.K., *The Heroine's Text: Readings in the French and English Novel 1722–1782* (New York, 1980).
Mitchell, J., *Psychoanalysis and Feminism* (Harmondsworth, 1975).
___ , *Women: The Longest Revolution. Essays in Feminism, Literature and Psychoanalysis* (London, 1984).
___ , and Rose, J. (eds), *Feminine Sexuality. Jacques Lacan and the 'école freudienne'* (London, 1982).
Moi, T., *Sexual/Textual Politics. Feminist Literary Theory* (London, 1985).
___ , (ed.), *The Kristeva Reader*. (Blackwell, Oxford, 1986).
Oakley, A., *Subject Women* (London, 1982).
Okin, S.M., *Women in Western Political Thought* (London, 1980).
O'Toole, L.M., *Structure, Style and Interpretation in the Russian Short Story* (New Haven and London, 1982).
Ponomareva, S.I., *Our Women Writers* (St Petersburg, 1891).
Porter, C., *Fathers and Daughters* (London, 1976).
Pratt, A., *Archetypal Patterns of Women's Fiction* (Brighton, 1982).
Praz, M., *The Romantic Agony* (Oxford, 1970).
Rich, A., *Of Woman Born. Motherhood as Experience and Institution* (London, 1977).
Richards, J.R., *The Sceptical Feminist. A Philosophical Enquiry* (Harmondsworth, 1982).
Roe, S. (ed.), *Women Reading Women's Writing* (Harvester, Brighton, 1987).
Rogers, K.M., *The Troublesome Helpmate. A History of Misogyny in Literature* (Seattle and London, 1966).
Rose, J., *Sexuality in the Field of Vision* (Verso, London, 1986).
Ruthven, K.K., *Feminist Literary Studies. An Introduction* (Cambridge, 1984).
Sargent, L. (ed.), *Women and Revolution. The Unhappy Marriage of Marxism and Feminism. A Debate on Class and Patriarchy* (London, 1981).
Satina, S., *Education of Women in Pre-Revolutionary Russia* (New York, 1966).
Sayers, J., *Sexual Contradictions. Psychology, Psychoanalysis and Feminism* (London, 1986).
Showalter, E., *A Literature of their Own. British Women Novelists from Brontë to Lessing* (London, 1979).
Snitow A., Stansell C., and Thompson S. (eds), *Desire. The Politics of Sexuality* (Virago, London, 1984).
Stites, R., *The Woman's Liberation Movement in Russia: Feminism, Nihilism and Bolshevism (1860–1930)* (Princeton, 1978).
Stone, L., *The Family, Sex and Marriage in England 1500–1800* (London, 1977).
Suleiman, S. Rubin (ed.), *The Female Body in Western Culture. Contemporary Perspectives* (Harvard University Press, Cambridge, Mass., London, 1986).
Tanner, T., *Adultery in the Novel: Contract and Transgression* (Baltimore and London, 1979).
Taylor, B., *Eve and the New Jerusalem: Socialism and Feminism in the Nineteenth Century* (London, 1983).
Thompson, P., *The Victorian Heroine: A Changing Ideal* (London, 1956).
Todd, J., *Feminist Literary History. A Defence* (Polity, Cambridge, 1988).
Vicinus, M. (ed.), *Suffer and Be Still: Women in the Victorian Age* (Bloomington, 1972).

Warner, M., *Alone of All Her Sex: The Myth and Cult of the Virgin Mary* (London, 1976).
Watt, I., *The Rise of the Novel* (Harmondsworth, 1968).
Weedon, C., *Feminist Practice and Poststructuralist Theory* (Blackwell, Oxford, 1987).
Williams, M., *Women in the English Novel 1800–1900* (London, 1984).
Woolf, V., *Three Guineas* (Harmondsworth, 1977).

Index

For all artistic works, see under relevant author

Althusser, L., 7, 8, 14
ball, society, 55–6, 58, 60, 63, 86, 93–4, 122, 141, 142, 155–6, 169, 176, 179, 180
Belinsky, V., 93, 139
Bible, The, 5, 28–9, 87, 124, 125–6, 135, 153–4
Brontë, C., *Jane Eyre*, 165, 167, 168–9, 238 n10
Byron, Lord, 12, 16, 17, 19, 39–40, 42, 43, 168, 171, 180, 182, 202; *Childe Harold*, 73, 115, 123
Chernyshevsky, N., *What Is To Be Done?*, 87, 110, 158, 176, 179, 186, 215, 217
Dostoevksy, F., 4; *The Brothers Karamazov*, 218–19; *Netochka Nezvanova*, 1, 6, 9, 214, 217–26
duel, 57–8, 61, 113, 122, 127, 142, 144
family, the, 15, 48–9, 54, 191, 218–19
father, the, 2, 3, 9, 46, 47, 49, 77, 89, 135–8, 144–5, 152–4, 157, 158, 203, 214–26
Foucault, M., 5, 7, 14–15, 32
Freud, S., 5, 128, 146, 221, 226, 249 n11; Oedipus complex, 13, 34, 35, 39, 42, 46, 47, 87, 95, 153, 214–26
Gan, E., 2, 3, 4, 6, 10, 50, 53, 55, 64, 85–138, 139, 140, 147, 159, 160, 179, 180, 183, 220, 241 n52; *A Futile Gift*, 6, 9, 85, 99, 102, 120, 131–8, 140, 178, 216; *The Ideal*, 9, 85–104, 105, 106, 110, 113, 114, 115, 116, 117, 118, 119, 120, 121, 123, 127, 128, 129, 130, 131, 134, 135, 148; *The Locket*, 9, 85, 104–17, 118, 121, 127, 128, 129, 134, 174, 243 n93; *Memories of Zheleznovodsk*, 104; *Society's Judgement*, 9, 63, 85, 86, 110, 113, 117–31, 140, 144, 148, 150, 216
Gaskell, E., *Mary Barton*, 167
gaze, the, 20, 21, 38, 61–2, 82–3, 90–1, 94, 100, 114, 116, 128, 174
gender, 6–8, 13–15, 42, 43–4, 49, 60, 67, 91–2, 101–3, 116, 132, 139, 145–6, 150–1, 153–4, 190
Gogol, N., 66, 87, 155, 174, 179, 180; *Dead Souls*, 60, 169, 187; *Ivan Shponka*, 65, 198–9, 235 n35, 236 n46; *Mirgorod*, 53, 95; *Old World Landowners, The*, 185, 192; *The St Petersburg Stories*, 1, 128–9; *Taras Bulba*, 53
Griboedov, A., *Woe from Wit*, 106, 184
Herzen, A., 1; *The Thieving Magpie*, 213; *Who Is To Blame?*, 9, 184–213, 217, 246 n7
images of men, in *Baron Reykhman*, 151–4; in *Dacha on the Peterhof Road*, 171–3; in *The Fountain of Bakhchisaray*, 37–9; in *The Ideal*, 91–3; in *The Locket* (Gan), 106–8; in *Princess Mimi*, 56–8; in *Princess Zizi*, 69–70; in *The Prisoner of the Caucasus*, 21–6; in *Society's Judgement*, 118–19; in *Who Is To Blame?*, 197–203
images of women, in *Baron Reykhman*, 146–51; in *Dacha on the Peterhof Road*, 175–83; in *The Fountain of Bakhchisaray*, 39–41; in *The Gipsies*, 42–3; in *The Ideal*, 85–91; in *The Locket* (Gan), 108–11; in *The Locket* (Zhukova), 161–17; in *Princess Mimi*, 61–8; in *Princess Zizi*, 74–84; in *The Prisoner of the Caucasus*, 15–21; in *Who Is To Blame?*, 202–13
Karamzin, N., 19, 133; *The Island of Bornholm*, 123; *Poor Liza*, 160, 167, 168, 182, 208
Lermontov, M., 93, 135, 138, 140, 157, 186; *Demon*, 19; *A Hero of Our Time*, 1, 3, 4, 9, 29, 98, 101, 104, 107, 113, 118, 123–4, 172, 175, 177, 180, 183, 184, 198, 202, 217, 234 n7, 240 n49, 241 n56, 242 n62
man, and feminine iconography, 114, 119, 198–200; and male bonding, 21, 51–5, 216; and masculinity, 8, 106–8, 119, 126–7; and military motifs, 22–6, 34, 36, 37, 94–5, 119, 121–2, 126, 142, 152; as *raisonneur*, 3, 193, 203, 216, 217; as rake, 9, 91, 92–3, 96, 98–9, 100, 106–7, 110, 112, 114–15, 171, 172, 189, 195–6, 201; the superfluous, 2, 3, 9, 104, 106, 107, 190, 202, 217

255

Odoevsky, V.F., 1, 3, 4, 6, 50–84, 139, 140; *Katya or the Story of a Young Ward*, 50; *New Year*, 51–5, 56, 69, 216; *Princess Mimi*, 9, 50, 52, 55–68, 69, 70, 81, 84, 143, 150, 216, 235 n26; *Princess Zizi*, 9, 50, 68–84, 216; *The Salamander*, 50; *Tales of How it is Dangerous for Girls to Walk in a Crowd along Nevsky Prospekt*, 50
patriarchy, 16, 17, 34, 36, 37–8, 42, 45–6, 47, 62–3, 146–7, 151, 156, 161, 167, 183, 187, 188, 190, 197–8, 204, 205, 206, 207–9, 214, 216, 217, 220, 226
Pushkin, A., 2, 4, 139, 140, 206, 227 n2, 234 n16; *Evgeny Onegin*, 1, 2, 4, 9, 11, 19, 57–8, 62, 68, 69, 70, 77–8, 80, 94, 95, 98, 100, 102, 106, 110, 111, 113, 135, 140, 155, 156, 158, 159, 161, 162, 172, 177, 180, 182, 184, 185, 187, 188, 189, 190, 194, 198, 199, 201, 202, 203, 207, 209–10, 211, 217, 236 n47; *The Fountain of Bakhchisaray*, 3, 9, 12, 16, 17, 21, 31–41, 110, 160, 216; *The Gipsies*, 3, 8, 9, 12, 16, 17, 42–9, 90, 203, 216, 217; *The Prisoner of the Caucasus*, 2, 11–31, 215–16; *The Queen of Spades*, 4, 123; *The Southern Poems*, 1, 3, 8, 9, 11–49, 229 n16; *The Tales of Belkin*, 96, 106, 123, 169; 'There was a Time', 54
Remarkable Decade, the, 3
Richardson, S., *Clarissa*, 70, 71, 73, 77, 92, 98, 101, 115
Romanticism, 7, 89, 131–8, 171, 174, 175, 177–83, 185, 186, 189, 190, 191, 193, 195, 199, 200, 203
St Petersburg, 59, 86, 90, 94, 97, 136–8, 155, 168, 175
sentimentalism, 19–20, 31, 40, 79–80, 88–9, 91, 95–6, 105, 116, 137, 155, 166–7, 168, 169, 170, 175, 178–83, 211
Slavophiles, the, 3, 155
society tale, the, 4, 55, 85, 93, 104, 122, 123, 140, 155–6, 216
'Sternianism', 3–4, 104, 131, 142, 143
Tolstoy, L., 155; *Anna Karenina*, 48–9, 97, 140, 143, 144–5, 191, 217; *War and Peace*, 212
Turgenev, L., 19, 50, 71, 147, 157, 184, 186, 187, 191, 209, 236 n47; *Asya*, 50, 51, 113, 234 n7; *Fathers and Children*, 188; *First Love*, 50, 51; *Home of the Gentry*, 1, 199; *Notes of a Hunter*, 155; *On the Eve*, 1, 75, 110, 158–9, 203–4, 207, 209–10, 211; *Rudin*, 194; *Spring Torrents*, 50
Westernisers, the, 3
woman, and *bildungsroman*, 6, 217, 218, 224; as child, 18, 39, 46–7; creative woman, 9, 85–6, 88, 120, 127–38, 216, 217; and dark Forces, 19; and desire, 17, 32–3, 36–7, 43, 44, 45, 46–7, 49, 62–3, 97, 156–8, 159, 170, 175, 196, 215, 216; and devil, 87; and discourse, 60, 63–5, 67–8, 77–8, 88, 102, 117, 131–8, 171, 179–80, 216, 218, 223–4; as enigma, 70–1, 76–7, 84, 88, 97, 108–10, 112, 124–5, 128, 133, 157, 170; fetishisation of, 62, 66–7, 82–3, 84, 88, 90, 147, 161–2; and gossip, 9, 59–60, 63, 86–7, 120–1, 143–4, 150; iconography of, 7, 9, 19–20, 40, 79–80, 88–9, 90–1, 108, 110, 112–13, 114, 119, 149–50, 164–5, 170, 178–9, 180, 181, 183, 195, 204, 208, 210–11, 212–13; as 'identikit heroine', 5, 16, 20–1, 78–84, 204, 216; and insanity, 6, 133, 170, 171, 175, 181–3; and instability, 18; and love, 6, 19, 78, 99–100, 116, 117, 133, 167, 181–3, 196; and marriage, 6, 58–9, 61–2, 64–8, 71, 73, 84, 89–90, 92, 97, 130, 145, 158, 173–4, 181, 190, 191–2, 195, 211–12, 217; as mother, 5, 16, 18, 28, 47, 72, 75, 80, 87–8, 96, 105, 110, 118–19, 121, 129, 137, 141, 147–8, 159, 160–1, 166, 190, 193, 200, 201, 204, 207–9, 211–12, 219–26; and mutism, 18, 88, 108; 'new woman', 9, 50; as Other, 7; as passionate, 3, 5, 9, 12, 39–40, 42, 43; as persecuted, 9; and power, 9, 58, 66, 84, 86; and religion, 40–1, 81, 89–90, 91, 95–6, 99, 100, 103–4, 116–17, 129–31, 135–8, 166–7, 216; rivalry between, 157–8; seduction of, 6, 72, 73, 82–3, 91, 96, 98, 100–1, 112–15, 116, 175, 189, 204–5, 207–9, 219–26; as seductress, 5; and self-sacrifice, 78–9, 166; and sexuality, 5, 16–17, 18, 37–8, 42–3, 58–9, 61–2, 67, 81–2, 150–1, 204–5; and 'sisterhood', 75, 110–11, 129–30, 158–61, 176, 238 n13; stereotypes of, 6, 17, 18, 19, 78–84, 92, 177, 179; as strong heroine, 2, 50, 74–84, 184, 189, 196, 203–4, 209–13; and suicide, 17, 30–1, 97, 215–16; as virgin, 3, 5, 16, 18, 28, 32, 33, 34, 35, 36, 40–1, 42, 80–1, 90, 91, 96, 98, 108, 129, 189, 209;

as vulnerable victim, 9, 18, 19, 40, 41, 83, 91, 106, 188, 204–6, 207–9; as whore, 5, 17, 18, 35, 36, 40; and 'woman question', 4, 50, 85, 139, 215, 216

Zhukova, M., 2, 3, 4, 6, 10, 50, 53, 55, 56, 63, 64, 89, 139–83, 220; *Baron Reykhman*, 6, 8, 140–54, 156, 157, 158, 165, 174, 175, 216–17; *The Dacha on the Peterhof Road*, 9, 140, 141, 147, 168–83, 217; *Evenings at Karpovka*, 140, 145, 154–5, 168; *The Last Evening*, 141; *The Locket*, 140, 141, 154–67, 170, 171, 173, 175, 176, 177, 217; *The Monk*, 140, 155, 245 n12

Zhukovsky, V., 78, 189, 199, 200